SMALL EFFORT

BIG RESULT

You Can Innovate

JOHN PURDIE-SMITH

John Purdie-Smith – Small Effort Big Result : You Can Innovate
ISBN: 978-1-7641269-9-1 (Paperback)

A catalogue record for this book is available from the National Library of Australia

All trademarks, product names, and company names mentioned in this book remain the property of their respective owners. They are used here solely for identification and illustrative purposes.

Editing: Kristina Proft
Internal design: Ronald Proft
Delphian Books
+61 2 8625 5530
delphianbooks.com.au

Printed in Australia

Contents

PREFACE

If you don't have time to read this book, this is what it says.

You can learn to innovate intentionally, with a specific purpose in mind. It does not require a timely lightbulb moment or a lucky break.

You can learn to innovate through problems, resolving them innovatively and relatively effortlessly.

When you innovate, you create Innovative Value. This value is the gap between the effort you put in and the worth of what you achieve. *Small effort→big result.* You don't need unique talent or specialized know-how to do this, because the value you generate already exists. You learn where to find it and how to release it.

The path to unlocking this value runs through the problem that is stopping you reaching your goal. Every problem contains within it the secret of how it can be overcome innovatively.

There are six ways to unlock this secret so you not only achieve what you are aiming for, but you also do so with an amount of effort that is strikingly small relative to the value of what you achieve.

This is innovating. This is what you will learn to do.

If you are still reading, I am glad you are here. Welcome on the journey. Let me introduce myself and situate myself within my topic.

I was educated in New Zealand. While gaining undergraduate degrees in accounting and marketing, I found university life was fun and worth prolonging. Completing an honors degree in marketing secured a further enjoyable year and then after that—campus life was still fun—I signed up for a post-graduate degree in marketing, but with a bonus—I got to do it in England.

When the inevitability of needing to work for a living finally arrived, I entered the business world and took a job in sales.

During my education in the ways and means of business, I observed others successfully "closing the sale" and sought to emulate them. As I moved further up the business ladder, I saw how a good idea could boost business success enormously. Sometimes, it seemed like hitting the jackpot, striking gold, uncovering some hidden treasure.

Hey, business life could be fun too!

Although not conscious of a potential underlying methodology back then—this was my pre-theoretical phase—I was developing an intuition for how *good* ideas worked. Over time, I began to draw from aspects of that intuition to achieve some unexpectedly excellent results as the leader of several challenging projects, including:

- Repairing more than 20,000 properties in record time after the 1999 Sydney Hailstorm—Australia's most expensive natural disaster

- Cutting through the immense logistical difficulties to successfully deliver tickets for the 2000 Sydney Olympics to every Australian household that ordered them

- Transforming the customer service of a major home builder to win the Australian Housing Industry Innovation Award in 2009

I will talk a little more about the first two of these shortly.

However, this book's genesis was in the first year of my business life. Fresh out of university, my mind was open, keen to soak up knowledge that would propel my career. I came across a story in a business magazine about the introduction of Hi-Fi systems which—in the 1970s—had only recently evolved to include stereo sound. This latest enhancement had breakthrough market appeal. Eager retail stockists were plentiful, and competition among them was fierce.

The article I happened upon told of the outstanding success of a Hi-Fi retailer who used publicly available information to send letters (yep, pre-email) to the parents of students who would shortly be graduating from university. After offering congratulations, the letter suggested a Hi-Fi stereo system—competitively priced, of course—would be a fitting graduation gift for their son or daughter, after a season of hard work and, presumably, some austerity.

While this initiative was not unusually brilliant, I liked its innovative simplicity. The retailer achieved an outsized market share in a crowded, local marketplace at low cost by tapping into information available to anyone.

I cut the story out of the magazine and popped it into a manila folder (yep, pre-home computer). Collecting stories containing what I felt were Innovative Ideas became a habit and before long the manila folder became quite fat, progressing over the years to a computer file. And ultimately to a largish computer file.

I collect such anecdotes still and add them continuously to a website containing thousands of categorized innovative ideas. There they can be searched by business or activity, by goal and by problem, with each idea containing hints of how to adapt it.[1]

Over this extended period, I became increasingly intrigued by innovative ideas.

Can they be generated routinely or do you only stumble upon them by chance?

Do they contain some common pattern?

Can you create them intentionally?

This fascination turned into my quest to learn how to innovate.

My challenge over the pages that follow is to demonstrate to you, the reader, that purposefully generating innovative ideas to solve problems is a skill that can be learned and applied with confident expectation of success. You will learn to innovate intentionally—anyone can.

---

1   If of interest, access to these ideas is freely available at Sebir.com

So, what does it mean to innovate?

There is no shortage of opinions on the subject, but if we are going to innovate, we need to know what success looks like in unmistakably clear terms. We need to use terms that distinguish the acts of innovation and innovating from the maelstrom of views we will encounter shortly in the Introduction.

In my study of thousands of compelling innovative ideas, I discovered that there is one characteristic they all possess. In fact, it was this defining characteristic that drew me to them. There was something surprisingly beneficial happening.

"What a great idea!" was my instinctive response when I came across an especially innovative act.

But on closer examination, what really caught my attention was that unexpected value was being created, value out of proportion to what you would normally expect under the circumstances. For some reason, the result towered over the apparent effort that had been expended to produce it. There was a gratifying inequality.

All the ideas I had collected and studied had this *Small effort→big result* quality.

This is not our normal experience in everyday life. Usually, we expect an outcome more or less commensurate with what we put into bringing it about. A common adage is: "Hard work pays off." Others include: "You get what you pay for" and "You reap what you sow." That sort of thing.

In fact, our aversion to the imbalance between effort and result is probably more ingrained than a mere expectation. In his 2001 book, *The Tipping Point: How Little Things Can Make a Big Difference,* Malcolm Gladwell claims we are socialized to make a kind of rough approximation between cause and effect. He asserts that we struggle with something where the effect is out of proportion with the cause.

We must break with any mental conditioning like this because what I found in studying many innovative ideas refreshingly shattered such a rule of commensurability. Achieving an appealing disparity between effort and result is exactly what we are about in these pages as we seek to innovate.

When we tackle a problem blocking a goal, we want to overcome it in such a way that what we achieve considerably outweighs our efforts. Achieving maximum effectiveness with Economy of Effort is the essence. Economy of Effort is the imperative saturating the entire approach to innovating that this book teaches. It is the framing foundation of the Innovative Value we generate.

For a relatively small amount of effort, we want a big result.

Small effort→big result.

Three Reasons for Reading On

A fair question at this stage would be:

Why should I have faith in the content of this book to teach me to innovate?

After all, perhaps the teachings put forward here are not much more than yet another perspective, by yet another commentator, on the crowded field of innovation?

To answer such a question, I advance three premises that I believe fortify the entire endeavor:

1. Theory not opinion

2. Empirical evidence

3. Ideal timing

Theoretical Foundation

The key principles underpinning the innovating model advanced in this book were derived scientifically through grounded theory. These principles emerged from empirical research that studied many successful innovative ideas. They are not simply the product of preconceived assumptions formed from my interest in innovation. Instead, the theory grew out of the data generated from the analysis of thousands of transformative ideas—deconstructing and reformulating them repeatedly—until reliable theoretical principles could be established.

This process involved observation, "data-driven" hypothesis development and testing, analysis of results, and conclusion drawing.

Ultimately, a cohesive theory has coalesced, comprised of Four Foundational Axioms. These are introduced in Chapter 2: How Should We Think to Innovate? They surface constantly and in-depth throughout the pages that follow, because they are the basis upon which the theory of how to innovate through problems has been constructed. The axioms encompass: the primacy of problems; the creation of the *Small effort➜big result* gap, which represents innovative value; the principle of releasing of value that already exists—rather than needing to create it; and the all-pervasive availability of untapped innovative value.

Real World Evidence

There are many stories scattered throughout these pages. They are short stories, but they are, for all practical purposes, true stories. They are real-life examples of innovative solutions generated to solve authentic problems—overwhelmingly in the field of business—and they anchor the theory upon which this book is based. These innovative ideas have worked in practical situations, are on the record and their efficacy has been verified. More precisely, the results the ideas achieved in each case are demonstrably worth significantly more than the effort employed to produce those results.

Thousands of such innovative ideas have not only enabled the compilation of a coherent theory but they self-evidently demonstrate that innovative ideas so formulated are powerful and extremely effective. Consequently, we can be confident if we are faithful to the process by which they were formulated, we will achieve comparable success.

There is however another dimension of this empirical validity: rather than applying the thinking being taught here to individual, isolated problems, it can be applied in a congruent and mutually reinforcing manner to major projects that contain multiple, interconnected problems.

I was able to test this myself during my business career.

I will limit my comments to two large projects that can be checked out on the public record. In one, problems were thrust upon me and my team; in the other we invented our own.

The two projects were:

1. The 1999 Sydney Hailstorm Disaster[2]

2. The Sydney 2000 Olympics Ticket Home Delivery Program[3]

In the first project—the 1999 Sydney Hailstorm—nature unleashed a host of problems in the manner that only natural disasters can. This made it easy to identify those problems of course. Embracing them and dealing with each of them individually and innovatively opened a path to successful restoration of the more than 20,000 damaged homes in record time.

With the Olympic Games to be held in Sydney the following year, the New South Wales State Government wanted the repair task completed in the remaining eight months of 1999, even though the damage to house roofs alone was equivalent to a year's work for a roofing industry already caught amid a pre-Olympic building boom. Thousands of homes visibly draped in tarpaulins when multitudes were flying in for the Olympics wouldn't do at all. Anticipating, preempting and innovatively addressing problems ensured the Government's goal of a pre-Olympic, pristine-looking Sydney was achieved.

In the second project—the 2000 Olympics ticket delivery—there was no crisis and therefore no overt problems to confront before the Ticket Home Delivery Program got underway. Nevertheless, prior to its commencement, a decision was taken to

---

2   The 1999 Sydney Hailstorm disaster was Australia's costliest natural disaster at the time, with giant hailstones—some over 9 cm in diameter—pummeling the city on April 14, 1999, causing widespread destruction to homes, vehicles, and infrastructure, and resulting in insurance claims exceeding 1.7 billion Australian dollars.

3   The Sydney Organizing Committee for the 2000 Olympic Games (SOCOG) launched 'Your Ticket Sunday', a massive home delivery program starting on August 6, 2000, to distribute Olympic tickets to hundreds of thousands of Australians, making it the largest and most complex delivery operation ever attempted in the country.

identify potential problems by holding a full-day workshop involving parties with relevant transportation and delivery experience. Their assignment was to brainstorm all imaginable problems that could conceivably arise before and during what would be the largest logistical exercise ever undertaken in peacetime Australia.

With only one ticket delivery attempt per customer possible prior to the commencement of the Olympics, coveted Olympic tickets had to be hand-delivered without fail to more than 400,000 customers across the length and breadth of Australia—including islands off the coast.

Once again, the strategy of first clearly identifying and then innovating through problems—mainly by ensuring they did not occur—was uncommonly effective. Just one example: two sequentially posted cards, an early non-digital form of 2-factor authentication, removed the need for on-the-spot self-identification by ticket recipients. All tickets found their way into all customers' hands prior to the Olympic Opening Ceremony.

For Our Times

The philosophical approach to innovating adopted here is right for our times. There are two reasons why, and both reasons are monumental on a world scale:

1. Environmental sustainability

2. Artificial intelligence

First, environmental sustainability.

As each year and each decade passes, the mandate increasingly adopted by national governments everywhere is the push for sustainability. It goes by many names—combating global warming, addressing climate change, shrinking environmental footprints, reducing pollution—and various related terms. But putting aside political or ideological differences, it can be boiled down to a stark proposition: the compelling obligation to do more with less.

This book's innovating model rests on doing more or better with what we already have. Or have access to. The entire premise is one of extracting latent or residual value from what already exists but is currently underutilized. Creating a new resource through which to innovate is, by definition, unequivocally excluded. Thus, adding to an environmental footprint, for instance, is an impossibility.

We take what we have inherited, what we have around us and—rather than discarding it or ignoring it—we harness it to innovate.

Second, Artificial intelligence (AI).

There have obviously been many technological developments over the decades since I first contemplated crafting a personal innovating skill. Paramount has been computerization and its progression into portable, personal devices. Generally, whenever a new technology bursts onto the scene, the impact is overwhelmingly positive, dramatically improving human productivity and the quality of life for many. Inevitably, in the early days, there is always the fear of downside and unintended consequences. Potential threats are identified but once the latest invention has gained traction and proved what it can do, the positives have tended to outweigh the negatives.

The latest electronic transformation is artificial intelligence (AI)—more a gorilla in the neighborhood than a new kid on the block. It is already obvious that the implications and ramifications of AI are immense. While enormous benefits are being forecast, there is also significant concern, particularly around job displacement.

There is however a reliable way to ensure we are not run down by AI.

AI's core strength is in performing mundane, repetitive tasks with ultra efficiency. It is especially good at processing and retaining vast amounts of online data, identifying common patterns and translating them into insights for specific subject areas. It can do this, in effect, instantaneously, with speed and accuracy astonishingly better than any of us can remotely hope to emulate.

But AI has limitations—especially when it comes to imagination, lateral thinking, and creative insight. The best way to avoid being overtaken by pattern recognition on steroids is to develop entirely new patterns through innovative thinking. If those patterns do not yet exist, AI cannot replicate or exploit them. In the generation of new innovative patterns and thinking imaginatively about the issues in our business and personal lives, we remain firmly in control.

This is where knowledge of how to innovate is so valuable. No need to fear AI. After all, it is just another tool, albeit a super-efficient one. By using it smartly, we can also become super-efficient, freeing up time to become super-effective through innovating.

We should therefore keep up to date with the advancements in AI and use AI to do what it is good at.

That will give us even more time to do what we are good at.

Innovating.

Not only will we acquire mastery of a supreme skill—we can brush off AI and save the planet as well.

John Purdie-Smith
Sydney, 30 September 2025

INTRODUCTION

You're not a scholar, you've no right to have ideas

EUGENE IONESCO

With an emphatic denial is a good place to start.

The personal ability to innovate on purpose—to think imaginatively to solve a problem in a timely manner—is not the privilege of an elite or select few.

It is not solely the prerogative of those with a creative bent, or those with a genius-level IQ, or those who are highly educated, or indeed—with a respectful nod to the Romanian-French playwright, Eugene Ionesco whom we have just met—those of an intellectual persuasion—scholars.[4]

You don't have to be a scholar to innovate.

Nor is it something that is only the right of organizations. Nor is it limited to the commercial sphere. Nor is it solely most prominent among those at the leading edge of technology.

Innovating can be practiced in any domain and—more specifically for our area of enquiry—by any person confronting a problem, whether it occurs in their professional or personal life.

It is a skill that can be learned and mastered by anyone. Both viewpoints—that the ability to innovate cannot be personally acquired and that such an ability is exclusively the purview of commercial organizations—are myths.

There are two other myths that subvert the notion of innovating as a personal, learnable skill. We might as well deal with them while we are at it.

Myth number three is that the act of innovating is not something you can control. This viewpoint sees valuable innovative ideas as mostly emerging from the brain's "black box" in a largely unpredictable manner. Any thought of launching beneficial imaginative thinking for a specific purpose is dismissed on the grounds that being able to do so would be akin to knowing exactly how the human brain works, and being able to direct it toward a required end.

This is a reasonable objection. We do not have such knowledge. Any allusion to some sort of precise regulation of the billions of neurons in the human brain to

---

4   In fairness to Mr. Ionesco, he placed the declaration that opens this chapter in the mouth of a character in a short play entitled *Maid to Marry*. He cast himself in the position of being on the receiving end of the assertion and tries to rebut its message. Nevertheless, we thank him for the contention; it is useful for our purposes. We don't agree with it and his response in the play indicates that he doesn't either.

produce an innovative solution for some pressing problem is simply not believable.

However—and this is the crucial point—between the diametrically opposed positions of precisely instructing the brain and attempting no thought guidance at all, there is a fertile void. As we will discover later, an appreciation of how successful innovative ideas are formulated can convert our thinking from an amorphous, undirected medium into an informed and purposeful force. The study of thousands of such ideas reveals principles and patterns common to them all, patterns which can therefore be brought together into a cohesive model that is readily understood, learned, and applied.

The fourth and final myth is the tendency to confuse innovation with invention.

This is hardly surprising, because all contemporary product breakthroughs—from the personal computer through laptops and handheld devices to the iPhone—are typically referred to as innovations rather than inventions. The misconception is reinforced by the common tendency to equate innovation with research and development (R&D) activities and spending when commentating on or evaluating it. Such a belief gives the impression that innovating is a big deal—that unless you come up with a revolutionary new product or service—you are not innovating.

This impression is also false.

A further, unfortunate offshoot of such inventive bias is the view that innovative effort is always applied to things you can see and feel, especially products that emerge as electronic technology advances. However, breakthroughs are just as plausible in social and behavioral settings as they are in hard-wired, product development ones. If innovating is seen to have relevance only when something tangible is being invented or enhanced, the option of tackling a problem involving human affairs is completely overlooked as an opportunity to innovate.

This is a great pity, because the scope of problem-solving prospects in social, everyday domains far outweighs the agenda for technical inventions at any given time. Further, accepting that innovation and invention are synonymous leads many people—who would never think of themselves as inventors—to conclude they cannot hope to innovate.

The ability to innovate is for anyone. Do not be put off by imagined intellectual constraints, the need for corporate muscle, or some sort of inventive DNA.

And especially, do not be put off by any thought that deliberate acts of the imagination are beyond you.

It is all mythical.

The Aim of This Book

There are reasonable grounds to argue that learning to innovate is the most valuable skill anyone can acquire. No one experiences a life without problems—either in one's personal affairs or occupational pursuits. Overcoming them is necessary to progress and to human flourishing. To be able to do this reliably and relatively effortlessly is therefore a precious talent.

This book aims to teach such mastery.

If you have begun reading it, you have either already decided to learn to innovate through problems or you are at least open to being persuaded it is worthwhile. The distinction is not an empty one. Arguably, the single most common reason why we do not become more proficient at solving problems with imaginative ideas is that we have little interest in doing so. We cannot be bothered. It requires committed intellectual effort for one thing but, perhaps more telling, there is no roadmap to guide our thinking—no obvious starting point. It shapes up as a probable waste of time.

Mostly we are content to muddle through the circumstances we face—taking things as we find them—and then, when we must, paying the inherent cost to resolve the situation.

Another thing that puts us off is when the problem we are confronting is large or complicated. The assumption is that if the problem is big, the solution will also have to be big—and almost certainly expensive. Typically, the answer arrived at through conventional problem solving is commensurate with the effort. A deep breath is needed, but the resolve required can dampen enthusiasm and stall the search for a solution.

At least in the short term.

This stance of holding off is however understandable. Oftentimes, ideas that resolve a situation we have been living with eventually emerge. It seems subconscious contemplation has a role to play. Sleeping on it is good advice, and many of us can attest to how well that works by recalling times when it did. We all get good ideas now and then—they just kind of happen.

This is not to say we always do nothing. Most of us are familiar with techniques such as brainstorming, and may occasionally try this, or something similar. We will look more closely at brainstorming and its cousins in Chapter 4.

This book argues for and demonstrates that there is a reliable alternative to just waiting and hoping—and not just for major, infrequent problems. If adopted, the way of thinking outlined here can be employed as a matter of routine, brushing aside minor problems that arise and overcoming major ones when they occur.

Helicopter View of the Road Ahead

Before we lift off for a helicopter view that gives us a big-picture understanding of what is to come, there are some terminology matters to clarify.

I have an aversion to jargon—an antipathy probably also shared by many readers. At the risk of inviting the charge that I only have an aversion to jargon that is not mine, I want to request your indulgence just twice: in establishing a succinct, memorable label for the three-stage, input-output model soon to be introduced, and in identifying its three major elements.

Admittedly utilizing a little specialized language makes it a easier for me, but I believe there is a genuine matching benefit for readers. You will be spared the tedium of overly wordy descriptions and constant elaboration.

In the Preface we clarified exactly what it means to innovate. We said that when we innovate, we achieve a result disproportionately beneficial to the effort that went into producing it. For a relatively small effort, we want a big result. *Small effort→big result*.

The gap between the two is proof of the Innovative Value we have generated.

To capture this kernel of what it means to innovate, for convenience, I have adopted *Sebir*® as a loose acronym for ***Small effort→big result*** and as a concise label for the pattern it describes.

Sebir: a result in which the value achieved clearly exceeds the effort invested.

For convenience, I will use the term to refer to the three-stage, input-output model (a clunky label), which we will soon come to know as the Sebir Model.

And it is expedient to adopt easy-to-use designations for the three main, sequential elements of the Sebir Model. I will be calling them the *Initiator*, the *Connector* and the *Responder*. These are not people or roles. In the Sebir Model, the Initiator, Connector, and Responder are resources—existing things that contain unused value relevant to the problem being addressed. We will be talking about them a lot later but, for easy reference, these terms are defined in the Glossary at the end of the book.

There is one final jargon indulgence I've resisted: referring to "innovative ideas" as "Sebirs." This is something I do on the website *Sebir.com*, but I have chosen not to foist that familiarity on readers here. Throughout these pages, innovative ideas remain simply "innovative ideas."

In addition to the terms I have coined, I also use some familiar words in nuanced ways—emphasizing particular aspects of their meaning. These terms are often capitalized, and when they are, they also appear in the Glossary.

Finally—a note on the word "goal." Behind every problem we seek to innovate through, there is always some aim, objective, or desired outcome—a goal—that remains unfulfilled because of that problem. Otherwise, we would have no need to innovate. Achieving that outcome lies at the heart of how to innovate, as taught throughout this book.

Rather than alternate between terms like *aim*, *objective*, or *purpose*, I have chosen to use "goal" almost every time. While repeated references to a goal being blocked or a goal being achieved may risk a touch of stylistic monotony, it is the lesser fault. There are important insights to be gained at many points in our journey toward personal innovating mastery—and these are best grasped without the distraction of varied terminology for the result we are seeking.

Our goal is the goal.

The Journey

Since we are seeking to acquire a cognitive skill rather than following the tangible steps that typically lead to a physical competency, knowing clearly how we are going to proceed is even more essential. No need to use any obtuse imagery. As we are looking to progress from a current state where something we want to do is being blocked, to a transformed state where our goal is fully achieved, the obvious metaphor is that of a journey.

Time to go up in our helicopter to gain a high-level view of that journey.

At first, we notice there is a single road from start to finish. We set about innovating by following the same route every time. This road is a three-stage model—the Sebir Model—that gives shape to the formulation and eventual generation of the required innovative solution. The stages comprise the three core elements of the Sebir Model and are well sign-posted. The Initiator points down the road to the Connector which, in turn, points further on to the Responder.

More on these elements—and the Sebir Model that forms the road—shortly.

An early view from our helicopter also detects a road of five distinct segments, or, as convention dictates for a book, five PARTS.

And look—some travelers are gathering supplies at the point of departure—provisioning for what lies ahead. These preparations are important.

Becoming equipped for the journey is the task of PART 1: A MIND TO INNOVATE.

Chapters 1 to 4 frame the way of thinking that must be learned and adopted before the journey of learning to innovate commences. Chapter 1 ensures that our innovating focus is precisely defined—a critical step, given the widespread tendency to engage the concept of innovation in a loose, undefined manner—whereas Chapter 2 makes the case for acquiring a completely different way of thinking. Chapter 3 reveals where innovative value is lying, waiting to be harvested, while Chapter 4 evaluates the existing, alternative approaches to generating innovative ideas, including brainstorming.

Then—from our elevated position—we observe the road has six lanes. These reflect the six different ways we can innovate through problems. PART 2: THE CENTRALITY OF PROBLEMS elaborates on what the central role of problems embodies. Problems are *the* pathway to all the innovative solutions that overcome them. Chapters 5 to 12 start by arguing the case for embracing rather than shunning problems, and then disclose, quite systematically—with a chapter devoted to each—the six ways (the six lanes on the road) by which problems can be dissected to reveal a path to the innovative solution.

A notable consequence of putting problems at the center of the Sebir Model is that we gain much more than a powerful strategic framework for innovating. We also acquire a rare and wide-ranging skill. We not only learn to innovate through problems that we *know exist*, but we also learn to innovate through problems that we *don't know exist*. And more implausibly still, we learn to innovate through problems that *don't yet exist*. While this may sound improbable now, by the end of the book, the full extent of this proficiency will feel both within reach and inevitable.

Bringing our helicopter down a little, we can detect there are two types of travelers on the road. One is using a form of public transport because they have chosen to Innovate through Copying, adapting from what already exists. The other is using private transport. They have decided to go it alone—to Innovate through Originating.

Please don't read any significance into this analogy between public transport (copying mode) and private transport (originating mode). It is rudimentary and not intended to do more than distinguish the two distinct modes of innovating. Certainly, you should not entertain the notion that Copying to Innovate is somehow inferior to Originating to Innovate. As we will discover, some of the most iconic products and services that are intrinsic to modern living such as Velcro, Post-it Notes and even the telephone, owe their creation to the copying mode of innovating.

And, since there is no limit to how many times we undertake the journey, we can switch between the two modes as often as we like.

PART 3: INNOVATE THROUGH COPYING, conveys in detail what is involved in the first of the two modes of innovating as we travel the road. Chapter 13 introduces the copying mode of innovating. It is followed by two more specific chapters (14 and 15) that deal respectively with copying by observing people and copying by observing things. The latter includes copying by observing best practice.

PART 4: INNOVATE THROUGH ORIGINATING, is an in-depth look at generating innovative solutions anew—without the leg-up of something existing that can be copied and adapted. This draws directly on the Sebir Model. Chapters 16 to 19 introduce originating and then unpack the three elements of the Sebir Model, with each element attracting its own chapter.

In Chapter 20: Originate by Renewing Processes, we reap an unexpected bonus. Whereas the bulk of the book's teaching relies on the identification and systematic analysis of specific problems, this chapter demonstrates how to innovate without knowing what the underlying problems are. We innovate anyway.

The more perceptive reader may have detected that PART 4: INNOVATE THROUGH ORIGINATING is anchored by the Sebir Model whereas it does not appear to feature in PART 3: INNOVATE THROUGH COPYING.

And yet we have been told the Sebir Model is the only road we travel to innovate. How do we reconcile this?

The answer is that the Sebir Model underpins both modes of innovating—copying and originating—but in the former, its three elements (Initiator, Connector and Responder) play only an incidental role. They are a consequence of Copying to Innovate whereas in the case of Originating to Innovate, they are the sequential launch points. This will become clear as we move forward.

The final segment of the book's main content is PART 5: THE SEBIR MODEL IN ACTION. Here we move from learning to doing, and the central component is a step-by-step "How To" Roadmap—the Sebir Ladder. Had we kept a travel diary—faithfully recording the practical implications of everything we learned along the way—we would now have a list of navigational instructions—some broad, with more specific ones nested beneath them. The pointers in this travel log chart a purposeful route forward—one that, when followed step-by-step, begins to resemble the rungs and steps of a ladder.

The structure that takes us from learning to doing is the Sebir Ladder.

Finally, the customary back-end extras make an appearance. There are two appendices: Appendix A, which contains a template for the *Problem PhotoBox*—the most essential tool in the entire book—and Appendix B, which offers some light entertainment in the form of collections of puns and paraprosdokians. As we will discover, puns and paraprosdokians are playful and revealing pointers to personal innovating. These are followed by a handy alphabetical Glossary of the key terms and distinctive language used in the book.

Lastly, there is a reasonably extensive Bibliography for the persistently curious.

The Sebir Model

The Sebir Model is a three-stage process in which each of the three stages (elements) is an input. When added together, they produce an innovative solution that is the output. Crucially, the value of the output of the model—the innovative solution—significantly exceeds the value of the sum of the inputs.

The end is *not* justified by the means—and the welcome difference is the Innovative Value that is generated.

As you would expect, the Sebir Model's three stages—containing the three elements—are sequential, moving through one, two, and three phases of the model to produce the sought-after innovative result.

The three elements are all resources. As we will come to thoroughly appreciate, *resource* is a term loaded with meaning—a veritable "holy grail" when we innovate.

The input resources we are talking about here are:

- The *Initiator*. This is the first input resource, the one primed to launch the act of innovating. It possesses value suited to resolving the problem being addressed. Chapter 17 is dedicated to innovating through the Initiator Resource and the options for priming it

- The *Connector*. This is the second input resource, the one that positions the Initiator in a manner that maximizes the likelihood that an interaction will occur between the Initiator and Responder (the third element). Chapter 18 is dedicated to innovating through the Connector Resource and the options for positioning it

- The *Responder*. This is the third input resource, the one behaving or performing in a manner that amounts to achievement of the goal the problem is blocking. Chapter 19 is dedicated to innovating through the Responder Resource and the options for stimulating the response desired

Each of the three stages embodies the imperative of Economy of Effort we introduced in the Preface. How this plays out will be seen as we progress, although we will provide a glimpse of what is involved in a moment.

The Sebir Model enables us to intentionally formulate an innovative solution to a problem. It is how we generate Innovative Value. We will learn much more about the Sebir Model in Chapter 2: How Should We Think to Innovate?

Compass Settings for the Journey

After a lengthy process of experimentation and refinement, the Sebir Model of how to innovate has emerged robust.

It has stood the test of time.

Some preparatory reminders.

Recall that we reject the hypothesis that Innovative Ideas are random and arbitrarily fashioned by our environment or circumstances. And we also deny that the capacity to innovate is narrowly distributed throughout the population. Any of us can innovate. We do not need to be an inventive brainiac and we do not need corporate clout.

Yet, it is an ability that must be acquired. It must be learned. This is not a practice we just fall into.

Nor does it involve some sort of magic mental capacity or the knack of cerebrally being in the right place at the right time.

This is not to say—in fact, emphatically not to say—that we ignore the role of our brains. The approach here is a measured attempt to steer a path between the unknowability of how the human brain has imaginative ideas and the passive, laissez-faire mental state in which innovative thoughts randomly spring to mind. There is a productive middle course that—while it does not precisely govern the brain—also does not leave it entirely to its own devices. Although not scientifically flawless, what can be achieved in guiding the brain is overwhelmingly superior to passively responding to random external stimuli.

This is the course we are following.

Naturally, I would like to say that if you faithfully follow the lessons taught throughout this book, you will never fail to come up with an effective innovative solution.

I would like to, but I can't go that far.

Nevertheless, if you assimilate the lessons taught as a total way of thinking, much will be accomplished. You will enjoy some significant triumphs. In a relatively short time, thinking innovatively will become second nature to you and the step-by-step directives you have learned will be supplanted by instinctive knowledge of how to innovate.

Although my personal odyssey has been long, I continue to uncover fresh insights into the nature of innovating. I have come to realize this adventure is never-ending, as learning to innovate means no matter how far you have come, there's always more to learn. And that is fine, because it is a gratifying quest—it has the thrill of the hunt—and I have no wish it should end.

What I would like, however, are some travel companions—others who can build upon and improve what is on the record so far. There are certainly areas that could benefit from being stretched beyond their current bounds. It would be encouraging to have someone else identify the inevitable flaws and oversights of the underlying theory, pushing on toward something better and gaining the mastery that comes with it.

Let's get started.

PART 1

A MIND TO INNOVATE

We are about to set off on a journey.

While most journeys involve physical movement from a point of departure to an intended destination, the journey down the road of the Sebir Model requires mental movement as well.

A core promise of this book is that it is grounded in tested theory, not opinion or wishful thinking. That is my contribution. Your contribution is to make any necessary shift to your mindset. Some of the foundational principles you will meet are counter-intuitive—challenging both common assumptions and habitual ways of thinking. For this reason, implementing the lessons of this book with mastery—why settle for less?—means learning to view challenges through a new lens.

A new mindset isn't optional; it's essential.

If you have a mind to innovate, have a *mind* to innovate.

1

WHAT DOES IT MEAN TO INNOVATE?

If you don't know where you're going, you'll end up someplace else

YOGI BERRA

In the 1913 edition of Webster's Unabridged Dictionary, the following observation was made about the word *idea*:

There is scarcely any other word which is subjected to such abusive treatment as is the word idea, in the very general and indiscriminative (sic) way in which it is employed, as it is used variously to signify almost any act, state, or content of thought

It is doubtful the situation has changed for the better since then. With the explosion in publications and communications, it is likely that the context within which the word *idea* sits is even more confused now. Given that the skill of innovating falls within the broader notion of idea generation, we must recognize where we stand and extricate ourselves from the maelstrom of uses and meanings that have attached themselves to innovating and ideas.

It is essential to stake out the territory that delineates the type of idea we are talking about when we are talking about innovating and what it means in this book.

We need to know what to aim for when we innovate, and we need to know we have succeeded when we have hit the mark.

But—before we get to that—we will conduct a quick survey of the vast terrain inhabited by *innovation* to better understand what we are up against.

What is Innovating?

For brevity and convenience, we will use the terms *innovating, innovation* and *innovative* more or less interchangeably.

The words *innovation* and its descriptor *innovative* have been among the most alluring terms used in business literature and communications over the past 75 years or so. The notion of *innovativeness* seems to conjure up everything a business desires to be in the eyes of its stakeholders—particularly its customers—and therefore claims to be actively engaged in innovation, or of being innovative, are prevalent.

The curious thing is that this situation has emerged without a single, widely accepted definition of what *innovation* or *innovative* means. This could simply be because the terms have so many forms and uses. Most commonly, they are used in relation to a distinctive new product or service that might typically be described as a breakthrough *innovation*. Personal computers first, then handheld devices, and then smartphones have attracted such a label.

But not all innovations are revolutionary. Innovation can also result from improved efficiency in processes, and from improvements that are incremental at the level of a single instance but impressively valuable in aggregate. The very way a business operates could give it an innovative edge, a powerful competitive advantage in many marketplaces. In the early 21st century—on its way to becoming the most valuable company in the world—Apple Inc would have made most people's lists as the consummate, innovative company.

Sometimes—on an even grander scale than breakthrough products and services—innovation has led to completely new industries. Many are in the "sharing economy." Airbnb facilitates the renting out of homes that are privately owned but amenable to sharing with others. It has become the world's largest provider of accommodation but doesn't own any real estate.

Uber enables the hiring of privately owned cars, a space previously occupied by taxis customized for such activity. Uber is likely the world's largest taxi service but doesn't own any cars. Both Airbnb and Uber have connected buyers and sellers on a massive scale by means of business models that are nearly capital free.

There are many variants less well known than Airbnb and Uber. Boat sharing and caravan sharing for instance. Tool libraries exist to allow users to borrow tools and equipment for home improvement or gardening projects, reducing the need to purchase seldom-used items. Pet sharing services connect pet owners with people who want to take care of a pet occasionally.

These novel, new services all exploit the connection between the internet and a smartphone to achieve greater use of assets that already exist as opposed to creating new ones for a specific purpose. In a sense, what was traditionally "work" has become digital orchestration—done innovatively. The physical form of something is enjoyed without the need to own it.

Also—within existing industries—innovation has enhanced customer satisfaction in major ways and moved almost relentlessly to address previously unmet needs.

A couple of examples.

Recognizing that some customers cannot readily afford the upfront cost of durable goods such as washing machines, manufacturers supply the machines at no cost, monitor usage and charge customers for each load of washing—rather than for the appliance itself.

And to reward good drivers, a car insurer utilizes in-vehicle telematics to charge drivers premiums that differ based on individual driving styles and associated risks, as well as on the amount of driving they do. Drivers can lower their individual insurance costs by proving they are a "good driver."

An innovative solution has also benefited the legion of property renters who face the cost of installing security systems every time they move—due to the permanence of such installations. A home security company has developed a battery-powered alarm system that requires no complex setup, works wirelessly with smartphones, and can be taken with them when renters relocate. Itinerant people can know the comfort of continuing, reliable security—without treating the purchase and installation as a sunk cost.

innovation

A ROUND OF APPLAUSE FOR THE INNKEEPER

WILEY'S DICTIONARY

WILEY'S DICTIONARY

With Permission by John Hart Studio, Inc.   7-17-06

But innovation has not been limited to business applications.

Environmental sustainability has also been a major beneficiary of innovation—as has society generally—in the areas of healthcare, education, and technological advancement.

Just one eco-friendly example.

To address the challenge of excessive packaging and the environmental issues it creates, an online retailer partners with others to design right-sized product packaging. Each item is packaged so it fits snugly within standard postal envelopes or typical courier boxes, eliminating the need for additional wrapping or padding. This initiative reduces packaging waste, avoids disposal and dumping issues, and significantly lowers transport volume and shipping costs.

All the above accounts are illustrations of innovating that a broad sweep through the field can uncover. If we cut through the many and varied new products, services, applications, and techniques that have been spawned, we can find two common threads applying to them all:

- Value that was not there previously is generated

- Value is created through the implementation of novel ideas

This sees innovating as the generation of value via the formulation and implementation of an idea that innovatively overcomes a problem and, in so doing, satisfies a previously unmet goal.

This insight into innovative value is fine as far as it goes, but it doesn't go far enough for our purposes. Certainly, our model is fundamentally about creating value as well, but from there we part company with conventional understandings of innovating.

It is not enough to merely create value.

Our model of innovating hinges on *how* that innovative value is generated.

(Incidentally, I prefer to use the term "generate" value rather than "create" value, as it better conveys the notion of deliberate intent. "Create" can imply some sort of unlearned talent. More on creativity versus innovation later in this chapter.)

Here is our litmus test for innovating.

We innovate when two conditions prevail:

- Our context always contains an obstacle stopping us from doing something we want to do. A problem is blocking a goal

- The idea solution that neutralizes the problem and clears the way to the goal generates value far greater than the effort expended

This imperative of Economy of Effort—where the result achieved is disproportionately favorable to the effort invested—has been emphasized and amplified already both in the Preface and the Introduction. The essence of our interpretation of innovating—the test by which we know whether we are truly innovating—is that the value generated is unexpectedly abundant.

Small effort → big result.

Enough said on that.

Going back to the diverse range of examples highlighted above, the message is clear: the fruits of innovation are ubiquitous, and the value generated is undeniable.

It is now time to look more closely at the genesis of innovating—the innovative idea that breeds the value that is enjoyed so widely.

What is an Innovative Idea?

As we have seen, ideas and innovating are inextricably linked. To disentangle ourselves from the chaotic world inhabited by the overlapping meanings and applications of the term *innovation* and its derivatives, we carved out a few examples of innovative value and the ideas that produced it.

Now we need to escape from the tangle of meanings attached to the word *idea*.

Our breakout starts with discarding the general notion of *ideas* and dedicating ourselves to ideas that are *innovative*.

It is axiomatic that if we cannot establish a clear profile of the Innovative Idea behind genuine innovating, it will be impossible to achieve any precision in our attempts to innovate. One of the most famous minds in history—that all-round clever person—Albert Einstein, is credited with saying:

If you can't explain it simply, you don't understand it well enough

It follows logically that if you don't understand something well, you will struggle to do anything worthwhile with it.

We do not want to be in that position.

So, what is an Innovative Idea?

To be practically helpful, we need a definition that recognizes the moments when we exclaim "What a great idea!"—when something surprisingly favorable has happened—way out of proportion to what the circumstances would suggest. The occurrence is unexpected—sort of magical and beneficial in a very satisfying way.

It feels good.

But this observation is not practically helpful. Einstein certainly would not regard it as a simple explanation of an Innovative Idea. It contains ingredients that are extremely difficult to measure and their existence or otherwise is likely to come down to feelings or opinion.

That said, I can now come at the issue from a much more reliable and illuminating perspective. In a sense, I have had a definition thrust upon me. Over many years of researching literally thousands of ideas I have judged to be innovative, I have gravitated to a set of criteria that could be word-smithed into a definition—or perhaps more accurately—into a *category* of ideas.

This of course does not make my definition or categorization superior to others, but it does have the empirical advantage of being founded upon thousands of successful ideas whose innovative efficacy in real life was—and often still is—obvious to everyone.

While these innovative ideas vary widely, they share several common features. One, however, stands above the rest. We have already encountered it, but because of its fundamental importance, it would be neglectful to proceed without revisiting it first. The innovative ideas share the common DNA of Economy of Effort. The value of each innovative idea dwarfs the effort that went into its generation. A relatively small amount of effort has caused a disproportionately big result. It's that *Small effort→big result* maxim—once again. This recurring imbalance between effort and value is the pattern I referred to earlier as a Sebir.

Most of the time, this characteristic is immediately obvious. Even if not explicitly identified, it is usually the aspect that prompts the instinctive "What a great idea!" reaction. We know intuitively we have just encountered something unusual—pleasingly out of balance—unexpectedly worthwhile.

But there is more to our Innovative Ideas.

In addition to Economy of Effort, my analysis uncovered four other attractive features they can possess:

1. Novelty

2. Simplicity

3. Unexpectedness

4. Inevitability

Adding one or more of these characteristics to economy of effort brings balance, harmony, and appeal to the innovative ideas, ensuring they are effective without being soulless.

Novelty

Innovative ideas usually contain a novel or fresh insight.

The roots of the word *innovation* go back to the Latin word "innovatio," which pertains to introducing something new or adding something new to what already exists. Novelty therefore is often intrinsic to innovative ideas.

A simple example of a novel addition to an existing product addresses the common frustration of finding washed cups, mugs, and glasses still wet after a dishwasher cycle. When placed upside down, the pooling of water in their bases prevents the dishwasher's drying cycle from working effectively.

The design fix is straightforward: standardizing a small notch in the rim of the bases of the vessels allows water to drain instead of collecting. With pooling prevented, the containers dry properly—and the irritation disappears.

Novelly innovative.

Simplicity

Often, after innovative ideas have been implemented, the solution is so obvious—so simple—we conclude it was bound to happen eventually anyway. It wasn't obvious before the event, but it is afterwards. Disarming simplicity in implementation—albeit identified in hindsight—is a common feature of innovative ideas.

One example conveying simplicity comes from the remote villages of a developing country, where mothers are supplied with tiny sleeping bags containing a paraffin-based pouch to keep their babies warm. Once heated, the sleeping bag can maintain its temperature for up to four hours.

However, a problem arises when the mothers—who trust Western medicines and devices to be unfailingly effective—warm the bags to only 30 °Celsius instead of the recommended safe level of 37 °Celsius. The numerical temperature is displayed on the sleeping bag's temperature indicator, inviting adjustment. Sometimes the mothers judge the number being displayed is too high and—even though the design of the bedroll ensures the temperature is always optimized—they reduce it to a lower temperature, putting their baby at risk.

To guard against this instinctive behavior, the temperature display is modified, removing numerical temperature levels, and replacing them with a reading that now reads simply "It's OK" when the optimum temperature is reached. This curbs the impulse for mothers to adjust the temperature to a lower level.

So effective. All that is changed is the form in which the information is displayed. The maximum desired effect is achieved with minimal effort.

Simply innovative.

Unexpectedness

Lots of innovative ideas produce unexpected or surprising results. When you think about it, a surprising result is not that surprising. If a needed solution is foreseeable and is easily predictable, it would be implemented already. The reasons for its unexpectedness are what has concealed the solution up until now.

A suburban barber with an established business is alarmed when a competitor sets up a shop nearby. The newcomer announces their arrival with a large prominent signboard advertising: "Haircuts Only $10." This price is significantly lower than that which the incumbent hairdresser customarily charges. Matching the $10 price will be costly and may prompt the newcomer to advertise at an even lower price level.

In response, the established barber does something unexpected.

He erects his own signboard with the following message: "We Fix $10 Haircuts."

Unexpectedly innovative.

Doing the Unexpected to Innovate

A microbrewery in Scotland, with a reputation for innovative and bold craft beers, launched a beer called "Elvis Juice," but soon faced a lawsuit from the Elvis Presley estate demanding they stop using the "Elvis" name. It was reported that one of the owners of the brewery changed his name by deed poll to "Elvis," making it possible to claim the beer was named after him and had no connection to Elvis Presley. The business eventually won the right to continue using the name "Elvis Juice." How influential their unexpected innovative maneuver was in this victory is unknown (to me).

Inevitability

A gratifying quality of some innovative ideas is that, once they are initiated, it is obvious they will not fail to deliver the intended result. They have an inherent, self-perpetuating quality that guarantees the outcome.

A reliable way of ensuring a desired result is achieved is to innovate in collaboration with physical or chemical laws—as they always do what they are supposed to do. A good example of this comes from a building operator who wishes to deal with the safety risk of fire doors not closing in the event of a fire because the mechanism that closes the fire doors is itself disabled by the fire. If this happens, the doors will not shut.

To ensure fire doors close automatically in the case of fire, a wedge of material is affixed to hold the doors open during normal operation. This wedge is so constituted that it melts when exposed to uncommon heat, allowing gravity to close the doors when fire liquefies the wedge.

The reliability of the fire door protection system—even in the unlikely event of a troublesome fire—is rendered inevitable by an idea that innovatively counters a potential weakness.

A comparable example is the use of bimetallic plates to control the opening of roof windows in a greenhouse, opening them only when conditions require. Bimetallic plates are comprised of two layers of different metals that react to changes in temperature by bending. When they are connected to the windows of a greenhouse, they bend causing a window to open when the temperature changes, inevitably ensuring the desired temperature control.

But inevitability in an innovative idea does not always require mechanical or immutable natural laws.

Consider the common problem experienced by commercial ventures undertaken by two or more people in partnership, where disputes or disagreements can result in a deadlock. This is particularly so where those involved have equal rights in an enterprise. An innovative mechanism to resolve ownership disputes and avoid expensive and protracted legal disputes sometimes found in partnership or shareholder agreements is a "shotgun clause."

The shotgun clause is a binding arrangement that forces a resolution of specified issues by allowing one party to propose a way forward that the other party must accept or counter with an equivalent alternative. For example, a joint venture agreement may permit one of the partners to offer to buy out the other at a considered price in the event of a major impasse. The other partner must either accept this offer or offer to buy out the first partner on the same terms. In either event, the innovative intervention means a stalemate is inevitably avoided.

Inevitably innovative.

And Where Does Creativity Come into It?

For the sake of completeness, it is worth touching on the concept of creativity and its relationship to innovation, because the two terms are often used interchangeably. That is not the case in these pages. They are not regarded as synonyms here. Innovating is seen to be different from creating.

Most commonly, creativity is associated with the "creative arts"—fields such as music, art, literature, design, fashion, and even culinary pursuits. There is often an implicit assumption that the creative skill involved is innate—unique to a particular individual. Something one is born with rather than something one learns. He is a gifted pianist. She is a gifted designer. That kind of thing.

In its natural form, creativity differs from our version of innovating because we do not regard the latter as something exclusive. The ability to innovate is not a talent that a person inherits. We can all do it.

However, innovation and creativity are related concepts. Both involve use of the imagination to birth something that did not exist previously and both are exercised in every field of human endeavor. Both rely on ideas that are new. A common distinction voiced on how they differ contends that creativity generates ideas that are essentially raw—regardless of their practicality—whereas innovation focuses on the implementation of ideas to realize a worthwhile benefit.

On this view, creativity is an integral part of the innovative process, the part that sparks the ideas that are put to valuable use.

This distinction doesn't affect us much because—as we will see—although creative thought does have a role when we innovate, there is one key area in which we diverge fundamentally. In being mainly about the generation of ideas—whether they are implemented or not—creativity nearly always involves what is called Divergent Thinking. This emphasizes the generation of the maximum number of ideas without initial regard to their quality.

Brainstorming is the best-known expression of divergent thinking.

The model we are developing here takes the opposite approach. It is based on Convergent Thinking. We innovate using a logical, systematic method to zero in on a single innovative idea that neutralizes a prevailing problem, not on many possible solutions.

We will look at brainstorming and divergent and convergent thinking in greater depth in the next chapter.

This Is Innovating

As full-time American baseball legend and part-time social commentator Yogi Berra reminds us at the beginning of this chapter, it pays to be clear about the destination before embarking upon a journey.

Otherwise, we could end up anywhere.

In our quest to innovate, we don't have to travel far to see evidence of innovation—or, more precisely pertinent to our interest—of *innovating*. The benefits are all-pervasive. Being conscious of the prevalence of these benefits is useful, because it leads to an appreciation of Innovative Value.

But there is certainly a fog of innovation. "Innovation" is a label applied to numerous and diverse endeavors. To distill practical lessons from the prevailing confusion, we must stake out our territory and clearly define the essential principles that will guide us.

Once we look more closely, we will usually see that whenever innovative value is evident, it has sprung from an original, imaginative idea. Such ideas have potency and appeal. They have efficiently resolved a problem blocking a goal or an unmet need. Generating them is the essential steppingstone to the realization of innovative value.

However, the generation of an imaginative idea is not sufficient for our purposes. Any such idea must genuinely deliver innovative value, and we have been quite explicit about what that looks like.

Small effort→big result.

Our innovative idea is one where a relatively small amount of effort produces a disproportionately large result.

Effort and result are incommensurable.

Although this imperative of economy of effort is always at work—and is always inherently obvious—it does not by any means render our innovative ideas unexciting. Someone could be forgiven for concluding this, especially when it is also remembered that our innovative ideas do not rely fundamentally on creative brilliance, but rather on a skill that is learned.

So, do we have something well fit for purpose but lacking vibrancy?

Certainly not.

Other striking qualities—novelty, simplicity, unexpectedness and inevitability—often accompany innovative ideas, bestowing upon them a sense of refinement and a subtle beauty.

These qualities don't drive the innovative solution; rather, they are attendant qualities—elegant, often exquisite in their own right, yet secondary to the result.

Interestingly, such qualities are reminiscent of a dimension of beauty celebrated in mathematics, because of its immutability. The English mathematician, G H Hardy in his 1940 essay, *A Mathematician's Apology*, expressed the belief that these aesthetic considerations—"unexpectedness, combined with inevitability and economy" alone justify the study of pure mathematics.

Perhaps we might be bold enough to say the same about our category of innovative ideas—and about the enriching reward that comes from mastering how to generate them?

2

HOW SHOULD WE THINK TO INNOVATE?

---

*The significant problems we face cannot be solved at the same level
of thinking we were at when we created them*

ALBERT EINSTEIN

On the short list—make that the *very* short list—of the greatest thinkers of all time, we will always find the name Albert Einstein, who lived from 1879 to 1955. He was one of the most influential scientists ever and is best remembered for developing the theory of relativity and "the world's most famous equation": $E = mc^2$.

It is therefore well worthwhile to not only note, but also to seek to understand the lessons he passed down to us—doubly so if we are seeking to think innovatively. He had specific advice about such thinking—such as the counsel opening this chapter. The implicit guidance it contains corresponds with Einstein's broader views on problem solving, the use of the imagination and innovating.

But more than just encouraging such thinking, Einstein insisted that to engage effectively in it, familiar ways of thinking need to be left behind. New modes of thinking must be adopted.

There is another less charitable quotation attributed to him that pertains to the realm of problem solving:

Insanity is doing the same thing over and over again and expecting different results

Even if it wasn't Einstein who said this, its message is still useful for our purposes. The critical point is that generating innovative solutions to problems is not going to happen if we think the way we always have, but just try harder. Fruitful acts of the imagination are rarely able to be conjured up at will.

First, our way of thinking must change.

Then our vision of what we can do can begin to change.

And only then can we begin the journey to innovate.

So, how should we think to innovate?

Our Cognitive Instructor—The Typical Process

When we acquire proficiency in a physical skill—say, like learning a musical instrument—or become competent in a handcraft like quilt making or woodworking, the learning path we follow is usually well illuminated. Music sheets or clear "How-To" instructions exist, and progress is easy to measure because there are unmistakable audible signals—the right notes—or visual evidence—appealing designs or the gradual emergence of a charming piece of furniture—that inform us of how we are doing.

We may even have a personal coach or instructor.

Acquiring proficiency in a cognitive skill like innovative thinking is not so easy. Plain instructions on how we should think to have a helpful idea are typically not available, and without them it can be impossible to know where to start or—even if we do—to know if we are making meaningful headway. As argued in the next chapter, even techniques like brainstorming—which produce a flurry of potential problem-solving ideas—are inherently unstructured and leave no clear trail to assess how close we are to solving the problem.

It is like traversing an unsign-posted terrain without a map or compass. If we are going to innovate with intent, we need some sort of *mental map* that reliably guides our thinking to our destination.

Good news: such a mental map is readily available—and acquiring it is as simple as thinking of the act of innovating as a process of inputs and outputs—rather than as a sudden burst of insight, a eureka moment, or a single, fortuitous event.

Comprehending and innovating through the lens of an input-output process is extremely powerful. After all, acting out an input-output process is a fundamental part of living. Much of what we do is an input-output process in action—from making a cup of coffee, to preparing a meal, to doing our jobs. Most of the time, we act in a purposeful way—the input—with a certain end in mind—the output. We train or study to become proficient in some field. We go out with friends to enjoy ourselves. We sleep to rest our bodies. These activities are all such a normal part of life that we don't consciously think of them as a process.

But, to innovate, we need to be intentionally process-minded.

The Natural Law of Action and Reaction

So how can we employ an input-output process as our mental compass to innovate?

To answer this question, we turn to another renowned scientist—who would certainly make the same short list as Albert Einstein. Although he lived more than 200 years before Einstein, Sir Isaac Newton exhibited innovative thinking, insight, and analytical reasoning comparable to Einstein's. His contributions extended into various fields such as universal gravitation, calculus, and optics.

But, first and foremost he is known for his three Laws of Motion.

Our interest lies with the final one.

The third of Sir Isaac Newton's Laws of Motion states that for every action there is an equal and opposite reaction. In the natural, physical world this is always true. The actions and reactions are equal in magnitude and opposite in direction.

We are going to take some license and treat this law as an input-output process. We will consider the action as the input and the reaction as the output. The way they behave can provide important, foundational instruction about how to innovate—no matter what circumstances we are dealing with.

When input-output processes are found in nature, they obey certain laws like Newton's Third Law of Motion without fail. Recognizing this and simultaneously recognizing that when it comes to human endeavors—such as when an action is initiated by people and a reaction eventuates—the incontrovertible Law of Nature does not necessarily hold. Equality of action and reaction is not assured.

It is often said that we tend to get out of life what we put into it and the notion has appeal because it seems fair. It seems natural. But, in human affairs—unlike in nature—the inputs and outputs are often *not* equal.

With every action we initiate, we seek to bring about a certain result, but our effectiveness in doing so can vary. For instance, we may well achieve what we are aiming for or, at least, obtain something commensurate with what we put in. Think of studying for an exam: if we prepare thoroughly, the result often reflects that effort. In this case—as in nature—the effort is matched by the reward it brings.

But then, unfortunately, sometimes disaster strikes—perhaps a failed business venture—and what we get back is negligible or even negative, compared with what we invested.

And finally, sometimes we get lucky—maybe a lottery win—where what we get back is significantly out of proportion to what we put in.

Successful innovative ideas are reflective of this last outcome—but we aim to generate them without waiting for luck to strike.

To help us innovate, we can compare the laws encoded in nature with the absence of similar laws in human activities. Frequently, processes and interactions initiated by people are unequal exchanges. When we bear in mind that the value on one side of the input-output process can exceed or fall short of the other, the possible effort and result outcomes can be represented simply in four quadrants:

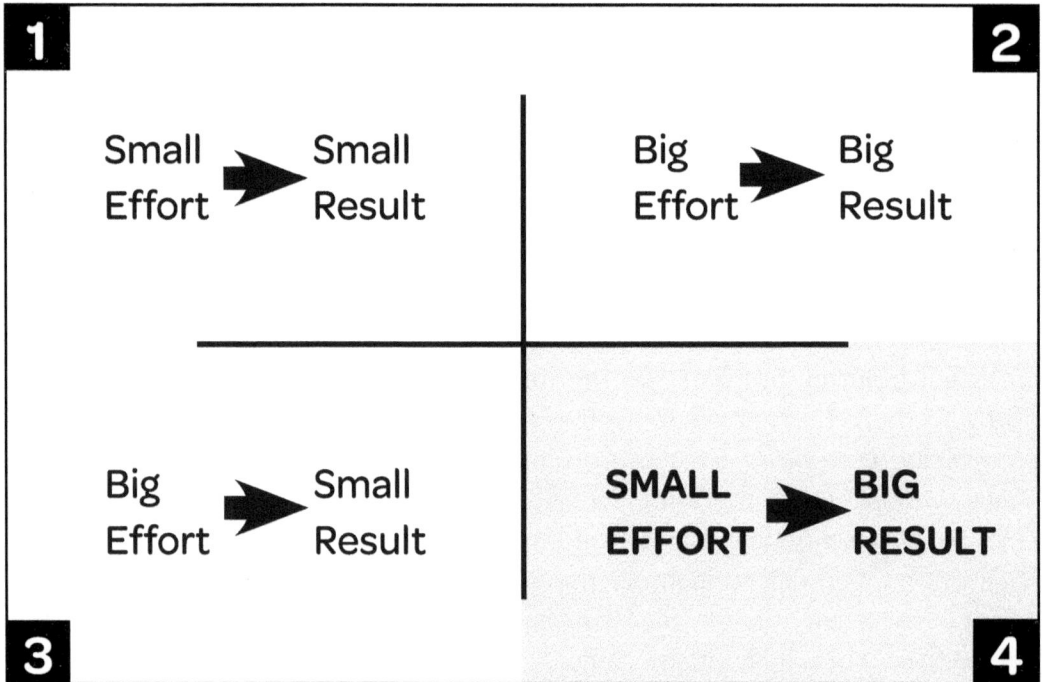

Quadrants 1 and 2—where the input efforts and the output results are essentially equivalent—accord with Newton's Third Law of Motion. And they align with the common sentiment that we should expect to reap what we sow.

Quadrant 3 is the failed business venture.

We are interested in Quadrant 4—the last scenario.

If human intervention can bring about unequal input-output results that are both good and bad, gaining insight into how to intentionally achieve a *beneficial* input-output result is theoretically possible.

This is the rationale that drives our adoption of an input-output process as our cognitive map.

Upsetting the Natural Order of Things

To think innovatively, we acknowledge the structure of the input-output process bestowed on us by nature with the sole aim of upsetting it—so the output produced significantly and beneficially exceeds the sum of the inputs.

Quadrant 4 in the figure above.

This *Small effort→ big result* consequence is what a successful innovative idea looks like. At its essence, it seems to create value out of nothing. It's as if two plus two equals five (or more). The imaginative manipulation of the inputs generates far greater value than conventional thinking assumes possible.

This is the mental picture we will retain in our minds to innovate. We will visualize a rewarding, unequal input-output process to direct our efforts.

Doing this is not as mentally daunting as it sounds. Once you are alert to the possibility, you will start to notice unequal input-output processes as a matter of course—and especially whenever innovating has occurred.

But don't take my word for it. Let's look at a common experience.

Be My Guest

Staying at a hotel brings with it a certain sense of freedom. We are paying for the privilege of course, but in return, we can relax and enjoy ourselves. We make the most out of what we are paying for.

Take our comings and goings. While not necessarily deliberate, when we leave our rooms, the liberty we are experiencing could lead us to neglect turning off the lighting, or the TV. Not such a big deal we would think. After all, we are paying.

Such understandable behavior does however cause a problem for hotel operators. They prefer that their guests use as little energy as possible in keeping with a comfortable stay. They prefer that lighting and TVs are turned off when guests are not in their rooms. They prefer that energy is conserved and costs minimized.

Of course they do.

Many hotel operators have solved this particular problem through intervening in an input-output process that is typically acted out by us, their guests.

When we leave our room, we take our room key (the input) so we can get back into our room on our return (the output).

This is normal behavior.

And for the effort of taking our key with us, we re-enter our room—the result—when we get back with relatively little matching effort.

Effort and result seem fair enough. They seem balanced.

Enterprising hoteliers have converted this seemingly equal input-output process into an unequal one—one beneficially unequal for them.

Building on the essential behavior of guests who usually take their keys with them when stepping out of their rooms, the hotel provides a tag that not only operates as a key to open the door, but also turns the power off automatically when it is removed from a wall slot by the door. And its reinsertion reactivates the power—which guests must do if they want lighting and TV—when they return.

So, the hoteliers innovate. They achieve a big result relative to the effort they invest. They do this by extracting unused value from the predictable conduct of their guests who take their key with them when they go out. In effect, the hotel operators coopt their guests to be custodians of the hotel's energy saving goals.

What was previously a relatively equal, proportionate input-output process—guests taking their room key to conveniently re-enter their room—has been transformed into an unequal input-output process, notably profitable to hoteliers, yet neutral in impact on their guests. The guests' behavior remains unchanged, but the *output* it produces is greatly amplified with relatively insignificant effort on the part of the hotel owner.

This is innovating: taking an existing input-output process, manipulating an aspect of it with economy of effort, and generating a new output that is disproportionately advantageous.

The natural order of things is upset.

We hope Mr Newton doesn't mind.

The Sebir Model

We will learn much more about how processes can be innovatively manipulated later but for now, the lesson is a simple one. When we set about innovating, we can do so most reliably when we envisage a process whose input and output are normally balanced and envisage changing it into one into one where the output value outstrips the input value.

Now is as good a time as any to return to our innovating model—the Sebir Model—we met in the Introduction.

This time, we will use a visual representation of the Sebir Model to facilitate a clearer explanation. This conceptual image deliberately contains minimal detail to help you focus on the overall structure. I want you to mentally retain this visual depiction, because discovering how to innovate through the lens of this image will do two things: deepen your grasp as we proceed, and accelerate your intuitive sense of where you sit within the complete framework at any moment in time.

The illustration of the Sebir Model below depicts an input-output process model that is unequal. The output visibly towers over the aggregate sum of the three input elements.

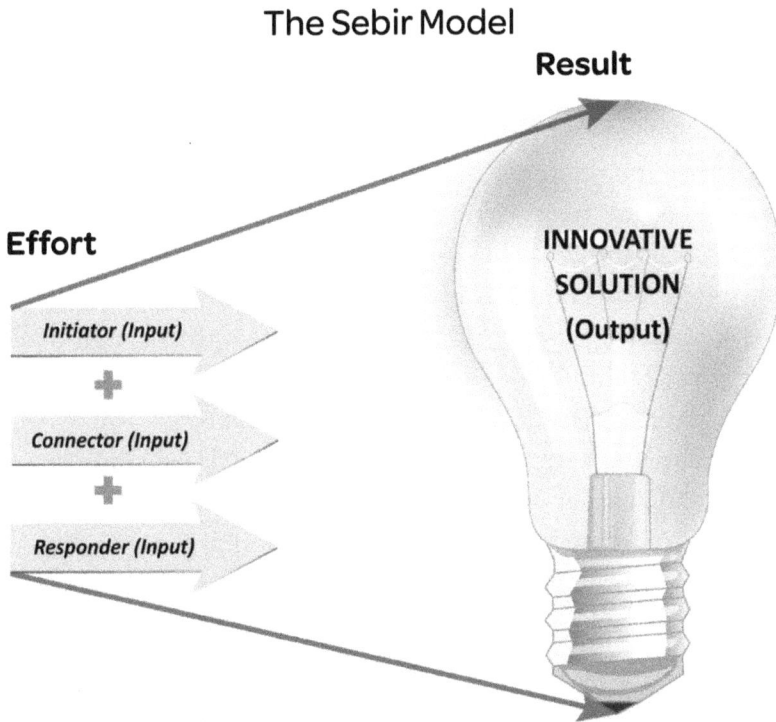

The Sebir Model

Result

Effort

Initiator (Input)

➕

Connector (Input)

➕

Responder (Input)

INNOVATIVE
SOLUTION
(Output)

As established in the Introduction, the three input elements are called the Initiator, the Connector, and the Responder.

Each represents one of the three sequential stages of the Sebir Model, and we will become proficient at navigating each stage as we move through this book. Although they each get their own chapter later, I will say some more about the Initiator, the Connector and the Responder now.

The Initiator is the first input resource that is manipulated to release the unused, residual value it possesses. Because this value does not have to be recreated, it is practically free. As will be explained much more fully in Chapter 17: Originate Through the Initiator Resource, there are three main ways in which the Initiator is manipulated. Without changing it much at all, the Initiator Resource can be primed to *do more of* what it normally does, *to do something in addition* to what it normally does and to *do something quite different* from what it normally does.

The Connector is the second input resource, and it facilitates the positioning of the Initiator and the Responder to maximize the likelihood that they will interact with each other without the need for additional coercion. Often this union can be guaranteed to occur. As will be explained much more fully in Chapter 18: Originate Through the Connector Resource, the three positioning strategies, in order of potency, *suggest, encourage* or *compel* interaction between the Initiator and Responder.

The Responder is the third input resource, the one ensuring completion of an innovative project and the realization of the value that solves a problem and achieves the goal. As will be explained much more fully in Chapter 19: Originate Through the Responder Resource, the behavior or performance that results is behavior or performance the Responder is already predisposed to deliver. It is poised to happen anyway. There are two degrees of response, depending on whether the Responder is a person or a thing.

With a person, choice is of course involved, and the responses range from what *is normal,* to what *is convenient,* to what the person *thinks is right* through to behavior in a person's *self-interest.* If the Responder is a thing, the thing always does what it normally does *physically, chemically, electronically* or *conceptually.*

As the descriptions of the three elements of the Sebir Model confirm, each is a resource—a fundamental concept when we innovate—with all the qualities we assign to the term. But more importantly, these three are not just any resources—they are the three core pillars upon which our entire model for innovating is built.

There are also Four Foundational Axioms that underpin the Sebir Model and our ability to innovate. All the logic and rules we harness to generate Innovative Value flow from these. The term Innovative Value is an expression we use most prominently in these pages. It appears more than 100 times. It is what we are aiming for; it is what we are formulating; it is what we will ultimately produce.

The four axioms are:

1. Problems are welcome and even desirable, because they reveal the path to Innovative Value

2. Innovative Value is the large but unwarranted, beneficial gap between effort and result

3. Innovative Value is uncovered, not created

4. Innovative Value is ubiquitous and readily accessible, not scarce and elusive

Axiom 1 is the pathway to everything we will learn with eight chapters devoted to problems and how we innovate through them. Sir Isaac Newton has helped us learn about Axiom 2. Axioms 3 and 4 are set forth more fully in the next chapter where the nature and source of Innovative Value are revealed.

Incidentally, I use the term "axiom" not so much for technical reasons but more to distinguish the four of them from the other principles, rules and insights that flow from them. The Four Foundational Axioms and the imperative of Economy of Effort underpin our entire approach to innovating.

Our Thinking Roadmap

So, this is how we should think to innovate.

We visualize what we are seeking to do through the transactional metaphor of an input-output process—but one initiated by humans.

Most significantly, we view success as an *unequal* input-output process—where the value of the output strikingly exceeds the sum of the inputs.

Only nature's processes produce equal inputs and outputs every time. These dominate the first two quadrants of the effort and result quadrant diagram we explored earlier. The third quadrant is a disaster—we want nothing to do with it.

But now we understand the secret of the fourth quadrant: *Small effort→big result.*

Admittedly, as a mental map, an unequal input-output process is still conceptual. To be reliable and practically useful, it must become more concrete. This is achieved through the Sebir Model. It identifies three sequential resource inputs—the Initiator, the Connector and the Responder—and these work together to forge the innovative output that is greater than the sum of their parts.

The Sebir Model is the dependable road along which we journey to innovate.

A final point.

Embracing an input-output model as our cognitive guide to successful innovating is a lot more than simply having a mental model versus not having one at all. It gives us an additional, compelling advantage—a process we can manage and shape. If we focus on a single innovative outcome in our efforts to innovate, we are engaging in an activity over which we have little—if any—control: a flash of inspiration, or a one-off, spontaneous solution to some problem.

It is a small, elusive target. A single idea.

We don't want to focus on tenuous, isolated outcomes which we cannot control. We want to focus on a process that we *can* control: the Sebir Model. This puts us in charge of a working framework with multiple points of leverage through which to innovate, not just a sole lever.

If we have a mind to innovate, then, let's acquire a mind to innovate.

Mr. Einstein would approve.

3

WHERE DOES INNOVATIVE VALUE COME FROM?

Perfection is achieved, not when there is nothing more to add, but when there is nothing left to take away

ANTOINE DE SAINT-EXUPERY

The line of argument we have been running until now is that, if genuine innovating has occurred, the beneficial value of the result clearly exceeds the combined value of the effort invested to achieve that result. *Small effort→big result.* An innovative maneuver has delivered extra, unexpected value. This value normally should not have materialized, but somehow it did.

Innovative Value is the gratifying gap between effort and result.

This brings us inevitably to the question that heads up this chapter: where does that innovative value come from?

A Perfect 10

This modern urban tale can help us.

If you are a visitor wandering the streets of Naples—Italy's third largest city—in the first decade or two of the 21st century, you soon become aware of the ubiquity of the Number 10.

Sometimes it is part of a poster, or part of a photo, or part of a painting. At other times, it simply appears on its own. It may be portrayed laterally on a flat surface or be represented three-dimensionally—as a one or two-part icon made from wood, ceramic, or some other material.

At first glance, the association between the Number 10 and the location in which it is displayed is not usually obvious. Most often, though, these locations will be commercial in nature, offering some sort of product or service.

But, what does it mean?

For the local populace there is no mystery. They are quite at home with Number 10. This is what they know.

10 was the number worn by one of the greatest players in the history of soccer, Argentinian Diego Maradona—while he played for Naples during 1984–1991. When he joined the Napoli football team, they were on the verge of being demoted from Serie A, the top tier of Italian football. During his time with them, Napoli enjoyed the most successful era in its history, winning the Serie A Italian Championship for the first time in 1986–87, again in 1987–88, and were runners-up in 1988–89 and 1989–90.

They also won the Union of European Football Nations (UEFA) Cup in 1989.

The effect on Naples and its people over this period was monumental. *La Dolce Vita* had come to the city. Gradually Maradona and his proxy—Number 10—came to be synonymous with ultimate success. It came to represent the epitome of excellence—of supremacy, of being at the pinnacle, and of succeeding with unmatched style. At minimal cost, Neapolitans could impute such qualities to their enterprise simply by incorporating the Number 10 in their business livery or communications.

And they still do. Sometimes Maradona is portrayed. Sometimes he is not.

The point is this. Number 10 is just a number among an infinite number of numbers. But, in Naples and its environs, it means a lot more. It has accumulated latent, unused value accessible by anyone who wants to tap into it. We could reasonably suppose that over time that value will eventually be exhausted but for the time being, it continues to be in demand and available.

The Number 10 is a good example of how any resource—even a conceptual or abstract one—can contain residual value that can be extracted and put to use.

And if that value already exists and can be retrieved with minimal effort, the conditions are ripe for innovating.

Everything that Exists is Underused

In Chapter 2: How Should We Think to Innovate? we acknowledged the symmetry of Sir Isaac Newton's physical Law of Nature where an action in one direction is normally offset by an equal and opposite reaction. We found it convenient to depart from that physical symmetry to embrace a non-physical asymmetry. Specifically, we embraced the notion of an unequal input-output process—where, impressively—a result is engineered that attractively exceeds the effort employed to achieve it. *Small effort→big result.*

This metaphor is useful, but, in truth, we cannot embrace it unthinkingly without confronting another reality.

Something cannot be created out of nothing.

So, where does the extra value come from?

After all, two plus two does not equal five.

The answer is one of those revelations that sits right under our noses, and it is derived from two of the Four Foundational Axioms that underpin how we learn to innovate—Axioms 3 and 4:

- Innovative Value is uncovered, not created
- Innovative Value is ubiquitous and readily accessible, not scarce and elusive

This is how the theory unfolds.

Whether shaped by human intention or arising within natural systems, everything that comes into being tends to serve a purpose—to provide value in some context. But for that value to be enjoyed, what is created must be used by someone or something else.

All this is obvious enough.

However—and this is important but usually overlooked—*there is always some value left over that is not used.*

Only if something is used perfectly—

- at the right time
- for the right time
- in the right place
- at the right rate, and
- for all potential uses

—is all of its inherent value exhausted.

And, as such perfection does not exist, there is always residual value that can be innovatively retrieved. As the French writer, poet, journalist and aviator, Antoine de Saint-Exupery, perceptively observes at the head of this chapter, perfection is not achieved until there is nothing left to take away.

This captures our conviction.

All resources are underused resources. Their value has not yet been fully harnessed.

Finally—and pleasingly—because unused value is embedded in any resource—effort that has been previously invested and does not need to be replicated for that left over value to be enjoyed—innovative value is lying there, just waiting for us to uncover it and make use of it.

Like Maradona's Number 10.

All of this might sound a little bit too good to be true but, it rests on a sound, theoretical foundation. Admittedly, proofs can be a little dry—but stay with me—this one is worth it.

Even Waste Possesses Innovative Value

To reinforce our central proposition—that all resources possess a residue of value that can be tapped to innovate—I will make the same point from the negative side of value. We have already shown that a resource does not have to be tangible to contain unused value; it can be conceptual, like the Number 10.

Let's push our theoretical contention further and test it against entities that have been discarded as *waste*.

If our basic hypothesis is that *all* resources are underused because they contain value not yet consumed, then surely a true test is that even waste must contain latent worth?

The term "waste" does not of course have favorable connotations. It is logical to think of waste as having no residual value—maybe even as having negative value—because usually there is a cost to dispose of waste. In fact, we probably would consider waste not as a resource, but as an anti-resource or non-resource.

Yet it can still prove valuable as this inspiring piece of history shows.

In May 1940, the World War II situation was a very depressing one for the Allies who had been driven back by the German army onto the beaches of Dunkirk along the north coast of France. Several hundred thousand British and French soldiers were trapped there and facing annihilation unless they could be rescued. While not as concerning as the potential waste of life, many thousands of items of military equipment would be *wasted* because they would have to be left behind.

In a striking example of how waste can be used to innovate, trucks initially destined to be abandoned proved to be of value—well beyond their original purpose when they were first shipped to France. The large-scale evacuation of the troops looked to be impossible due to relentless bombing by the German Luftwaffe and a shortage of jetty facilities. As part of Operation Dynamo, hundreds of small boats—fishing boats, pleasure craft, lifeboats, and even civilian vessels—had arrived to ferry soldiers from the beaches of Dunkirk to larger ships waiting offshore, but had nowhere to dock.

To address this lack of docking capacity for the multitude of small vessels, the British troops went back to their previously deserted trucks, started them up and drove them progressively deeper into the surf, parking them side by side. In doing so, they effectively created an improvised jetty—a platform of trucks—that provided much-needed docking space. This "truck jetty" allowed multiple small boats to come alongside the chain of *waste* trucks, greatly speeding up the loading and ferrying of the soldiers from the beaches.

In an operation often referred to as "miraculous" in historical records, 338,000 soldiers were evacuated. Although ostensibly of no value at all, the detritus of stranded trucks proved to be a source of innovative value that was literally lifesaving.

Waste as a Source of Innovative Value

In 2021, a German brewer based in Dusseldorf was facing significant losses due to a massive surplus of unsold beer nearing its expiry date. This had accumulated because of the Covid-19 pandemic restrictions that kept restaurants and bars closed. Instead of dumping the excess, unsold beer, the beer maker entered a partnership, collaborating with craft bakers who baked loaves of bread with beer rather than water. The resultant product was well received and went on to become an established offering. Expensive loss due to waste was avoided when that waste was recognized as possessing latent value, which could incorporated in another product of saleable value.

Anywhere and Everywhere

We began this chapter with a question: *Where does Innovative Value come from?*

Because really good ideas tend to be scarce, our natural inclination is to conclude that the circumstances that give rise to them—the wellspring of Innovative Value which emerges—must also be difficult to uncover.

The reality could not be further from this assumption. There is no need for special circumstances to exist. The nub of the issue is that innovative value is not dependent on the quality or otherwise of a selected resource. All it needs is for a resource to *exist*. Every resource contains latent, unused value, because every resource has been consumed or utilized only partially. None has been perfectly used because such usage is impossible.

To put it the other way, logically, it is *not* possible for a resource to exist that has zero residual value.

And, not only can a resource be something abstract like a number—the Number 10—but it can also be something that has negative value in a conventional setting—like waste.

Innovative value comes from anywhere and everywhere—from any resource that exists.

Internalizing this insight reveals why the wellspring of innovation is far more accessible than we might think.

4

BRAINSTORMING AND OTHER DIVERSIONS

Do not be so open-minded that your brains fall out

Often attributed to G.K. CHESTERTON

One of the world's largest advertising agency networks, Batten, Barton, Durstine & Osborn Inc., or BBDO, as it quickly became known (no surprise there), has been around for more than 100 years, but it almost didn't make it past its first 20. In 1939, profits were declining and one of its co-founders, Roy Durstine, left to start up an independent advertising agency that would be in competition with BBDO.

Things were not looking good.

A second cofounder, Alex F. Osborn, had a passion for creative thinking and turned to BBDO's employees for ideas to arrest the downturn in the agency's fortunes. As a result of this collaboration, he produced a manual entitled *How to Think Up* and this notion of "thinking up" evolved into the process we now know as Brainstorming.

Osborn's initiative worked spectacularly well for BBDO. By 1951—with its refreshingly novel approach to its clients' needs—BBDO surpassed $100 million in annual billings, becoming only the second USA-based advertising agency to achieve that milestone. In 1953, *Applied Imagination* was published and in it Alex Osborn popularized the process of brainstorming, convincingly illustrating its effectiveness with BBDO success stories.

From that time, brainstorming has evolved into the most common method used for creative idea generation in the business world and in academia. By 1958 eight out of ten of the largest corporations in the USA were using brainstorming to generate ideas. It also became a focus of research in business-oriented universities and institutions seeking to make it even more effective. That research continues today—with recent efforts exploring how AI tools can augment the brainstorming process.

At its core, brainstorming operates through intensive and free-wheeling group discussion, although there are rules Osborn instituted. For instance, every participant in a brainstorming session is encouraged to think aloud and suggest as many ideas as possible—no matter how outlandish or bizarre they may seem at the time. Judgment is deferred with priority being given to the quantity rather than the quality of ideas. Review of the ideas generated is allowed, but only when the brainstorming session is over.

Although brainstorming has easily been the most popular method, it is by no means the only one. Other creative thinking techniques have been formulated and are in use. Among the best known are those created by the Maltese physician Edward de Bono who coined the term Lateral Thinking. This technique encourages approaching problems from different perspectives and breaking with established patterns of thought to generate creative solutions.

One of his most widely used methods is *Six Thinking Hats*, which systematically guides group discussion in a parallel fashion—where everyone metaphorically "wears" the same hat at the same time—focusing on one specific mode of thinking before collectively moving to the next.

For instance, when the white hat is being worn, objective facts and data about the subject are called for. Donning a red hat allows emotions, feelings, and instinctive reactions to be expressed. A black hat introduces critical thinking—emphasizing risks, problems and all possible reasons why ideas might not work. Its opposite, the yellow hat encourages optimism—highlighting opportunities, benefits, and ways to make sure the ideas succeed. The green hat promotes creativity and imaginative thinking about the matter at hand, while the sixth and final hat—the blue hat—focuses on the structure and strategy of the session—ensuring participation by all and keeping the thinking process on track.

Depending on how widely you wish to cast the net, there are many schemes and frameworks that can be called upon as aids to creative thinking. A 2005 book by David Moseley, *Frameworks for Thinking: A Handbook for Teaching and Learning*, evaluated 42 of them. These included de Bono's lateral and parallel thinking tools, as well as others like Bloom's taxonomy for hierarchical learning, Gardner's theory of multiple intelligences and Paul's model of critical thinking.

But we should pause here, as we risk straying too far from what is most helpful to us.

Staying closer to home, we need to limit our survey to specific idea generation— and confine it to the commercial sphere—to avoid drifting into artistic pursuits.

There are many business idea generation options out there although they vary dramatically in their essence and their practical fitness for the task at hand.

A comprehensive analysis of existing idea generation *products* was completed by Brian Glassman at Purdue University in a 2009 dissertation that lists and reviews *22 Activities and 25 Techniques/Tools*. He isolates nine *Full Idea Generation Processes* which he studies in greater detail. Of the nine, four exist in the form of books and had not at that time been converted into systematic how-to guides or software-driven processes; rather, they tended to be delivered by special-purpose consulting firms. Another four are based on research described in public articles (e.g., via the *Harvard*

Business Review) and merely describe the processes involved.

In addition to providing an exhaustive list of the available idea generation techniques—two findings that emerged from Glassman's work—and later research in 2023 when he was joined by James Hornitsky—are pertinent to our efforts to innovate.

The first was the conclusion that there was no model that could be harnessed to manage the entire idea generation process. Those that existed tended to deal with discrete aspects of the total activity, not the whole.

The second discovery was that the focus of idea generation efforts was organizational. There was a conspicuous gap in the market for tools that could be utilized by an individual.

This latter finding resonates with me. I recently did an AI-assisted review of the more than two million Groups on the professional networking platform LinkedIn, specifically searching for a community focused on exploring how to innovate personally—the mindsets, methods, and practical intricacies involved. Although there are at least several dozen well-known groups specifically focused on innovation themes, I found nothing at all in the individual "How to Innovate" niche.

It would appear that the gap identified by Glassman and Hornitsky still exists. Perhaps this book will help seed the beginnings of such a community—and the shared knowledge it implies.

Outside of serious research efforts such as those discussed above, there are literally hundreds of websites that have some connection—however tenuous—to business innovation and business ideas.

Finally, there is one other methodology I would like to mention. It goes by the name of TRIZ. For those of a Russian persuasion (or just plain curious), TRIZ spells out *Teoriya Resheniya Izobretatelskikh Zadach* and translates to *Theory of Inventive Problem Solving*. It is a problem-solving methodology developed by Genrikh Altshuller from his position as a clerk in a patent office in the former Soviet Union. He began work on the methodology around 1947 and continued to develop it with colleagues over the following years.

Although it was developed decades ago, I have a sentimental as well as strong intellectual attraction to the TRIZ system. While Altshuller deconstructed thousands of commercial patents to discover inventive principles and generic rules that could explain new, patentable inventions, I deconstructed thousands of innovative business ideas to discover patterns and principles that provide a foundation for innovating. I was also encouraged by Altshuller's belief in the premise that there are universal precepts underlying acts of the imagination that can be discovered, learned and systematically applied.

Another parallel is the concept of *ideality* that TRIZ embodies. My principle of AFTI—*Aim for the Ideal*—and *ideality* overlap in the sense that both seek to achieve the maximum—or *ideal* benefit—with minimal resources.

AFTI– *Aim for the Ideal*–is introduced in Chapter 6.

As a methodology, TRIZ is quite technical—appropriate for scientific problem solving—and is mainly used for fine-tuning inventions and resolving complicated engineering problems. These days it is practiced by specialist consulting firms around the world. Due to its technical complexity, it is more suited to those with professional expertise—especially in engineering fields—and who have had exclusive training in the use of TRIZ. This reduces its practical usefulness for those of us who are less technically inclined, even though it is exceptionally well grounded.

Divergent Versus Convergent Thinking

Except for TRIZ, a common feature which most idea generation techniques share is that they are ways of stimulating the brain to come up with lots of ideas. They are therefore relatively unstructured and tend to treat the brain as a "black box." Because we do not know with any precision how the brain has imaginative ideas, we tend to fall back on stimulating its "black box" *from the outside*. Even the label "Brainstorming" could be seen as confirming this. While a "storm of ideas" may be envisioned from the exercise, there is also the sense—more like a hope—that by "storming" the brain, it may give up some of its secrets.

Such techniques as brainstorming are examples of Divergent Thinking. They aim to generate as many creative ideas as possible. The expectation is always that among the sheer number produced, one or more of them will lead to a practical solution. The resulting ideas may be unique—and even innovative—although they will vary widely in terms of their usefulness. Some may be truly intriguing but entirely impractical from a resource, cost, or time point of view.

By way of illustration—just picking one at random—typical brainstorming sessions occasionally include a discussion about how to reduce food-related waste during consumption. The idea of developing edible plates and cutlery almost always surfaces, but concerns about taste, hygiene, and usability quickly and inevitably follow—leading to the conclusion that replacing traditional disposable or reusable utensils is impractical.

Back to Divergent Thinking.

The term was first coined in 1956 by the psychologist Joy Paul Guilford—he, despite the cheerful first name. At the same time, Guilford, almost inevitably, also identified an opposite approach which he called Convergent Thinking. Rather than spawning many potential solutions, convergent thinking follows a process that zeroes in on just one workable solution.

The difference between the two approaches can be represented visually like this:

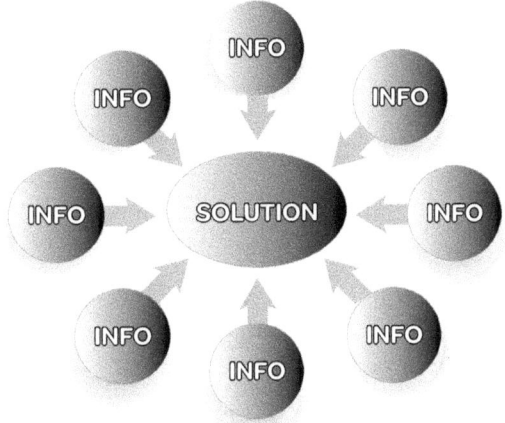

In contrast to divergent thinking, the Sebir Model described and taught throughout this book channels an overwhelmingly convergent thinking method. Instead of seeking to generate as many ideas as possible with the chance one will prove to be a practical solution to the prevailing prozblem, we will be unpacking components of the inherent problem and its context and using them to converge on a single, workable remedy.

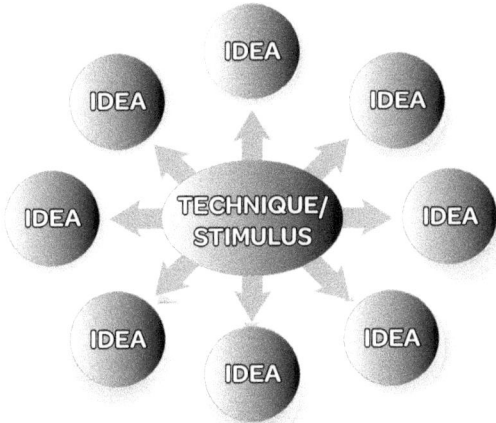

Our Lens

Opening up our thinking through techniques like brainstorming is a common way to generate imaginative ideas. After all, throwing off the shackles has an innate appeal. It is an implicit recognition of the unknowability of the human mind and seems to be a worthwhile initiative in such circumstances.

If we cannot precisely direct the brain, we can at least rattle it to see what falls out.

But we don't want the whole brain to fall out of course—as warned in a line often attributed to G.K. Chesterton, though its true origin is uncertain.

Being too open to every new idea can have the effect of steering us away from a coherent framework for innovative thinking rather than drawing us toward one. We are seeking a balanced approach that does not completely discard techniques such as brainstorming, but sees them as potential aids on the path to formulating a single innovative solution.

Indeed—as evident in PART 5 of this book where implementation of the Sebir Model is demonstrated—brainstorming can be very useful in generating possibilities and options to be considered as we move from learning to doing, and climb the Sebir Ladder.

Our brains are wholly capable of following logical rules, of building upon them and of adapting them. We are not limited to those that open the mind. We can just as readily accommodate those that concentrate the mind. Although counter-intuitive, intentionally limiting our thinking can be more effective than opening it up to endless possibilities.

As a rough analogy, divergent thinking and the techniques it accommodates are akin to using a shotgun to hit a target.

We prefer a rifle.

PART 2

THE CENTRALITY OF PROBLEMS

Arguably the most challenging proposition in this entire book is the argument that problems should be seen as friends rather than enemies. This is more than a rhetorical flourish or a mindset trick for staying positive. It's a practical truth rooted in an apparent paradox: problems not only block the path to some desirable goal but also contain the key to unblocking it.

Inevitably, embracing problems as partners and allies involves getting to know them intimately. They have a structure and follow a trajectory. By studying their anatomy and tracking their cause-and-effect movement, we equip ourselves to choose which of six distinct ways is best for tackling any problem.

But their contribution when we innovate runs far deeper than providing a menu of strategies. These are powerful but they only hint at the multi-layered mastery we acquire when we fully embrace problems:

- We can innovate through problems that we know exist

- We can innovate through problems that exist, but we don't know what they are

- We can innovate through problems that don't exist and so we invent them

Which is just another way of saying: the secret to innovating through problems … is to innovate *through* problems.

5

SEE THE PROBLEM AS THE PATHWAY

Problems are just opportunities in their work clothes

HENRY KAISER

Late in 208BC, General Xiang Yu, a brutal Chinese warlord from the Chu state, had a problem.

Xiang Yu had recently rebelled against the first dynasty of Imperial China, the Qin Dynasty, but the pivotal Battle of Julu was not going well. He sent an advance force across the Yellow River but on joining them a little later, he discovered those troops had been nearly starved by a prolonged siege. And even with those weakened fighters added to the men he had brought with him, Xiang Yu's Chu army was still heavily outnumbered.

His combined forces were inferior numerically and physically.

But Xiang Yu's response was remarkable. He deliberately gave himself and his men more life-threatening problems. He ordered the destruction of all their supplies and cooking equipment, except for what would be sufficient to sustain them for just three days.

This created an additional problem (self-inflicted)—a serious shortage of provisions.

And, while his men slept, Xiang Yu oversaw the sinking of all the boats they had used to cross the Yellow River.

Yet another problem (self-inflicted)—no escape route.

He told his men the next day that their choice was to fight and win quickly against overwhelming odds, or die without any hope of a retreat.

Faced with that persuasive incentive, Xiang Yu's army was spurred to fight with extraordinary fierceness and resolve. They found ways to defeat the Qin forces in nine consecutive engagements to ultimately win the Battle of Julu.

When and how Xiang Yu acquired such astonishing perspicacity is impossible to say. Maybe this insight developed over the course of his victories in the many battles that won him power over large tracts of China. Or perhaps his mentor was the Chinese general, military strategist and philosopher, Sun Tzu, who authored the book *The Art of War* about 300 years earlier. Xiang Yu could have been drawing upon

Sun Tzu wisdom such as:

Battles are won before they are fought

But whatever the reason, Xiang Yu certainly exhibited an insightful and radically different approach to problems. Instead of trying to minimize them—or overcome them, or avoid them—he embraced them. And not only that, he magnified them. In doing so, instead of being overwhelmed by problems, he was able to turn them to his advantage. He saw problems as friends and formidable operational allies.

Xiang Yu teaches us two valuable lessons about how to innovate through problems:

1. Cultivate the right problem mindset

2. See the inherent difficulty starkly and succinctly

We learn the first lesson from simply observing what Xiang Yu decided to do. We learn the second one from inferring how he arrived at that decision.

The Problem with Problems

An attitude toward problems such as Xiang Yu's is rare. Although a negative reaction to problems is normal—probably even in ancient times—this sentiment is possibly even stronger in modern times. For most of us, problems are something we prefer not to experience. We don't like them; we don't want them.

Out of sight, out of mind is an ideal category in which to lump them.

A quick dictionary-check experiment can make the point:

COMMON DICTIONARY DEFINITIONS OF "PROBLEM"
WIKTIONARY
A difficulty that has to be resolved or dealt with
OXFORD ENGLISH DICTIONARY
A thing that is difficult to deal with or understand
MERRIAM-WEBSTER
A question or difficulty calling for a solution or causing concern
COLLINS ENGLISH DICTIONARY
A situation that is unsatisfactory and causes difficulties for people
DICTIONARY.COM
Any question or matter involving doubt, uncertainty or difficulty

If Xiang Yu were to travel forward through time (presumably not by boat) and looked over our shoulders at this dictionary survey, I don't think he would find a description he would agree with. Although one of the dictionary definitions does also encompass the notion of a problem being something that requires a solution, the striking common thread of all of them is their tenor: they are overwhelmingly negative.

And that is the problem with problems—we are conditioned to regard them pessimistically. Our experience is reinforced by how problems are presented to us. They are not something we welcome.

They are usually seen as harbingers of bad news.

As human knowledge has increased—and more tellingly—as the communication and sharing of knowledge has increased—the undesirable role of problems has been amplified. Almost by definition, any explaining or recounting of the ebb and flow of human affairs must acknowledge the part played by problems. Progress is described and celebrated in its achievements *in spite of* the many and varied problems encountered along the way.

Rarely is advancement recorded as having occurred *by virtue of* those problems.

This worldview is not compatible with our model of personal innovating.

If we want to innovate intentionally, we must start with the problem stopping us from doing something we want to do. Therefore, the more intimately we know and understand that problem, the more likely it is we will be able to innovate through it. Instead of harboring a negative view of problems, we embrace them as we would a friend or helpmate. Even indifference to problems can hinder innovative efforts.

Our attitude toward problems must be unmistakably welcoming.

This is the first lesson from Xiang Yu.

The Opportunity with Problems

Problems are the pathway to an innovative solution.

Despite the prevailing prejudice against problems, there are some more enlightened views around. In his stimulating book, *The Obstacle Is The Way*, Ryan Holliday establishes his entire thesis on a few words written by the Roman Emperor, Marcus Aurelius, in the year 170AD. After a short prefatory discourse, Marcus Aurelius concludes with:

The impediment to action advances action. What stands in the way becomes the way

It would be a mistake to regard what Marcus Aurelius wrote about problems as merely a shrewd comment based upon the sweeping experiences his lofty position had afforded him. He wasn't just reflecting on the past—he was arguing for the need to see problems as the key to progress. Ryan Holiday elaborates on this from multiple perspectives in his book. Problems should be searched out rather than shunned. They should literally be embraced because they contain the hidden means to otherwise unobtainable ends.

From research I have completed into thousands of business problems that were solved innovatively, the path to an eventual solution invariably passed through the inherent problem. This is not to say those involved knowingly focused on the problem right from the start. Sometimes the solution was achieved through trial and error. Or, people stumbled upon an answer serendipitously. Occasionally, a known, parallel situation proved to be adaptable to the one at hand and a satisfying answer was put together by copying the essence of that analogous solution.

But even though what transpired may have been clumsy or lucky, a forensic look after the event reveals that—even in diverse circumstances—there is inescapable symmetry between the intrinsic problem and the ultimate solution. The negative and the positive co-exist.

This knowledge invites a contrary perspective on the nature of problems, a constructive, confident one. Oscar Wilde captured it well:

> *Between the optimist and the pessimist, the difference is droll.*
> *The optimist sees the doughnut; the pessimist the hole!*

We must be optimistic about problems to innovate.

And, once an understanding is gained of the essential, facilitating role a problem plays in the generation of a successful innovative solution, it becomes obvious that the problem truly is the pathway.

To build on this insight, a prerequisite to adopting this fresh view of problems is to settle upon a definition of them that recognizes both their negative and positive features. One that Xiang Yu would agree with.

This should suffice:

OUR PROBLEM DEFINITION

A problem is a difficulty that blocks the achievement of a goal and contains the means of achieving it

We are now oriented to evaluate any problem standing between us and a goal.

Undress Problems to Reveal the Opportunity

People from various fields have long discerned the Jekyll and Hyde character of problems and taken advantage of this sensitivity. Henry Kaiser, a 19th century industrialist and shipbuilder in America, opens this chapter with his optimistic take on problems being opportunities in their work clothes and Marcus Aurelias obviously saw them in a positive light almost 2000 years ago.

And we have Oscar Wilde's cheery, doughnut juxtaposition of the two perspectives.

Another American, John Gardner, a public official and educator, observed in the 20th century:

We are continually faced with a series of great opportunities brilliantly disguised as insoluble problems

Although the interpretation has perhaps been stretched a little, the ancient Chinese symbol for crisis has also been widely used to highlight the alluring contradiction that can be found within problems:

危機

The symbol is made up of two characters, and the argument that the first represents *danger* (or difficulty) and the second *opportunity* is a preferred representation used frequently in business education and, at times, in political communications. It was a favored rhetorical device used by US President John F. Kennedy in campaign speeches. Although some assert the explanation employed is apocryphal and that, strictly speaking, the second character really means *change* rather than *opportunity*, this hasn't detracted from the popularity of the device—nor its expository value.

It engages.

Whatever metaphor we prefer, the common theme running through all these depictions is that the beguiling underside of problems needs to be sought and found. We must undress problems. We must peel off any disguise.

In the end, we want to work with Dr. Jekyll, not cower before Mr. Hyde.

So how do we do that?

To make a problem work for us, we must be able to see it starkly and succinctly. This involves not only an unadulterated description of the obstacle but also visualizing what it can look like once it has been radically overcome.

It is important to avoid being dragged into an arm wrestle over how a problem should be defined or described. Intellectually rigorous explanations of what constitutes a problem are not helpful. This can be a complex area, and many books have been written about problem definition. How is a problem described? What is the root cause of the problem? And how do you know you have found it? Probing of that kind.

This is not for us. We have our definition—a problem is a difficulty that blocks the achievement of a goal and contains the means of achieving it.

And so, to the second lesson handed down from Xiang Yu.

When confronted with a formidable enemy relative to his own forces, Xiang Yu did not analyze his strengths and weaknesses.

Nor did he conduct a brainstorming session to lay bare all his options. He saw through to the actuality of his inferior, weakened army who were facing a seemingly unconquerable foe and focused solely on how he could overcome that brutal deficiency.

Xiang Yu's uncomplicated approach can be translated into a useful template for breaking a problem down into its primary components—simply, clearly, and nakedly. We will build on this later so we are fully primed to innovate, but for now, we'll start with the identification of the three primary components of a problem:

THE THREE PRIMARY PROBLEM COMPONENTS	
Problem Obstacle	This phrase contains one or more nouns that identify the barrier that blocks the reaching of a goal
Problem Cause	This phrase contains the Problem Obstacle qualified by one or more adjectives that identify *how* it blocks the reaching of a goal
Problem Solution	This phrase, which is exactly opposite to the Problem Cause, uses one or more adjectives to reframe the Problem Obstacle once a problem is solved and a goal achieved

To see this routine in action, we return to Xiang Yu and the situation his Chu army faced at the Battle of Julu:

XIANG YU'S STARK PROBLEM STANCE	
Problem Obstacle	**Chu Army**
Problem Cause	**Defeatable Chu Army**
Problem Solution	**Undefeatable Chu Army**

Although we cannot of course know for sure, here is a possible interpretation of what happened. To win the Battle of Julu with the reality of a weakened army—one susceptible to defeat—Xiang Yu seems to have acknowledged his own parlous state—a "Defeatable Chu Army"—and then visualized and focused on its victorious opposite—an "Undefeatable Chu Army."

How could he bring this about?

How could he ensure his men would not be defeated?

As we now know, he was boldly innovative and created irresistible motivation for his men to fight.

And they did so. In fact, they fought so fiercely that history records "Every Chu soldier taking on ten foes."

A credible conclusion is that it was the unembellished Problem Solution that Xiang Yu visualized which caused him to become so audacious and inventive. After all, conventional battlefield thinking wasn't going to transform the Chu army.

But, regardless of the accuracy of our supposition, we have a lesson we can use. Acknowledging the stark reality of a problem—the Problem Cause—enables us to see through to a dramatically contrasting reality—the Problem Solution.

Such a crystal-clear vision equips us to innovate. We not only see the problem—we see through to a diametrically opposite solution state that inspires us like never before. We consider the Problem Cause and do a mental 180—a radical reversal.

Incidentally, this is where the necessity of describing a Problem Cause succinctly becomes evident—a point that has been emphasized already. Mentally reversing a Problem Cause of two or three words is easy enough to handle. Achieving the same when a Problem Cause is fully articulated as a longer phrase or sentence can pose a much tougher mental challenge.

Let's pause here for a moment and take stock of what we have just done, because this exercise is the essential early step every time we innovate. We must be able to remember and apply the routine, and—as we will see in the next chapter and later—it has other important uses.

So, we will give the problem identification routine an apt name. There are various possibilities, but we will go with this: as we have achieved transparency by inverting a negative image (the Problem Cause) into a positive one (the Problem Solution)—something we have in common with the standard photographic process—we will refer to the problem encapsulation—the way the problem is captured and presented—as the *Problem PhotoBox*.

We will begin by constructing a Preliminary Problem PhotoBox—the foundation upon which the complete, fully operational tool will be built in the next chapter.

As will become increasingly clear over the coming chapters, the *Problem PhotoBox* is the indispensable tool when we innovate. For now, we will focus on its progressive formulation.

An early and fundamental challenge that arises during the building of a *Problem PhotoBox* is this: how do we know we have evaluated the problem sufficiently well to innovate?

Very easily. We use a single question. To determine if we have described Xiang Yu's circumstances adequately—or the circumstances of any problem we are confronting—we apply the following litmus test:

PROBLEM SOLUTION TEST

If the Problem Solution—which radically reverses the Problem Cause— is attained, does this mean that the goal has also been achieved?

If the answer is "Yes," our problem framing is adequate for innovating purposes.

It is obviously important that this test question can be answered with ease. If the Problem Solution is accurately described and is genuinely the reciprocal of the Problem Cause, the answer to the question testing the adequacy of a problem description will always be "Yes."

Once again, the virtue of succinctness demanded by the *Problem PhotoBox* justifies itself.

Building a *Problem PhotoBox*—initially by identifying the Problem Obstacle, Problem Cause, and a radically inspiring Problem Solution—can be done for any problematic situation.

Some Guidance with Expressing the Problem

A practical prerequisite to populating the *Problem PhotoBox* is expressing the prevailing problem in clear and simple language so the *Problem PhotoBox* components can be identified, extracted and described. But often, the fog enveloping a problem appears as an amorphous mass, making it difficult to isolate what the problem really is.

To cut through this confusion, we can borrow a little from metaphysical thinking— viewing the problem in terms of what the Problem Obstacle *is* or what it *does*. This sounds more abstract than it really is. We are simply using a different lens—one that gives us some helpful structure—to see a problem clearly, so that breaking it down into its component parts is easier.

There are four basic forms a problem statement can take. These fall into two opposing pairs.

The first pair relates to *being*—the state of the Problem Obstacle:

- It *is* something undesirable
- It *is not* something desirable

The second pair relates to *doing*—the action of the Problem Obstacle:

- It is doing something undesirable
- It is not doing something desirable

This can be illustrated by re-visiting Xiang Yu's problem stance from earlier. As we have not yet illustrated how the complete *Problem PhotoBox* is built, we will refer to our summation of the situation facing Xiang Yu as a "Preliminary" *Problem PhotoBox*:

XIANG YU'S PRELIMINARY PROBLEM PHOTOBOX	
Problem Obstacle	**Chu Army**
Problem Cause	**Defeatable Chu Army**
Problem Solution	**Undefeatable Chu Army**

If we were to transport ourselves back in time to just prior to the Battle of Julu—and gain an appreciation of the situation—we could express Xiang Yu's problem in four different forms.

We might begin with *is* or *is not* and state:

- the Chu army is *defeatable* in the Battle of Julu, or

- the Chu army is *not undefeatable* in the Battle of Julu, or

We might choose *is doing* or *is not doing* and state:

- the Chu army is *losing* in the Battle of Julu, or

- the Chu army *is not winning* the Battle of Julu

Each of these four statements approaches the expression of the problem in a different form but, in the end, all converge on the same core Problem Cause—"Defeatable Chu Army"—which leads to the same Problem Solution—"Undefeatable Chu Army."

Even if you don't consciously use one of these four forms and find stating what the problem is a relatively simple matter, the chances are you are emulating one of them intuitively.

However, if the problem feels fuzzy or hard to pin down, start by identifying what the Problem Obstacle is or does. Then use one of the four forms as a guide to express the problem clearly and simply. That clarity will make it easier to populate the Problem PhotoBox—and ultimately, to innovate by means of it.

This thought framework is not mandatory, but if the guidance proves useful, it is there to be drawn upon.

Follow the Problem Pathway— Even When There's No Problem

Having finished reading this chapter, you could be forgiven for thinking I am advocating the practice of inventing problems for the pleasure of solving them.

In homage to Xiang Yu.

Well, in a practical sense, I am.

Our opportunities to innovate are not limited to situations where we are faced with one or more problems. If they were, the entire approach we are advocating would be purely reactive—restricted to innovating only when we are on the back foot, under pressure or playing catchup.

We are about far more than that.

Take, for example, a new project you are about to embark upon. It hasn't had time to accumulate any problems yet because it hasn't commenced. When you are in this position, spend a measured amount of time—either on your own account or with a team of fellow stakeholders—to literally brainstorm anything that could conceivably go wrong once the project is underway. This will produce a sizable list of *invented* problems. With the problem-tackling techniques you will learn in the following six chapters, make plans to either preempt each hypothetical problem (best) or prepare innovative remedies to deal with any problems should they occur.

Befriend problems before they become enemies.

Then you can innovate on the front foot as well.

Back to Xiang Yu.

He was of course engaged in much more than an academic exercise. He invented a problem that enabled him to innovate in the face of a life-or-death situation.

And, at the fundamental level, he also demonstrated that provided a problem is diagnosed without fuss—looked at stripped bare—it compels concentration on what is needed to achieve a desired state that is a perfectly opposed utopia.

Our emerging *Problem PhotoBox* technique works by first clearly articulating the Problem Cause. We then define the Problem Solution as its ideal, mirror opposite. As we will see, this both sharpens focus and channels our thinking toward a narrow set of tightly defined options that align with the sought-after Problem Solution.

Finally—going back to the history books—it would be possible to gain the impression Xiang Yu was a solitary pioneer in employing the option of self-inflicted marine sabotage as an innovative military strategy. That it was a quirky one-off.

But this is not so.

More than 1700 years later, in 1519AD, the Spanish conquistador Hernan Cortes did the same thing. He led the first expedition that caused the fall of the Aztec empire, but after he and his men landed at Veracruz, on the East Coast of Mexico, he sank his own ships. Although his men longed to return home—with all their options for doing so eliminated—they quickly re-focused on helping Cortes follow the problem pathway to achieve his expeditionary goals.

There are probably other such stories, albeit untold. The legacies of innovating are not newly discovered phenomena, but riches now recognized, comprehended and preserved for our instruction.

For now, we have constructed the Preliminary *Problem PhotoBox*—sufficient to frame a problem with clarity and direction. In the next chapter, we complete the *Problem PhotoBox* by adding the remaining components and transforming it into a fully operational innovating tool.

6

SIX WAYS TO NAVIGATE THE PROBLEM PATHWAY

If your only tool is a hammer, all your problems will be nails

MARK TWAIN

Folklore from the Puglia region of southern Italy, sometime during the 14th to 17th centuries, remembers an innovative tax dodging maneuver that is impressive.

Even by today's standards.

It concerns the trulli (singular trullo), the traditional, limestone huts in the Apulian town of Alberobello that characteristically feature pyramidal, domed, or conical roofs. Trulli were built using dry-stone masonry, without any mortar or cement. This style of construction is also found in the surrounding countryside where most of the fields are separated by dry-stone walls.

A popular belief is that there was a clever purpose in the mortar-less hut construction. Technically, the absence of mortar cement combined with the interlocking stone formation meant the trulli huts could be demolished with ease. Simply removing the pinnacle keystone in the conical roof was enough to reduce the dwellings to a pile of stones. This design of the "now you see it, now you don't" feature of the huts was apparently a stunning riposte to a building completion tax for which the local feudal lords would be liable. When the king's tax inspectors were scheduled to visit from Naples, the dwellings could be collapsed quickly.

No building, no taxes due.

And once the taxman had passed through, the stone huts could be readily re-erected.

After some polite applause perhaps, of pertinent interest to us is this question: how did such an extraordinary option even enter the thinking of those local property owners? After all, there is something about the gravity of buildings—something about their permanence—that automatically disqualifies any thoughts of their routine disposability. They are here to stay! Admittedly, the long-proven practice of local dry-stone wall construction supplied the means of building such dwellings, but it is still quite a step from there to seeing such construction as suitable for a house design that is reversible.

How did it happen?

While we can speculate about how the overlords arrived at their audacious solution, we cannot know for sure. Perhaps a belligerent comment or thought by one of the landowners along the lines of: "I'll destroy any property I own before I pay taxes on it!" may have led to literal consideration of such a possibility. Being prone to outbursts like this when confronted with an infuriating dilemma is not uncommon for any of us.

But—while it can be fun to indulge in a little guesswork—we don't need to know exactly how the Italian landowners got there. We need to know how *we* would get there. What we want is confidence that any path we are following to innovate can ensure that a brilliantly novel Problem Solution comparable to the collapsible trulli huts shows up among our options. We want this as a matter of course—not through a stroke of serendipity.

To do this, we return to our preliminary, partially-built *Problem PhotoBox*, which we met in the previous chapter. This time we will use it to ensure we frame our Problem Solution in a manner that leads to the exposure of the most innovative ideas.

Adding Perfection to the Problem PhotoBox

By way of a quick recap, the preliminary *Problem PhotoBox* encapsulates any problem in a snapshot of three components: the Problem Obstacle, the Problem Cause and the Problem Solution. The Problem Obstacle is the barrier blocking any goal, the Problem Cause describes what the Problem Obstacle is or is doing that makes it a barrier, and the Problem Solution describes the Problem Obstacle when it has been vanquished and is no longer a barrier to the goal being achieved.

A partial *Problem PhotoBox* capturing the tax problem faced by the landowners in Puglia would look something like this:

TRULLI HUTS PRELIMINARY PROBLEM PHOTOBOX	
Problem Obstacle	Property Taxes
Problem Cause	Property Taxes Due
Problem Solution	No Property Taxes Due

In a mimicking of the intrinsic process in photography—where a negative image is transposed into a positive one—the pivotal action in the compilation of any *Problem PhotoBox* is describing a Problem Solution that is the mirror-reverse image of the Problem Cause. Although we did not dwell on the matter in the previous chapter, this maneuver is our device for ensuring all solution options—even ones as outrageous as the collapsible trulli huts—are considered.

But seeking to describe a Problem Solution that is the antithesis of the Problem Cause goes beyond finding an informative phrase in contrast. It is much more than simple opposition. The Problem Solution must represent a result that is *perfect*—an outcome that cannot be bettered. The ideal.

When a Problem Solution is not only vividly conceived—but perfectly conceived—it excites the imagination to a far greater extent than the mere bringing of analytical prowess to bear on a problem. It is the catalyst for radical, innovative thinking about the remedy.

To demonstrate how this can be done, we introduce another empowering device, known by the acronym of AFTI. The term "AFTI" will become an essential part of our innovating vocabulary.

AFTI stands for *Aim For The Ideal*. It designates the mode of thinking that must be employed to achieve the required description of the target state that epitomizes the Problem Solution. The phrase is self-explanatory. Whenever we confront a problem blocking the achievement of a goal and begin to build our *Problem PhotoBox*, the final description of the Problem Solution is what we envisage a perfect result to be.

Although visualizing an ultimate outcome—setting an AFTI Goal—before tackling a problem might seem an unnatural diversion, it is not new behavior for most of us. We resort to it quite naturally—when we are negotiating for instance. Although not an exact analogy, we will often begin a negotiation with a claim or demand far exceeding what we are prepared to accept. We seem to know instinctively that we will eventually obtain the best result if we start by boldly exaggerating the boundaries of our expectations to extreme positions.

Similarly, envisaging a Problem Solution that represents an ideal—or extreme—outcome has the effect of maximizing the scope of the potential ideas generated. Setting a goal that is arguably outrageous forces the contemplation of possibilities that should be considered but do not normally enter our thinking because they are so outrageous.

Even though they may not be recognized as such, AFTI Goals are a reality of life anyway. On the global stage, they are employed to propel the cause of climate change. References to "net zero" have become a common AFTI Goal catchphrase in the drive for climate-related carbon reduction. An *ideal* sounding outcome. In innovating to achieve this AFTI Goal, the aim is to seek to achieve a *perfect* balance between the amount of greenhouse gases emitted into the atmosphere and the amount removed.

The world-wide sustainability mission also promotes a "zero waste" AFTI Goal. This lofty objective has spawned impressive innovative initiatives such as where major industrial producers create a "closed loop" system. Inside this, all materials are treated as "nutrients" that can be reused in the production process or returned without harm to the environment—a far cry from the early days of the industrial revolution.

Not surprisingly, the tantalizing appeal of a perfect—or "nil"—outcome has extended to the notion of an AFTI Goal of "zero cost" in business settings. While superficially implausible, businesses have adapted and innovated to achieve a costless state in aspects of their operations.

A famous and enduring example from Japan's manufacturing heyday is "Just-in-Time" manufacturing.

At the dawn of the 1970s, car manufacturers in Japan focused intently on significantly reducing production lead times while simultaneously lowering the costs of manufacture—an impressive AFTI Goal because it seemed to defy conventional trade-offs. Doing things better usually costs more. The major problem standing between them and their goal was inventory. Having all components unfailingly available when needed meant very high inventories were required and, inevitably, these were associated with high costs.

The ultimate solution was not a conventional one—such as using coordinated purchasing power to secure the lowest possible component prices. The latter would reduce inventory costs. While such a strategy has clear value, it pales in comparison to eliminating inventories altogether—completely removing their cost.

By partnering closely with suppliers, car manufacturers pursued precisely that goal. They arranged for those suppliers to hang on to all components and deliver only what was needed, exactly when it was needed, to the car factories. Deliveries were made daily, tailored to the specific requirements of each day's production schedule.

What initially seemed an overly ambitious AFTI Goal—shortening lead times while cutting inventory costs—was, in the end, successfully realized. A previous significant cost effectively became no cost.

So, with AFTI we are in good company. The range and quality of the solution options we consider in the final analysis depends solely on the extent of our aim. If we *Aim For The Ideal*—set an AFTI Goal—we unshackle our thinking so conventional mental constraints no longer apply. And the vibrancy of that vision motivates us and gives us the necessary momentum to achieve a gratifying innovative result.

William Ellery Channing, an American preacher in the early 19th century encapsulated the sentiment well when he said:

Fix your eye on perfection and you make almost everything speed towards it

Those are the conditions we want to create.

Building the Trulli Stone Huts

Although we cannot know precisely how the local rulers of Alberobello arrived at such an intrepid solution to their tax problem, what we can do after the event is revisit their preliminary *Problem PhotoBox* and—crucially—expose their AFTI Goal.

Before we do that, we must remember that a typical and entirely understandable response when we are confronted with a problem is to be proactive and immediately set about seeking solutions. This seems logical and it feels right. Getting on with the job of resolving the difficulty as soon as possible appeals. But—in omitting the step of setting an AFTI Goal—we are inevitably limiting the range of options within which an innovative result might be found. Radical, audacious possibilities are lost, never to be considered.

That's not for us.

Here once again is the preliminary *Problem PhotoBox* with the AFTI Goal highlighted:

TRULLI HUTS PRELIMINARY PROBLEM PHOTOBOX WITH AFTI		
Problem Obstacle	Property Taxes	
Problem Cause	Property Taxes Due	
Problem Solution	No Property Taxes Due	AFTI Goal

The Problem Cause the landowners faced is clear: "Property Taxes Due." In keeping with its essence, the AFTI Goal envisages the perfect situation of *no* property taxes being payable. With their dismantlable trulli huts, the feudal lords achieved this result.

But what if the landowners had responded in a more conventional fashion? All would not have been lost. They still could have conceived of several measures that would improve their situation—maybe sharing the taxes with a neighbor, requesting a contribution in kind from tenants who live in the huts, seeking to delay the payment of taxes due by agreeing to pay more later, negotiating some sort of reduction, finding a technical loophole in the ownership particulars, or even organizing a political protest—and so on.

All these options could potentially reduce the burden of the new settlement taxes, but all are predictable, run-of-the-mill courses of action. Because they are just that, none meets the requirements of the *Problem PhotoBox*, as the AFTI Goal envisages that zero taxes will be paid.

Deliberately seeing the Problem Solution as a perfect result—as an AFTI Goal— does not, however rule out any of these more obvious possibilities. We get them anyway. Compellingly, in a classic win-win scenario, the *Problem PhotoBox* exercise forces us to consider innovative alternatives in addition to conventional ones.

But, if the step of setting an AFTI Goal is not taken first, it is unlikely our minds will extend to possibilities that are radical enough to be innovative. Our thinking will remain necessarily orthodox.

Incidentally, in settling on the AFTI Goal wording of the Problem Solution, don't worry about right grammar or technically accurate antonyms. Often inserting "No" or "Non" as prefixes before the Problem Cause—as we have done with "No Property Taxes Due" in the preliminary *Problem PhotoBox* above—is sufficiently effective. Or the adjective "Nil". And—as pointed out in the previous chapter—being succinct when describing the Problem Cause pays off. It is far easier to imaginatively reverse a two- or three- word descriptor than an entire sentence that encapsulates the problem.

Now that we have adequately framed the Problem Solution, we stay with our emerging *Problem PhotoBox* and turn our attention to the Problem Cause and its derivation.

Adding Causality to the Problem PhotoBox

As we will discover later in this chapter, the decision about which of the available ways should be employed to solve the problem pivots on the problem's anatomy and trajectory. To gain a workable insight into the nature of the Problem Cause and how it performs its goal-blocking role, we check out the concept of cause-and-effect.

Cause-and-effect is rooted in the principle of causality. This is where a person, thing, process, or concept—all are a *cause*—influences the behavior or performance of another person, thing, process, or concept (all are an *effect*).

An effect is the direct result of a cause.

To put it another way, a problem exists because something gives rise to an action, phenomenon, or condition (the cause) which produces a result or consequence that has an undesirable impact on something else (the effect).

The cause of a problem always has an effect.

Understanding the cause-and-effect relationship—specifically, how the Problem Cause impedes the achievement of the AFTI Goal—is essential for identifying the most effective problem-solving strategy in any situation.

There are six ways of dealing with a problem.

But, before we can decide which one to use, we must identify both what *caused* the problem and the harm that is being *effected*. We do this by exposing the anatomy of the problem and the cause-and-effect trajectory in play.

We return once more to the *Problem PhotoBox* and will now expand it. For convenient recall, definitions of the three primary components identified in the previous chapter are shown below, along with two additions. Together, these form all five problem components—the complete set required to capture and understand the cause-effect chain that illuminates the full extent of the problem:

ALL FIVE PROBLEM COMPONENTS	
Problem Obstacle	This phrase contains one or more nouns that identify the barrier that blocks the reaching of a goal
Problem Cause	This phrase contains the Problem Obstacle qualified by one or more adjectives that identify *how* it blocks the reaching of a goal
Problem Solution	This phrase, which is exactly opposite to the Problem Cause, uses one or more adjectives to reframe the Problem Obstacle once a problem is solved and a goal achieved—**but now a *perfect* reframing**
Problem Object	**This phrase contains one or more nouns that identify the object that is harmed by the Problem Effect**
Problem Effect	**This phrase contains the Problem Object qualified by one or more adjectives that identify *how* it is harmed by the Problem Effect**

Now we will add the two new components to the *Problem PhotoBox* that we previously built for the landowners of Puglia and their mortarless, trulli stone huts. This gives us a complete *Problem PhotoBox*:

TRULLI HUTS COMPLETE PROBLEM PHOTOBOX		
Problem Obstacle	**Property Taxes**	
Problem Cause	**Property Taxes Due**	
Problem Solution	**No Property Taxes Due**	**AFTI Goal**
Problem Object	**Landowners**	
Problem Effect	**Tax Liable Landowners**	

The expanded—and complete—*Problem PhotoBox* is now much more useful to us. In addition to exposing the ideal Problem Solution, it also encapsulates the anatomy and cause-and-effect trajectory as they relate to the problem blocking the goal.

We are now capable of selecting from the six ways available to us for innovating through a problem. Intrinsic to this selection decision is clarity about what caused a problem and the harm being done. The *Problem PhotoBox* gives us such clarity. (For readers who wish to make use of this tool immediately, a template of the *Problem PhotoBox* with instructions on how to populate it is contained in Appendix A.)

A final comment on the formulation of the AFTI Goal.

As we will see in our "How-To" guide in PART 5—The Sebir Ladder—the path to an AFTI Goal spans two steps on the Ladder. When we first encounter a goal-blocking problem, what it prevents us from doing draws attention to a goal we are currently unable to reach. This is our Preliminary Goal. But don't dismiss it because of the word "preliminary." It plays a vital role: it helps us identify and describe the five components making up the Problem PhotoBox, especially the Problem Cause.

Our ultimate destination is the AFTI Goal, but we cannot define it until we have clearly identified the Problem Cause. That Cause is, in effect, the inverse—albeit an unwelcome one—of the ideal we aim to achieve. Inverting the Problem Cause into the ideal Problem Solution gives shape to the final expression of the AFTI Goal.

The AFTI Goal then eclipses the Preliminary Goal.

Six Ways

Each of the six ways to innovate through problems is dealt with separately and in detail in the next six chapters. Accordingly, I will just introduce them here and add some brief descriptive comments for each. I use short names to label each way—with the accent on the type of action it involves. The comments that follow each way highlight its distinctiveness, noting whether the focus is on the cause (mostly) or on the effect of the problem (once).

To maximize the prospect of generating an innovative solution to achieve an AFTI Goal—an ideal state as radically removed as possible from the current, undesirable state—the six ways are necessarily aggressive. Accordingly, I have found it useful to think in terms of a military metaphor—seeing the problem as the enemy—and adopting action terms found in military planning and operations. In giving each way a label—for the sake of clarity—I have deliberately over-simplified and not yet differentiated each in terms of its specific relationship to the cause-and-effect trajectory. That will occur over the upcoming six chapters.

The four military ways for dealing with the Problem Cause are:

- PREVENT the Problem
- AVOID the Problem
- ELIMINATE the Problem
- TRANSFORM the Problem

The fifth way, the one that deals with the Problem Effect, is:

- NULLIFY the Problem

A sixth way operates outside the cause-and-effect trajectory:

- PREEMPT the Problem

To limit repetition of the individual terms and enhance readability as we progress, *way* and *strategy* will be used interchangeably.

We will dive deeper into each of the six ways in the chapters that follow but for now, here is a brief description of what each entails.

PREVENT the Problem

This way is designed to *Prevent* the cause of the problem from having its undesired effect.

The distinguishing mark of this strategy is that it is employed when the cause of the problem embarks upon its usual trajectory but doesn't complete it. The goal being blocked is achieved through *preventing* the cause from producing its typical effect.

AVOID the Problem

This way is designed to *Avoid* the undesired effect produced by the cause of the problem.

The distinguishing mark of this strategy is that it is employed while the cause of the problem continues to operate and produce its usual effect. However, the blocked goal is still achieved by sidestepping the impact of that effect, rendering it harmless.

ELIMINATE the Problem

This way is designed to *Eliminate* the cause of the problem so there is no possibility of an undesired effect.

The distinguishing mark of this strategy is that it removes the cause entirely, so the effect never occurs. The blocked goal is achieved by extinguishing the source of the problem, rendering both the cause and its effect non-existent.

With the benefit of hindsight, we can say that this is the way adopted in the case of the trulli huts. Rather than tackling the problem cause or its effect, the feudal lords had to deal with neither. Both were effectively neutralized by eliminating the cause of the problem—the trulli huts that gave rise to the liability for property taxes.

TRANSFORM the Problem

This way is designed to *Transform* the negative cause of the problem into a positive cause, remedying what is happening so no undesired effect occurs.

The distinguishing mark of this strategy is that the cause and the effect are fused together, and the blocked goal is achieved by changing the nature of the cause—so instead of producing harm—it secures the desired result.

NULLIFY the Problem

This way is designed to *Nullify* the undesired effect produced by the cause of the problem.

The distinguishing mark of this strategy is that—like the Avoid way—it is employed while the cause continues to operate and produces an effect. However, the blocked goal is achieved by fortifying the object of the effect, so the effect no longer causes the harm it typically would.

PREEMPT the Problem

This way is designed to be implemented before any cause-and-effect trajectory is set in motion.

The distinguishing mark of this strategy is that it reshapes the conditions leading to a Problem Cause so they are no longer capable of giving rise to that cause and its resultant effect.

Which Way?

As we explore the six ways of innovating through problems and learn how to choose the most eligible one, we will find—unsurprisingly—the conditions making each way optimal vary from one situation to another.

Therefore—in the interests of both clarity and recall—we will dissect the cause-and-effect of a problem the same way every time, using the same mechanism.

Except for the sixth way—the Preempt way—our go-to device for deciding which strategy—or way—we should choose to innovate is the Problem Way Decision Matrix. This framework enables us to assess the extent to which a Problem Cause or Problem Effect can be modified. A potential way is either in or out, depending on whether the cause or effect can be manipulated, controlled, or influenced. If none of these actions can be taken, that way is ruled out.

This is what the Problem Way Decision Matrix looks like:

PROBLEM WAY DECISION MATRIX		
	MODIFIABLE	NON-MODIFIABLE
PROBLEM CAUSE (contains Problem Obstacle)	Prevent	Avoid
	Eliminate	
	Transform	
PROBLEM EFFECT (contains Problem Object)	Nullify	Avoid

The following notes explain and illustrate how to interpret and apply the Problem Way Decision Matrix:

- The two large left-hand sections differentiate between the cause of a problem—which inherently embodies the obstacle causing the problem—and the effect of a problem—which inherently embodies the object of the effect. The smaller rows that flow from them label five eligible ways

- The two right-hand columns indicate whether the Problem Cause and Problem Effect can be modified

- Each of five problem-solving ways is placed within one of the four outcome zones, reflecting the conditions that favor its use

The Avoid way appears in two zones by default, when neither the Problem Cause nor the Problem Effect is modifiable.

Reminder: as we will see later, the sixth way—the Preempt way—operates outside the Problem Way Decision Matrix.

Again—at the risk of stating the obvious—comprehending the trajectory of a Problem Cause through to its Problem Effect is essential. This understanding must include a clear view of the Problem Obstacle and why it is deficient, and of the Problem Object and how it is being impacted. Once this familiarity is gained, the modifiability of the Problem Obstacle and the Problem Object can be assessed. As recommended in the Sebir Ladder in PART 5, inserting the names of the identified Problem Obstacle and Problem Object in their respective sections in an operational Problem Way Decision Matrix is practically helpful.

Much more detail awaits as we work through a Problem Way Decision Matrix step by step in the next five chapters. Once we see the Problem Way Decision Matrix in action, we will realize it is easily handled and instinctively intuitive. For the moment, grasping generally what is involved will suffice.

There are three final preparatory comments that are worth noting. They relate to how we interpret the information that populates the Problem Way Decision Matrix.

First, even though we usually mention just a cause or an effect, it is important to keep in mind that we really mean the Problem Cause and the Problem Effect. Further, *cause* or Problem Cause inevitably includes the Problem Obstacle, and *effect* or Problem Effect inevitably includes the Problem Object.

Second, to evaluate the content of each Problem Way Decision Matrix and draw conclusions based on the context of the problem we are addressing, we use a Logical Reasoning Routine. In the spirit of Aristotle, who stressed reasoning according to circumstances, we assess what the Problem Way Decision Matrix recommends by testing it against the specific circumstances—the Situational Background—that comprise the context of the problem and its ramifications. Such analysis enables us to decide which way is the best choice, especially when more than one way is a viable candidate.

Third, an explanatory comment on *modifiability*—the pivotal concept in evaluating the anatomy and trajectory of a problem through the lens of the Problem Way Decision Matrix. Modifiability is interpreted broadly. A Problem Cause (including its obstacle) or a Problem Effect (including its object) is considered *modifiable* if it can be manipulated, controlled, influenced—or even replaced—in a practical and effective manner. Ultimately, that assessment depends on what the Situational Background realistically allows. Cost, time frame, and impact on the total system within which the innovative project is being undertaken are factors that will have a bearing. Such constraints are usually obvious to the owner of the problem.

Modifiability is a seminal concept in our efforts to innovate. It can categorically rule out one or more of the available ways to innovate through a problem and therefore its identification is a crucial step—especially when there is a choice of Problem Obstacle. Here, we can take a tip from our warrior friend—Xiang Yu—whom we met in the previous chapter.

This is a straightforward and powerful pointer.

Recall that Xiang Yu faced formidable foes at the Battle of Julu. Regardless of how Xiang Yu framed his problem, he had two choices for identifying the Problem Obstacle: his own army—the "Chu Army,"—or the enemy's army, against whom he was fighting. Both were certainly "obstacles". But note this: in hindsight, we can conclude that he chose a Problem Obstacle over which he had considerable control—his own army. Had Xiang Yu focused on the enemy army and concentrated on how he might "modify" them to achieve his goal of victory, it is doubtful that he would have succeeded.

So, here is the message: if you can choose from more than one Problem Obstacle in pursuit of an innovative solution—not always the case admittedly—anticipate and mitigate the modifiability challenge by choosing the one over which you have the most influence and control.

More Than a Hammer

When we encounter a problem, setting a goal that is at the antithetical extreme of the undesirable situation caused by the problem can effectively break the shackles of conventional thinking. This stimulates us to consider possibilities whose sheer audacity—so bold or unlikely as to seem absurd—would have previously hidden them from us.

The wider the spectrum between the Problem Cause and the identified Problem Solution, the more all-embracing are the potential remedies. When we set a seemingly outrageous goal, it has an infectious impact. It transfers its bold energy into the thinking we employ to achieve it. This is why we must *Aim For The Ideal*—set an AFTI Goal—when we articulate the Problem Solution for a Problem Cause.

To innovate radically, we require the full armory of problem-solving strategies and not much will be accomplished with the default setting of normal thinking. With homage to Mr. Mark Twain who opened this chapter, if your only tool for addressing problem-solving is the hammer of convention, all your problem-solving nail fixes will propel you toward mediocre results.

Nothing innovative will be considered or achieved.

Problems are not amorphous. Regarding them as constituting a formless obstacle blocking the attainment of a goal is a recipe for limited and undirected effort. Classically, a Problem Cause invokes a cause-and-effect relationship. A subject inflicts an undesirable action on an object. Understanding this trajectory and the different roles of cause-and-effect in different situations inform decisions about how to tackle a particular problem and the course of action that should be adopted.

The six ways of addressing a problem can be considered much like how an army might plot the downfall of an enemy. Therefore, intelligence about that adversary is essential if a chosen strategy—or way—is to be successful. The executed way might *Prevent* the enemy from acting or advancing, or it might *Avoid* a direct confrontation or an unfavorable situation. It might *Eliminate* one or more threats posed by the enemy; or it might *Transform* conditions that favor the enemy into conditions advantageous to itself. Changing tack, an army could *Nullify* its own capabilities against a potential breach by the enemy. Finally, and perhaps most impressively, an army could *Preempt* a battle—for example, by launching a targeted strike to destroy the enemy's weaponry, crippling their capacity to fight and winning the battle without it even needing to take place.

Discerning readers may detect a paradox has surfaced. In the previous chapter, considerable emphasis was laid on the importance of embracing problems as friends. In this chapter, we are turning on them and treating them as enemies.

But we are neither inconsistent nor contradictory. We are simply moving beyond an intellectual recognition that problems have two sides—the difficulty and the opportunity—toward a deeper acceptance of both to determine how we deal with their duality in practice. Contrary to how they are typically perceived, problems can be potent allies when we innovate, Getting to know them as friends is an essential first step before we disarm them as potential enemies.

To understand more precisely when and how the six ways should be employed at the practical level, we need to see them in action in different situations. These illustrations—in which each way will be made to run a gauntlet of logical reasoning— will illuminate what is involved and lead to the required proficiency.

The next six chapters are charged with this responsibility. One is dedicated to each way.

7

THE WAY TO PREVENT A PROBLEM

Intellectuals solve problems; geniuses prevent them

ALBERT EINSTEIN

Notwithstanding the penetrating observation above from the reputable Mr. Einstein, achieving an innovative result by way of *preventing* a Problem Cause from delivering its harmful effect is one of the lesser-used strategies. We discuss it before the remedial ones because logic dictates prevention now is always superior to remedy later.

Given its relative scarcity, examples of the Prevent way are harder to find than the other five ways of innovatively tackling problems.

There is a reason for this.

If something is prevented from happening, it is a non-event. Non-events are typically not very newsworthy and most of the time—unless something quite spectacular is involved—they fail to rate a mention. Life takes them for granted and goes on with barely a nod in their direction. There is little glamor attached to prevention. Not many medals are awarded for preventing something harmful from occurring. The cavalry always arrives after the need for deliverance is well and truly established and receives the plaudits once the rescue is completed.

Arguably, it is more glamorous to put out a fire—even if you are the one who started it.

This is not a new strategic insight. Our ancient mentor—Sun Tzu—whom we met in Chapter 5, acknowledged it in the 5th century BC in his treatise *The Art of War*. Much of what he advocated revolved around the notion that victory by *preventing* direct fighting was the paramount way to win battles. He then went on to note that the inevitable consequence for the successful protagonist of such a *preventive* strategy was:

> *Inasmuch as his victories are gained over circumstances that have not come to light, the world at large knows nothing of them, and he wins no reputation for wisdom; inasmuch as the hostile state submits before there has been any bloodshed, he receives no credit for courage*

Blood and guts are the stuff of heroes. Victories achieved over circumstances that have not come to light—because they have been prevented from doing so—are not heroic, as they are rendered invisible.

Accordingly, many well-deserved honors and celebrations remain unknown and uncrowned.

Fortunately, there are some exceptions—as the following story about some resolute animal rights activists illustrates.

When Prevention is the Cure

Seal hunters in the Arctic were after the beautiful, soft sealskin coats worn by young seal pups and in this quest were killing thousands of them, usually by clubbing the pups to death. Knowledge of this activity and concern for the plight of the pups was genuine among animal defenders but tackling the hunters directly was daunting to say the least. Most of the predators were tough, uncompromising individuals, operating in remote locations far from the usual security and law enforcement safeguards.

And there were lots of them. Even if one or two of them were persuaded to desist, the positive impact on the pups would be minuscule.

Eventually, those wanting to stop the killing traveled all over the seal pups' natural habitat with spray cans of paint, applying a splash to the coat of every seal pup they could catch and restrain for a moment. The pups were completely unharmed and were not physically conscious of the marking they received.

But their sullied pelts were no longer of any value to the hunters.

The hunters stopped killing seal pups.

Although it is not clear exactly how they came up with their strategy, submitting the situation faced by the animal crusaders to the *Problem PhotoBox* is potentially enlightening:

SEAL PUPS PROBLEM PHOTOBOX		
Problem Obstacle	**Seal Pup Killers**	
Problem Cause	**Motivated Seal Pup Killers**	
Problem Solution	**Unmotivated Seal Pup Killers**	**AFTI Goal**
Problem Object	**Seal Pups**	
Problem Effect	**Slain Seal Pups**	

Now that we know what happened, seeking a Problem Solution—"Unmotivated Seal Pup Killers"—that is directly antithetical to the Problem Cause—"Motivated Seal Pup Killers"—makes perfect sense.

We can see that our heroic defenders were able to prevent the killing of seal pups by removing the incentive behind the Problem Cause—effectively stopping its effect in its tracks. The Prevent way proved highly effective.

Conditions that Point to the Prevent Way

Preventing the cause of a problem from having its undesired effect is the essence of the Prevent way. While the Problem Cause embarks upon its usual trajectory, it doesn't finish the job. What could previously happen cannot now happen because the Problem Cause is *prevented* from doing harm.

The Problem Way Decision Matrix below highlights the placement of the Prevent strategy and stipulates the conditions that represent the best environment for implementing it:

PROBLEM WAY DECISION MATRIX		
	MODIFIABLE	**NON-MODIFIABLE**
PROBLEM CAUSE (contains Problem Obstacle)	**Prevent**	Avoid
	Eliminate	
	Transform	
PROBLEM EFFECT (contains Problem Object)	Nullify	Avoid

To make the comments that accompany each Problem Way Decision Matrix as practically useful as possible, we will always start the evaluation of the way in focus— the Prevent way right now—by talking about any conditions that automatically rule it out. After all, if we are going to encounter a "Stop Sign" on any *way*, it's better to do so early, rather than initially enjoying favorable conditions only to hit impassable ones later.

If the Problem Cause cannot be modified—cannot be manipulated, controlled or influenced—the Prevent way is not an option. The cause must be *modifiable* (as delineated more fully in the previous chapter).

Except for the obvious situation where an effect has already permanently manifested, there are no other pre-conditions excluding the Prevent way.

We can also see from the matrix that when the cause of a problem is modifiable, the Eliminate and Transform ways are available to us as well. And if the effect of a problem is also modifiable, the Nullify way is an option too. This means we have three problem-solving options to tackle the cause and a fourth to tackle the effect.

So, which one do we choose?

Once the Problem Way Decision Matrix has prescribed which ways are eligible, practical considerations drawn from the background circumstances—affecting either the cause or the effect—will help us narrow down the available options.

Stage left, enter our Logical Reasoning Routine.

We reason by analyzing the cause (mainly) or the effect (sometimes) embedded in the situation. We evaluate their practical susceptibility to each of the ways that are eligible, and we do this in the light of the prevailing circumstances.

Usually, pragmatic realities will guide us home.

To demonstrate this, let's revisit the *Problem PhotoBox* that illuminated the story of the seal pup killers earlier in this chapter:

SEAL PUPS PROBLEM PHOTOBOX		
Problem Obstacle	**Seal Pup Killers**	
Problem Cause	**Motivated Seal Pup Killers**	
Problem Solution	**Unmotivated Seal Pup Killers**	**AFTI Goal**
Problem Object	**Seal Pups**	
Problem Effect	**Slain Seal Pups**	

The Problem Cause—"Motivated Seal Pup Killers"—was resolved utilizing a Prevent way, because it was possible to influence the hunters. However, we know from the Problem Way Decision Matrix that the Eliminate way and Transform way are also available when the Problem Cause can be modified or—more precisely in this case—influenced.

Why not one of them to deal with the "Motivated Seal Pup Killers"?

First, why not the Eliminate way?

Granting that passionate emotions may have been in play, we will give the activists involved the benefit of the doubt and assume the Eliminate way—somehow exterminating the "Motivated Seal Pup Killers"—may have been a thought but was never a serious consideration.

It's out.

What about the Transform way?

Again, it is highly improbable that reasoning with determined, unscrupulous, "Motivated Seal Pup Killers" would result in them reforming and changing their behavior.

Not likely at all. It's out also.

That leaves the Prevent way as the sole, compatible strategy for tackling the

Problem Cause of "Motivated Seal Pup Killers."

However, for the sake of completeness, we should acknowledge that—since the Problem Effect is also accessible to modification—there is still the option of dealing with the "Slain Seal Pups" via the Nullify way. It is worth noting, though, dealing with the effect of a problem should be a last resort—appropriate when no other way is available or workable. Common sense tells us it is always preferable to neutralize the cause of a problem so it cannot have an effect at all. Only if the cause cannot be stopped, should we shift our focus to the effect.

Interestingly—with the seal pup illustration—the Prevent way and the Nullify way can both be discerned as possibilities after the event. The activists discouraged (prevented) the hunters from doing their normal thing by rendering the seal pups unattractive to them. But this can also be seen as an application of the Nullify way—which we will unpack in Chapter 11—that of protecting the object of the effect from harm.

Such overlaps of technique—where it is apparent looking back that more than one way could have been used to innovate through a problem—are not uncommon. When talking about the features possessed by innovative ideas back in Chapter 1, we looked at the often-present symmetry—such as inevitability and the quality of self-reinforcement. This is recognizable in the protection of the seal pups, where buttressing them from harm also results in that harm being prevented.

But, a caveat. Don't let the possibility of two or more ways potentially overlapping cloud your thinking about which way you should choose. Whether or not they overlap is largely academic. Always follow the priority of your Logical Reasoning Routine.

Other Stories of the Prevent Way

Despite the many impressive advances in medical treatment, ongoing intervention is often still required. For instance, although the insertion of metal stents in narrowed human arteries is frequently a life-saving procedure, over time the stents typically need to be replaced—because the artery contracts around them, weakening their effectiveness.

The stents—the Problem Obstacle—are clearly modifiable by their makers. But it is illogical to consider eliminating them and there is no obvious way to transform them without impairing their technically precise function.

They are a classic candidate for the Prevent way.

An innovative initiative is launched to tackle the stent replacement problem. It involves adding a protective coating to the metal stents. The coating's ingredients inhibit artery contraction (the cause) for an extended period and effectively prevent the usual impairment of the stents (the effect), resulting in massive patient benefits.

Just as engineers can prevent a medical problem before it occurs, organizations can use similar thinking to tackle challenges in knowledge management. A common problem faced by businesses is the loss of valuable knowledge and expertise when long-term employees finally retire. This cost is exacerbated when those who follow them make mistakes due to their inexperience.

To prevent this double whammy—immediate loss of expertise and the cost of consequent errors—a postal organization reaches an arrangement with those approaching retirement whereby they retire gradually—say, over 6–12 months—reducing their number of workdays on a progressive basis until they stop entirely. During the phased shortening of their workweek, they shadow and guide their replacements, imparting essential understanding and preventing many costly mistakes from occurring.

Geniuses Not Necessary

Although it would be nice if Albert Einstein regarded us as genius-level innovators because we have successfully prevented a problem from wreaking its usual havoc, the compliment would be undeserved given what we know now. We willingly join the company of the many uncelebrated heroes who have ensured a potentially damaging event never occurred and remained anonymous because of what they did—because they were so effectively innovative.

While a lack of romance and recognition comes with the territory when we prevent to innovate, it is offset by the quiet gratification of knowing what could have been—and knowing the part we played in so elegantly frustrating the potential aftermath. Prevention carries the appeal of minimalism and the sort of effortless harmony that goes with it.

Preventing problems instead of fixing them is its own reward.

Yet—despite its undoubted effectiveness and aesthetic appeal—the Prevent way of innovating through a problem is not always a choice. It relies entirely on the cause of the problem being modifiable—manipulated, controlled or influenced. If we can tick this box, we can plausibly innovate by intervening and preventing the cause from delivering its usual effect.

8

THE WAY TO AVOID A PROBLEM

After 25 years of buying and supervising a great variety of businesses,
Charlie and I have not learned how to solve difficult business problems.
What we have learned is to avoid them

WARREN BUFFETT

The conviction expressed above by Warren Buffett, Chairman of the Board of Berkshire Hathaway Inc, appeared in his Letter to Shareholders following the 1989 business year. He is known as the most successful investor the world has ever seen. From starting his own investment company in 1956 and then in 1965 acquiring Berkshire Hathaway—which was a struggling textile manufacturing company—he has grown Berkshire Hathaway to be one of the world's most valuable companies, worth around $1000 billion in 2024 (one trillion dollars, according to the American system of naming large numbers).

The "Charlie" referred to is Charlie Munger, who was Warren Buffet's partner from 1978 until Munger's death in 2023.

In his annual Letter to Shareholders, Buffet likes to pass on lessons and insights distilled from his success leading Berkshire Hathaway over many years. In amongst this treasure trove of advice and wisdom is where we find the second way to innovate through problems—by avoiding them.

It has certainly worked for Buffet.

It can work for us also.

Like many of the principles we draw upon in these pages, the strategy of avoiding problems is not a recently developed practice. All six ways of tackling problems innovatively have roots in the history of warfare.

Students of military antiquity might refer to the strategy of achieving a goal by avoiding the problem as the "Fabian Strategy"—which takes its name from a Roman general, Fabius Maximus—who lived during 280–203 BC.

When up against the Carthaginian general, Hannibal Barca—who had a formidable reputation as a strategist and who had previously crushed the Romans at the Battle of Cannae in 216 BC—Fabius Maximus adopted a strategy of non-confrontation, avoiding pitched battles with what he regarded as a superior army. He focused instead on minor skirmishes to harass the Carthaginian forces and disrupt their supply lines.

While lacking initial popular acclaim—especially from those who favored a more Romanesque, more overtly macho response—this line of inaction eventually succeeded. Hannibal was unable to draw the Romans into a conventional battle and as time went on, logistical complications mounted up, wearing Hannibal's forces down. Rome's relentless attrition eventually secured victory over Hannibal.

Without quite realizing it, most of us encountered innovation based on avoiding problems during the early decades of the 21st century. Simply engaging with—or even just noticing—entirely new businesses that seemed to appear from nowhere and rapidly scale to global size would have brought us into contact with it.

We met some of these companies in Chapter 1.

Uber, Airbnb, Facebook and Alibaba built large businesses by avoiding the problem of raising the heavy capital investment that usually accompanies rapid growth in their industries.

Uber became the world's largest taxi operator by avoiding owning any cars.

Airbnb became the world's largest hotel chain by avoiding owning any real estate.

Facebook became the world's largest media company by avoiding owning any content.

Alibaba became the world's largest retailer by avoiding owning any inventory.

Myriads of other companies have followed a similar "capital-free" model in numerous different industries. Although less well-known than Uber, Airbnb, Facebook or Alibaba, they all employ software and smartphones to connect customers with resources that already exist, avoiding the problems of cost and complexity that go with ownership.

To dispel the impression that the Avoid way is confined to larger, strategic problems, a micro example will suffice.

A producer of plant-based milk has an intractable problem. It has developed what it believes to be an appealing consumer alternative for traditional milk—a drink derived from plants rather than animals—with enticing health and nutritional benefits. However, in certain markets, the maker of the product is blocked by legislation from using the term "milk" to describe its offering. With the cause of the problem being entrenched legislation, the Problem Obstacle is technically accessible but extremely difficult to modify. A protracted season of expensive lobbying to change the applicable laws or gain an exemption is conceivably possible, but has a low chance of success.

The only acceptable option is the Avoid way.

And so, the company innovatively avoids.

For marketing and packaging purposes, they design and utilize an image depicting a cow amidst plant greenery adjacent to a glass of what looks exactly like milk—

and they use terms like "beverage" and "drink" rather than the word "milk," which is nowhere to be seen. It is obvious the product is essentially a milk product—albeit plant-based—even though this is never stated.

Although the prohibiting legislation still exists, the use of imagery instead of words ensures the letter of the law is respected but its effect is innovatively avoided.

The Avoid way contains an element of finesse that is satisfying. It represents innovating *despite* the problem, not because the problem has somehow been neutralized. After all, the problem still exists, but we don't need to tackle it to blunt its effect. In taking an innovative sidestep to avoid it, we can then ignore it.

Let's take a quick look at what happened in the proxy milk story through the lens of the *Problem PhotoBox*:

PROXY MILK PRODUCT PROBLEM PHOTOBOX		
Problem Obstacle	**Product Legislation**	
Problem Cause	**Blocking Product Legislation**	
Problem Solution	**Non-Blocking Product Legislation**	**AFTI Goal**
Problem Object	**Milk Product Name**	
Problem Effect	**Disallowed Milk Product Name**	

As with the previous, backward-looking analyses via the *Problem PhotoBox*, we cannot know how the plant-based milk producer came up with their innovative solution. But when the diametrically opposite—but ideal—echo of the Problem Cause is visualized—"Non-Blocking Product Legislation"—it is possible to understand how the solution could be arrived at—especially given the unyielding nature of legal regulations. Very plausibly, the product creator's thoughts ran to considering tactics that would ensure the legislation was rendered harmless even though it could not be changed. Avoiding the legislation made better sense than directly confronting it.

Conditions That Point to the Avoid Way

The Avoid way avoids the undesired effect of a Problem Cause. The Problem Cause follows its normal trajectory but the goal being blocked by it can now be achieved because the usual harmful effect of that cause is avoided.

Consequently, an Avoid way can be employed even though the Problem Cause is alive and its Problem Effect is still in play. This can be especially useful if there is nothing practically that can be done about a Problem Cause and the effect it produces. When this is the case—and it commonly is—both the cause of a problem and its effect cannot be modified.

Again, for ease of reference, the conditions under which the Avoid way can be implemented are highlighted in the Problem Way Decision Matrix:

PROBLEM WAY DECISION MATRIX		
	MODIFIABLE	NON-MODIFIABLE
PROBLEM CAUSE (contains Problem Obstacle)	Prevent	**Avoid**
	Eliminate	
	Transform	
PROBLEM EFFECT (contains Problem Object)	Nullify	**Avoid**

In line with the approach we used at this point in the previous chapter when evaluating the Prevent way, we begin by identifying any conditions that categorically exclude the Avoid way as an option.

Unlike the other ways, there are no absolute exclusion criteria—no "Stop Signs," for the Avoid way. It is the ultimate default option. That is why it appears twice in the Problem Way Decision Matrix: as a fallback strategy for tackling either the Problem Cause or the Problem Effect.

The matrix makes the choice of the Avoid way straightforward in situations where modification is not viable. It is especially valuable in such cases—offering clear guidance—without ambiguity.

Let's do some logical reasoning to clarify how we arrive at a choice of an Avoid way—other than arriving at it by default. We can do this by means of a hindsight assessment of Fabius Maximus, our innovator earlier in this chapter.

We learned how the Roman military leader persistently avoided any major battles with Hannibal Barca and eventually he was able to weaken Hannibal and his forces. The primary motivation for Fabius Maximus was not drawn from an astute understanding of military strategy. Rather, he recognized that Hannibal was a fearsome foe with a string of impressive victories under his belt. Faced with such an intimidating Problem Obstacle, Fabius Maximus wanted to avoid direct confrontation under any circumstances.

We can take an important lesson from this. When we come up against an unassailable Problem Obstacle in our innovating endeavors—like a Hannibal Barca on the battlefield or a prohibition enshrined in law that the plant-based milk producer encountered—we are likely to—or should—conclude spontaneously that tackling it head-on is downright unwise. There is no need to analyze the options for doing so. Instinct takes over and we revert automatically to the Avoid way.

The Avoid way is a clear choice when the Problem Obstacle not modifiable. But if the Problem Effect is modifiable, the Problem Object can be nullified.

So why didn't Fabius Maximus avail himself of the Nullify way and buttress the Problem Object—his army?

Based on what he knew and respected about the military capabilities of Hannibal and his hordes—their fearsome battlefield prowess—it is almost certain that Fabius Maximus, in his thinking, had exhausted all the potential combat strategies—including defensive ones—that would protect his soldiers. The Nullify way offers him nothing militarily different from what the other ways would if they were available.

Avoid was his only option.

And, as we saw, it was very effective.

Other Stories of the Avoid Way

A supplier of photocopying and scanning equipment to small businesses often loses potential sales because the capital cost of a machine is beyond the means of some of its small business customers.

To avoid this problem, the vendor supplies and installs the equipment at nil upfront cost in return for agreement by the customer to pay a monthly usage fee calculated from the metered throughput of the machine. A large, unaffordable initial cost is replaced with a small day-to-day cost—effectively payment per copied or scanned page.

This problem-avoiding initiative removes a common barrier to equipment sales and simultaneously increases the size of the market available to the office equipment merchant.

Similarly, we heard earlier back in Chapter 1 how a washing machine manufacturer avoids the problem of losing customers for whom the full cost of the appliance is prohibitive, by setting up a lease arrangement for such customers. Instead of buying and owning the washing machine, people can commit to a regular payment determined by how frequently they use it.

In essence—and in practice—they pay per load of washing.

Admittedly, with the decreasing cost of business and personal appliances, such initiatives are much less necessary now, but their past practice clearly illustrates the Avoid way in action.

A distribution business faces a continuing safety challenge because many of its workers injure themselves lifting items into and out of delivery trucks. Employees loading transport vehicles frequently make up for any gap in the truck-feeding conveyor system by picking up packages and manually moving them as required. Inevitably, this results in injuries. By installing sensor-guided conveyor belts—that automatically extend into the trucks, or shorten, depending on the position of the workers—the temptation for manual handling and the injuries it causes are innovatively avoided.

The Avoidance Doctrine

A casual web search of the concept of avoiding problems overwhelmingly comes up with observations that are negative. Cowardly rather than clever seems to be the verdict applied to someone who avoids. I guess it comes down to what is more important amid life's challenges: succeeding or succeeding with style?

I suspect the most popular answer is both.

Perhaps.

However, most of the time, we can't have our cake and eat it too. We must choose. The best choice in terms of fully realizing a goal may not be the most romantic or heroic.

But it could be the most innovative and therefore the most effective.

We started this chapter listening to some wisdom from Warren Buffet. It is no surprise he subscribes wholeheartedly to the doctrine of avoidance when it comes to contending with problems. Despite his prodigious success and wealth, he maintains a very simple, modest lifestyle and, at this time, still lives in the same house he purchased in 1958 in Omaha in the USA. When he speaks in public, he often pokes fun at himself. This humble and self-effacing demeanor translates into a down-to-earth attitude toward the problems he encounters through his business. If avoiding problems works best, that is what he does.

Warren Buffett doesn't need to be noticed.

The Avoid way is a disciplined, business-like strategy. If the Problem Obstacle is undeniably daunting, instinct takes us to the Avoid way—usually without much hesitation. But even if we don't embrace it immediately, Avoid is the ultimate fallback option when all else fails.

Learning how to employ it is therefore a prized ability.

What Warren Buffett and his partner Charlie Munger also learned to avoid is dying young. Charlie Munger died on 28 November 2023, at the age of 99. He would have been 100 just over a month later. Warren Buffett turned 94 on 30 August 2024.

I didn't uncover this aspect of their avoidance philosophy in my research on how to innovate through problems.

9

THE WAY TO ELIMINATE A PROBLEM

*I once knew a chap who had a system of just hanging a baby on the
clothesline and he was greatly admired by his fellow citizens for
having discovered a wonderful innovation on changing a diaper*

DAMON RUNYON

Damon Runyon (1880–1946) was an American journalist and short-story writer
known for his distinctive style of humor and satirical pronouncements on human
nature and society in general. Among the social phenomena he railed against was
the prevailing attitude to innovation at that time. The observation attributed to him
above was apparently intended as a witty if sarcastic critique of the then tendency—
and perhaps still so now—to celebrate innovations when they were impractical—and
even when they were nonsensical.

He probably makes his point.

Nevertheless, his parody does betray an insight—perhaps a begrudging one—
integral to what we will unveil in this chapter: innovating by eliminating the cause
of a problem. Obviously writing in a period before the arrival of disposable nappies,
Runyon hints at the Utopian state where a baby's diapers can be cleaned without the
unappealing step of removing the soiled ones from the baby first. In envisaging such
a shortcut, Runyon is recognizing the potential of innovating to improve the quality
of an intended result by eradicating one or more of the ordered stages that normally
make it happen.

Problems can be daunting, and we gain an extra dimension of satisfaction in
overcoming them if the cause of the problem can be eliminated.

So, imagine how much more we would relish such a result if the method of
removing the Problem Cause is both permanent and free.

I have a favorite story that satisfies both criteria.

The gist of it appeared in a 2003 paper by Jack Hipple, an innovation specialist
based in the USA, presented an InfraGard meeting—a partnership program between
the U.S. Federal Bureau of Investigation (FBI) and the private sector.

The tale is as follows.

To remain competitive—and indeed to survive—a family-owned firm that manufactures metal products must automate. Unless it decides to invest in a multi-million-dollar transition to robotic automation of its production processes, it will gradually lose its place in the market due to the steadily increasing make-cost-per-unit of the metal items it fabricates and the increasing efficiency of its competitors.

The automation decision is made, money is borrowed and the conversion to robots is completed.

Then disaster.

Offcuts of metal waste build up on the machinery, regularly jamming the equipment and bringing the robots to a standstill. In the pre-robot environment, a watchful machinist effectively intervened by brushing such waste offcuts away as they built up.

Typical engineering solutions for this unexpected problem involve a workaround, some sort of "fix"—an automatic broom, a protective hood or guard, perhaps a powerful blower, and the like—but these all exacerbate complexity, potentially adding to maintenance costs and slowing throughput.

There is also the possibility that the overall rate of production will be even slower than it was originally.

The investment in robots—aimed at achieving uninterrupted automation and competitive fabrication costs—is being repeatedly undermined.

Another problem is funds for further upgrading the factory are exhausted.

Let's have a look at their problem through the *Problem PhotoBox*:

METAL OFFCUTS PROBLEM PHOTOBOX		
Problem Obstacle	**Metal Offcuts**	
Problem Cause	**Disruptive Metal Offcuts**	
Problem Solution	**No Disruptive Metal Offcuts**	AFTI Goal
Problem Object	**Production Output**	
Problem Effect	**Disrupted Production Output**	

The ideal answer is "No Disruptive Metal Offcuts"—but without adding to operating costs or impeding productive output.

Otherwise, the solution is counterproductive.

A challenging expectation.

Seemingly impossible?

Not if we tackle the Problem Cause in an Eliminate way—which is what the owners of the firm did.

They focus on removing the activity that generates the metal offcuts altogether. The metal chip offcuts are accumulating because they have something to accumulate on—a flat area designed into each machine. If that flat area is not there, the metal waste has nothing to pile up on.

Following this line of thinking, the proprietors realize that they can achieve the desired outcome by taking advantage of the law of gravity. Gravity of course is a quintessential free resource—available to everyone. They remove the machines and reinstall them upside down. The inevitable result is that the residual metal offcuts fall immediately to the factory floor as they are generated. They can be disposed of from there later, when convenient.

This innovative maneuver does away with the compliant flat zones, shutting down any possibility of the flow of production being impeded due to waste buildup.

This insight provided the pathway to the ideal solution: "No Disruptive Metal Offcuts."

Admittedly, there is a one-off reinstallation cost with this initiative, but achieving an innovative solution that makes use of a free resource to achieve a clearly permanent fix would almost certainly be worth the cost.

Innovative breakthroughs like this demonstrate that the need to *Aim For The Ideal* cannot be over-emphasized. Had the Problem Solution *not* been described in terms of perfection—"No Disruptive Metal Offcuts"—attention would likely have turned to conventional ways of managing the offcuts instead. But such options would have remained limited by the usual thinking of those who knew the factory and its problems best. It is only when the radical vision of "No Disruptive Metal Offcuts" is contemplated that focused, innovative effort is directed toward making the seemingly impossible a reality.

This is what an AFTI Problem Solution delivers.

Conditions that Point to the Eliminate Way

The Eliminate way removes the cause of the problem so there is no possibility of it progressing to deliver an undesired effect. That cause is extinguished; it no longer exists and plainly it cannot give birth to a harmful effect.

Although all six ways of innovating through problems have their pros and cons, one notable advantage of the Eliminate way is its potency. Except for the Preempt way, the other strategies—either overtly or tacitly—acknowledge the Problem Cause still exists. The Eliminate way eradicates it—often permanently. If a Problem Cause can still deliver its harmful effect in the future, it is clearly best that it no longer exists.

As we highlighted in Chapter 6, the Eliminate way was employed very effectively by the landowners in the Puglia region of southern Italy, who ensured they would not be liable to pay any property taxes because the cause of the taxes—their trulli stone huts—no longer existed. The huts were dismantled.

It is self-evident that to follow the Eliminate way, both the Italian feudal lords and the metal products manufacturer must have had access to the Problem Obstacle—the mortarless hut structures that gave rise to the property taxes and the pile of metal offcuts respectively—to bring about their eradication.

And both items needed to be amenable to removal—to be capable of being modified as required. For the Eliminate way of innovating through a problem to be employable, the Problem Cause—more precisely, its built-in obstacle—must be able to be manipulated, controlled or influenced.

Once again, we can represent the conditions that favor the Eliminate way in the Problem Way Decision Matrix:

PROBLEM WAY DECISION MATRIX		
	MODIFIABLE	NON-MODIFIABLE
PROBLEM CAUSE (contains Problem Obstacle)	Prevent	Avoid
	Eliminate	
	Transform	
PROBLEM EFFECT (contains Problem Object)	Nullify	Avoid

We have already seen that the Problem Cause must be modifiable for the Eliminate way to be viable. However, before we can choose it, there is another "Stop Sign" to consider—a simple, rational check.

If it fails, there's no point going further.

This check pivots on a single, decisive question:

ELIMINATE WAY EXCLUSION TEST

If the Problem Obstacle is eliminated, can the AFTI Goal still be achieved?

We must be able to answer "Yes" to proceed.

If the system or essential process that contains the Problem Obstacle is necessary to achieve our AFTI Goal, the Eliminate way must be ruled out if it impairs either of them. We cannot blow up the engine and still expect to drive the car.

We can work through how to apply this test by revisiting the *Problem PhotoBox* from our metal products story:

METAL OFFCUTS PROBLEM PHOTOBOX		
Problem Obstacle	**Metal Offcuts**	
Problem Cause	**Disruptive Metal Offcuts**	
Problem Solution	**No Disruptive Metal Offcuts**	**AFTI Goal**
Problem Object	**Production Output**	
Problem Effect	**Disrupted Production Output**	

The Problem Obstacle is the "Metal Offcuts." If these disappear—are eliminated—can the metal products fabricator continue to pursue its automation and production goals?

Clearly the answer is an unqualified yes. The metal offcuts are an unwanted side effect of the production of metal products and—as waste—are superfluous. They have no immediate value. Getting rid of them is not only an option, but also a necessity. This means the Eliminate way is both possible and sensible.

Having ensured the Eliminate way is a viable strategy, our Problem Way Decision Matrix instructs us that *if* we can modify the Problem Cause (and Problem Obstacle), the Prevent and Transform ways are also contenders.

We will now engage in some logical reasoning by continuing with a post-event analysis of the metal products offcuts story. We will look at what we know about the background situation and examine the alternatives for dealing with the modifiable Problem Cause via the Prevent and Transform ways in the light of that knowledge. As we have already learned when evaluating the Prevent and Avoid ways in the previous two chapters, the practical realities embedded in the situation we confront will normally indicate whether a particular way is viable or not.

Because they are generated as part of the production process, we know the "Metal Offcuts" are clearly physically accessible by the metal products manufacturer.

So, why not prevent the "Disruptive Metal Offcuts" from having a detrimental impact?

The content of the narrative addresses this possibility. Any sort of preventive initiative is likely to involve significant investment and will probably necessitate expensive workarounds that potentially slow the rate of production even more. Automatic brooms, protective hoods, physical guards and the like are possibilities but are likely to be operationally limiting ones.

So, why not transform the "Disruptive Metal Offcuts"?

As the metal offcuts are essentially waste, employing the Transform way to convert them into a positive contributor to productive output is dubious. Probably the best that could be hoped for is that the offcuts are of value in their waste form as scrap metal or could be converted into something else of disposal value. That said, it is doubtful any such conversion would generate value or worth exceeding the damage caused to production by the offcuts.

To be thorough, we should acknowledge that, under the "Modifiable" column and adjacent to the Problem Effect row, the Nullify way is also available to us if none of the three strategies in the top left-hand zone is viable and the Problem Effect is accessible (which it is). However—as already pointed out—it should be seen as a last resort because clearly, tackling a Problem Cause early is a decisively smarter strategy than letting it do its thing and dealing with its resultant effect later.

Other Stories of the Eliminate Way

A shared problem of virtually all businesses is the need to reduce their climate footprint. This can be an ongoing struggle. A moment's thought reveals that the best response to all eco-unfriendly causes is, ultimately, to eliminate them completely. No need for ongoing monitoring, remedial initiatives and maybe even countering unwelcome publicity.

A producer of household items focuses on the pollution disposal problems caused by the residual internal cardboard tube within items such as paper towels and toilet rolls. This necessitates separation, collection and recycling of the inserts.

At worst, they may end up in landfills.

Pursuing the Eliminate way to innovate through the problem, the manufacturer implements design improvements that result in products whose utility is unchanged despite removal of their inner packing cylinder. The redesign negates the need for internal support.

Stripping materials from products in this manner without impairing their functionality is a straightforward example of innovatively eliminating a Problem Cause. It is a favored innovative eco initiative—a form of eliminating waste—but clearly incorporating a much more insightful view of all that *waste* entails.

The Eliminate way is prevalent in all spheres of business. It often appears as a response to the setting of a perfect AFTI Goal. When applied to a frequent target area in business—cost reduction—the goal becomes eliminating costs altogether, not just lowering them.

This may sound like a fantasy for most businesses, but once the first step of setting the AFTI Goal of achieving zero costs is taken, possibilities inevitably start to emerge.

A supplier of electronic items to consumers must maintain a large, expensive customer contact service center to adequately respond to the thousands of phone enquiries it receives daily about its products. Over time, its telephone operators have become proficient at navigating such customer interactions adeptly. Still, the large overhead cost of the contact center is a major strain on profitability. Reducing the expense involved is hazardous because inevitably the quality of the service provided to customers—a distinct source of competitive advantage for the business—will deteriorate, triggering an even more serious set of problems.

Given the dilemma any sort of reduction in the scale of the contact center poses, the management dare to envision eliminating such overhead cost completely rather than attempting to scale it back.

The initially daunting vision of a *no-cost* contact center evolves into thinking which spawns a game-changing innovative initiative. The effort is built on the back of the organization's phone-based expertise in serving its customers. They discover—because of the sporadic nature of inbound calls—their operators often have spare work time when the phones are not ringing constantly.

This realization prompts the electronics supplier to pitch their call-handling proficiency as an attractive amenity, offering it to organizations that need it but either cannot afford it or handle it well themselves. They offer inbound and outbound call services at competitive rates to other firms. To the extent they are successful, they transform their customer service cost center into a profit center—or at least into one that meaningfully covers its own costs—thereby eliminating much of the overhead expense they previously incurred.

Another overhead expense example that illustrates the Eliminate way well comes from the 1990s when many of the efficiencies of online shopping we take for granted now weren't on the radar. A retailer of men's clothing found the overhead cost burden associated with a well-located retail outlet a constant threat to financial viability. He was deeply aware that many men did not like shopping and visited his shop infrequently—only when they had to. He found it frustrating that he had to carry the overhead cost of remaining continuously open in a prominent location so that he was on hand for the infrequent visits which matched his customers' habits.

This frustration led him to ponder how he might eliminate such overhead costs, bearing in mind that without a physical location—more than 30 years ago remember—he could not survive.

Ultimately—by harnessing his understanding of many men's aversion to shopping—he closed his shop permanently and adopted the following model. He rented warehouse space for just ten days at a time, four times each year, during which he displayed men's clothing, advertising the event to "men who hate shopping." To encourage them, he offered bulk pricing bundles—for instance, two or three suits, six shirts, three pairs of shoes—each available for an attractive, fixed price. Men could get the dreaded task done quickly, most economically, and at a scale that postponed the need for another shopping trip for quite some time.

The retailer's overhead costs were effectively eliminated—replaced by what amounted to just over one month's rent of a warehouse per year.

Boosting Personal Efficiency by Eliminating a Cause of it

Personal efficiency is an area where significant improvements can be gained by eliminating the cause of a time-wasting problem. While overtaken somewhat by texting, a classic instance of this is phone tag: a person and an acquaintance repeatedly fail to engage with each other to hold what they consider to be a necessary conversation. Returned messages result in returned messages. The cause of this problem can be eliminated very simply by installing the following message on each phone: "Please leave a detailed message and I will get back to you if you need me to." This instruction encourages callers to explain the purpose of their call, including if they require a response, and, if so, what it needs to be. This tactic usually leads to the remote but satisfactory—and much less frustrating—completion of a discussion.

Press Delete

Although Damon Runyon clearly had his tongue firmly in his cheek when he launched us into this chapter with his observation, it is still passably entertaining to speculate about the practical implications of his conclusion. He proposed that hanging a baby—still clad in its soiled baby undergarments—on a clothesline could be an efficacious method of cleaning the undergarments.

What exactly was the remedy he had in mind?

Perhaps he was looking to the rules of nature—as did our metal offcuts champions above—who invoked the law of gravity?

Perhaps he saw rain doing the cleaning and gravity taking over once the contents of the diapers had been flushed out?

I suspect he stayed away from such details and even though they might amuse us, they are not what we recognize him for. What we welcome is his insight that innovating thrives when one or more of the steps that contribute to a required result are eliminated. The resulting simplicity invariably unleashes innovative value.

The Eliminate way reduces complexity while simultaneously unlocking worth. It is probably the most muscular of the six ways—lacking the subtlety of the others—because it completely extinguishes a Problem Cause, often doing so permanently.

The Eliminate way can be a triumphant way to go.

10

THE WAY TO TRANSFORM A PROBLEM

A pessimist sees the difficulty in every opportunity; an optimist sees the opportunity in every difficulty

WINSTON CHURCHILL

In 1993, spectators and participants gathered at the start of the Leadville Trail 100 Ultramarathon were intrigued by what they saw. There was a group of around six middle-aged runners dressed in togas, standing around, butt-smoking while they waited for the race to begin. Covering 100 miles over steep, rugged trails in the Colorado Rockies in the USA, the Leadville 100 is one of the most grueling ultramarathons in the world. The bafflement at these runners only deepened when it was noticed that most of the group were preparing to run the race in sandals made from old tires.

They were Tarahumara Indians from the Copper Canyons region of Northwestern Mexico.

Ultimately, the winner of the Leadville was 55-year-old Victoriano Churro, who was a farmer and the eldest of the Tarahumara runners. He was followed by Cerrildo Chacarito in second and Manuel Luna in fifth. The three Tarahumara were still bouncing along on their toes as they crossed the finish line.

Their performance was no fluke. A year later, another Tarahumara runner, Juan Herrera, won the Leadville, finishing in $17\frac{1}{2}$ hours and chopping 25 minutes off the course record. Then in 1995, three Tarahumara finished in the top 10 of the rugged Western States 100 in California.

Among these runners, injuries were notable only by their complete absence.

Increasing awareness of the exploits of the Tarahumara—running vast distances in sandals made from discarded tires—found its way into how running injury was thought about. It led to a striking realization: legs, not shoes (or feet for that matter), are the body's best shock absorbers. The way the Tarahumara Indians run—their running gait—not what they wear—is the reason they do not incur any injuries. Most jogging traumas do not originate from shoes or feet: the real culprit lies further upstream. The offending cause is the runner's style. In running lightly on the front of their feet, the Tarahumara employed a gait that minimized the stresses traveling up their legs, stresses that cause Achilles injuries and similar complaints.

In refining the mechanics of how they run, the Tarahumara people transform a potential cause of injuries into a catalyst for an injury-free running style.

This is the essence of the Transform way of innovating through a problem—inverting a harmful element into a source of benefit.

Conditions That Point to the Transform Way

The Transform way transforms a negative cause of a problem into a positive cause. Note the wording change from the other four ways. The really distinguishing feature of the Transform way is that the effect disappears even though the cause stays. The cause is converted from a bad to a good force.

In addition to its remarkable efficacy, the Transform way possesses gratifying, redemptive symmetry: something essentially detrimental transitions into something undeniably beneficial. That of turning a problem into an opportunity, a liability into an asset, a cost into income, a minus into a positive. The obstacle blocking a goal becomes an active catalyst, ensuring the same goal is now unblocked and achieved.

This is how the Problem Way Decision Matrix portrays the Transform way:

PROBLEM WAY DECISION MATRIX		
	MODIFIABLE	**NON-MODIFIABLE**
PROBLEM CAUSE (contains Problem Obstacle)	Prevent	Avoid
	Eliminate	
	Transform	
PROBLEM EFFECT (contains Problem Object)	Nullify	Avoid

So, what are the "Stop Signs"? What are the criteria that automatically block the Transform way?

Just like the Prevent and Eliminate ways, if the Problem Cause cannot be modified—cannot be manipulated, controlled or influenced—the Transform way must be ruled out.

Seen from another angle, the Transform way turns the Problem Cause on its head—so the first requirement is that the Problem Cause must be able to be modified.

And remember, the Problem Cause always contains the Problem Obstacle which—to be more precise—is what we really need to reach and modify. We cannot focus on the Problem Cause without focusing on the Problem Obstacle.

Let's return to the Tarahumara Indians to flesh out the choice of a Transform strategy.

The *Problem PhotoBox* recording the injuries experienced by the Tarahumara runners can be represented like this:

TARAHUMARA INDIANS PROBLEM PHOTOBOX		
Problem Obstacle	**Running Style**	
Problem Cause	**Injurious Running Style**	
Problem Solution	**Non-injurious Running Style**	**AFTI Goal**
Problem Object	**Feet and Legs**	
Problem Effect	**Injured Feet and Legs**	

Once again, we apply logic to the available information to reach a conclusion about whether the Transform way is best. We will also vet the other eligible ways when the cause or effect is modifiable—Prevent, Eliminate and Nullify—to assess their viability in the context of the Tarahumara Indians' exploits.

We will start with the Prevent way. Why is this not an option?

Given the millions of research dollars ostensibly spent on the design of running shoes with the aim of preventing injuries, common sense suggests a fresh investigation of those possibilities is unlikely to come up with any new discoveries—at least in the short term. We are entitled to stand behind the investment and expertise of running shoe manufacturers and leave the Prevent way to them.

The Eliminate way is next, but can be ruled out immediately, because eliminating "Running Style" is irrational. It fails on the grounds that the Eliminate way can never be employed if the Problem Cause—and its innate obstacle—must remain in existence. Runners cannot run without a "Running Style."

The final available option in the Problem Way Decision Matrix is turning to the Problem Effect and somehow buttressing it. But here—probably even more so than with the earlier discussion of the Prevent way—the Nullify way is essentially what all running shoe manufacturers have been attempting for a long time. The shielding of "Injured Feet and Legs" by means of specially designed footwear is very close to protecting feet and legs in other ways.

I think we can conclude the prospects for employing a Nullify way have been exhausted as well.

Although it is unlikely that they would have had any intellectual appreciation of the fact, the Tarahumara Indians wisely adopted the Transform way—by running lightly on the front of their feet—to overcome the potential Problem Cause of "Injurious Running Style."

Other Stories of the Transform Way

The Transform way can be thought of as "turning a problem on its head." The cause of a problem is inverted—undergoes a form of reversal—so it no longer blocks progress toward a particular goal, but—in a pleasing twist—propels progress toward that goal.

We will look at some real-world examples where this sort of thing has happened. The result is usually impressive.

Every present-day business—regardless of the essential activities that underpin its market offerings—has a tangible obligation to the environment. This is an unavoidable social commitment and obviously brings with it an additional cost of doing business. This compliance cost is much more significant for certain industries—especially those involved in activities like mining and exploration—and especially if the sweeping mandate is reducing greenhouse gas emissions.

It is a difficult and seriously expensive problem for those involved.

One oil producer goes down the Transform way when confronting its eco obligation to reduce carbon dioxide emissions. It does this by capturing carbon dioxide from its industrial processes and injecting the gas deep underground for long-term storage. This initiative—known as carbon sequestration—satisfies its environmental obligation. But—in an innovative twist—the captured carbon dioxide is injected into depleted oilfields in a highly targeted way. The pressurized gas reactivates the reservoir, forcing out residual oil previously inaccessible using conventional extraction methods.

Here, the Problem Cause—having to incur the cost and effort of reducing emissions—is transformed into a process that—without changing its core purpose—also releases hidden value in the form of newly recoverable oil.

Transforming a Nightmare into a Dream

A recurring difficulty at a children's hospital is that many child patients—who must have a magnetic resonance imaging (MRI) scan—find the experience of being placed inside the MRI machine frightening. Managing them through the process can be challenging. Meaningful machine redesign is impractical, and sedation is regarded as a last resort.

The hospital decides to reinvent the experience. They paint the equipment to resemble a spaceship, provide the machine operators with a script, and reframe the scan process to have the operators lead young patients through a space adventure. "Listen for when the craft moves into hyperdrive!" This reimagining transforms a normally terrifying experience into something resembling a visit to a theme park. The numbers of patients needing to be sedated reduces dramatically and children look forward to the experience rather than fearing it.

Consider another example.

A worrying possibility for any organization is complaints made publicly about it—especially if they have been exaggerated, or worse, fabricated. This risk is now much greater with the advent of the online world. But instead of attempting to ignore them and hoping they go away, you can make those complaints work for you—by dealing with the problem in a Transform way.

Here is how the owner of a popular nightlife venue did it.

A club operator is subject to adverse, social media comments which are nasty and threaten to discourage customers. Recognizing the complaints are very few—especially in relation to the level of patronage being enjoyed—the venue proprietor incorporates the following message into their online advertising—"Come and see why less than 1% of our customers don't like us"—making sure it populates the web channels and sites where the abuse has been occurring.

Their innovative response transforms complaints that are potentially harmful into a playful and engaging communication that is capable of boosting their business.

Echoing the initiative of the nightclub owner, there is a story about Elvis Presley's manager, Colonel Tom Parker, that indicates he was a practitioner of the Transform way. He apparently also believed that negative entertainment publicity could be turned to profit. Colonel Parker was very energetic in selling Elvis records, photos, badges, buttons—all the usual paraphernalia—but he also spied an opportunity among those who disliked Elvis. In fact, he sold "I Hate Elvis" badges alongside the fan merchandise. The tale is likely exaggerated, but for us, it's the thought that counts.

And here is a story that—while tangential to usual notions of operational efficiency—offers an inspiring example of the Transform way. It is a classic illustration of flipping adversity to advantage.

The tale concerns an American college football team—but this is not your usual football team. Every player is deaf.

Relying on heightened visual abilities from lost auditory input, the players excel through sharp field awareness, quick hand signals, and no pauses for discussion. They follow the Transform way to innovate—they convert a collective hearing disability into an unmatched locational strength on the playing field.

And it pays off. The record shows they built an undefeated streak in the competition they played in.

This last story is, at a broader level, reminiscent of the Transform way as it has unfolded in neurodiversity education, an approach that recognises natural brain differences but, in doing so, shifts the focus from deficits to strengths. Unique perspectives are celebrated and directed into activities where their essence is a distinct advantage.

Looking in the Mirror

The story of the Tarahumara Indians that opened this chapter is a perfect illustration of both the power and subtlety of the Transform way as a problem-solving strategy. The juncture at which the Transform way operates often lies some perceptual distance from where its benefit is ultimately felt. In the Tarahumara case, a different use of hip flexors and gluteal muscles leads to better protection and preservation of what lies some distance below them—the legs and feet.

And protection and preservation like this are generated—not by creating something new—but by taking what already exists and precipitating a metamorphosis: converting a detrimental Problem Cause—in this case, impact strain—into a factor that literally fosters the reaching of a previously unattainable goal—long-distance running without injury.

This is the essence of the Transform way.

Before we met the Tarahumara, we heard from Winston Churchill—the British Prime Minister best known for his leadership during the Second World War—arguing in favor of optimists. But his deeper message is this: the lens through which we view adversity matters. What he champions is what we are about—a mindset geared toward seeing possibility in adversity.

This insight echoes what we talked about in Chapter 1—the role of symmetry in innovative thinking.

Many Transform solutions rest on a particular kind of symmetry—mirror symmetry. The image is identical, but reversed. The Problem Cause remains the same, yet—in a Transform solution—it reappears—flipped—and now serves the goal it once obstructed.

We can think of the Transform way as a method of holding the Problem Cause up to a mirror. In that reflection, we glimpse what the cause might look like—essentially unchanged—but turned to advantage.

From there, we begin the work of making that redemption real.

11

THE WAY TO NULLIFY A PROBLEM

When you can't work through a problem, go over its head

CHRIS CRAWFORD

On 20 April 2010, the oil drilling rig Deepwater Horizon—which was operated by British Petroleum (BP)—exploded and sank in the Gulf of Mexico, resulting in the death of 11 workers and the largest accidental spill of oil into marine waters in history. The scale and devastating impact of the incident ensured it attracted the maximum adverse publicity. BP's response to the disaster was criticized on many fronts and its public relations efforts and communication failures exacerbated what was already an unmitigated catastrophe.

BP's image was massively tarnished, and the oil spill became a moment that redefined the company, overshadowing its impressive accomplishments in growing to be one of the world's largest corporations since its origins in 1909.

It is a matter of record that BP paid billions of dollars in fines and community reparations. What is much more difficult to estimate with any precision is the cost and destructive ramifications of the reputational damage they suffered.

BP became Deepwater Horizon.

But it wasn't always.

Although it is virtually unknown, BP was involved in an earlier oil spill—this time in California, USA—and the impact on the company and its reputation was entirely different.

We would probably not even know about it if it wasn't for Dr Peter Sandman, a risk communication expert to whom we are indebted for the report on what happened. Sandman's thesis is that the fallout from environmental disasters—or any disasters for that matter—is made up not only of the physical damage done, but also of the public outrage that erupts around it.

Arguably, it is the latter and its reverberations which are responsible for the most enduring harm done to an organization that goes through such an experience. His memorable maxim—"It's the outrage, stupid!"—indicates that he certainly believes so.

Back to Dr Sandman's account of BP's first oil mishap.

The fuel spill in California in the early 1990s was, strictly speaking, not BP's doing, as the episode involved a contract carrier whom BP had engaged. Nevertheless, when asked on television if BP was responsible, their then CEO replied:

> *Our lawyers tell us it is not our fault. But we feel like it is our fault,*
> *and we are going to act like it is our fault*

This unusually candid response—when leaders and officials, both then and now, almost turn themselves inside out to avoid saying anything that could be construed as admitting liability—punctured the steadily inflating balloon of public outrage. The balloon crumpled.

Sandman ruled a line under the incident by saying:

> *Six months later they did a survey and found that BP had gained stature*
> *because of how they handled the spill*

There are plainly huge contrasts between how BP handled the 1990s California oil pollution matter and the 2010 Deepwater Horizon one. Reasoning that the earlier one was smaller does not explain the difference.

In backgrounding the story, Sandman explains that the potential for public anger at the time of the California episode was very high because just a few years earlier, in 1989, the notorious Exxon Valdez oil spill had occurred in Alaska. The response by the oil giant, Exxon, had infuriated people around the world. Despite the severe and lasting environmental impacts, Exxon were criticized for a delayed response, with cleanup efforts perceived as inadequate, and for contesting the extent of compensation owed to all affected parties.

People everywhere were accordingly primed to attack large oil companies for the slightest reason.

No further prompting was needed—but BP provided it.

Yet how BP handled this one is instructive and a perfect example of how to *nullify* the effect of a problem—to negate the expected repercussions of a Problem Cause. The California oil pollution event was undoubtedly a serious problem and had it followed its normal trajectory, the physical and public reputation consequences would have been monumental for BP.

Conditions that Point to the Nullify Way

The Nullify way buttresses the Problem Object that lies directly in the path of the Problem Cause against the undesired effect of that cause. It nullifies or cancels out the effect of the effect on the object.

As a result, any goal being impeded by that problem is now attainable.

The distinguishing mark of this strategy is that—in common with the Avoid way—it is deployed while the Problem Cause continues to exist in its entirety. Unlike the Prevent, Eliminate and Transform ways, the focus is on the Problem Effect rather than on the Problem Cause.

Back to our go-to Problem Way Decision Matrix—with the scrutiny this time on the Nullify way. We will look at the bottom, lower middle zone representing the modifiable Problem Effect and its inbuilt object:

PROBLEM WAY DECISION MATRIX		
	MODIFIABLE	**NON-MODIFIABLE**
PROBLEM CAUSE (contains Problem Obstacle)	Prevent	Avoid
	Eliminate	
	Transform	
PROBLEM EFFECT (contains Problem Object)	**Nullify**	Avoid

These are the "Stop Signs".

Firstly, for the Nullify way to be implemented, the Problem Effect (and Problem Object) must be modifiable—able to be manipulated, controlled or influenced. This is confirmed in the matrix.

Otherwise, it is out.

Additionally, the Nullify way is automatically excluded under the same conditions that rule out the Eliminate way when dealing with a Problem Cause and its associated obstacle. Just as the ongoing, essential existence of the Problem Obstacle disqualifies the Eliminate strategy, the Nullify way is not viable if modifying the Problem Object would compromise achieving the AFTI Goal. The Nullify way becomes entirely counterproductive when it undermines the host system and its intended objectives.

More specifically, and similar to the Eliminate "Stop Sign," the Nullify way must survive this question:

NULLIFY WAY EXCLUSION TEST

If the Problem Object is nullified, can the AFTI Goal still be achieved?

A "Yes" answer is required to proceed.

We can illustrate this hypothetically by returning to the seal pup story in

Chapter 7: The Way to Prevent a Problem. By way of a quick recap, this involved wildlife activists protecting seal pups from hunters who were killing them for their pelts. The seal pup defenders did this by defacing the pups' fur coats with a splash of paint. This prevented the young seals from being killed and did not harm them at all.

Strictly speaking, while the Prevent way was recognized as the primary means that achieved success for the activists, an alternative, hindsight-based interpretation could claim the Nullify way was used as well. This view holds some merit but consider this: the Nullify way would have failed if the activists had damaged the seal pups' coats to the extent that their natural fur protection was compromised, leading to their death.

In such a scenario, the Nullify way would not have succeeded because the Problem Object (the seal pups) needed to survive the protective treatment. Killing the seal pups before the hunters reached them would indeed have *nullified* them but would clearly have been self-defeating. As it turned out, they were not harmed and the Nullify way remains a plausible alternative account of what happened, since the Problem Object survived.

For the Nullify way to be viable, what is done to the Problem Object must allow the original purpose of any innovative undertaking to prevail.

Once the Nullify way has passed its practicality test, for the sake of completeness, let's examine when and why it might take precedence over the three other options—the Prevent, Eliminate and Transform ways. This is particularly relevant when dealing with a Problem Cause where both the Problem Cause and the Problem Effect are modifiable.

Usually, the answer to this question is self-evident as we can see if we return to the earlier oil spill story and populate the *Problem PhotoBox* with it:

OIL SPILL PROBLEM PHOTOBOX		
Problem Obstacle	**Public Disaster**	
Problem Cause	**Outrageous Public Disaster**	
Problem Solution	**Praiseworthy Public Disaster**	**AFTI Goal**
Problem Object	**Corporate Reputation**	
Problem Effect	**Devastated Corporate Reputation**	

Not much need for profound logical reasoning here when we set the contents of the *Problem PhotoBox* against the Problem Way Decision Matrix.

As the Problem Cause BP is confronting—"Outrageous Public Disaster"—has already happened, it cannot be modified. It is already a fact of life. We cannot modify or influence the Problem Cause by any of the Prevent, Eliminate and Transform ways. It's too late for them. The oil spill disaster is a fait accompli.

And the same logic applies to the Avoid way even though it is not really in contention based on the Problem Way Decision Matrix. Avoiding an effect that is already a reality is an impossibility.

We don't know how he got there, but the CEO of BP at the time gravitated to the only strategy that could successfully mitigate the problem—the Nullify way.

And he did an excellent job of employing it. By being explicit and unusually candid with the communities affected and the public at large—by taking them into his confidence—BP's leader succeeded in neutralizing a level of potential outrage that, once unleashed, could have decimated his company's reputation.

A comment yet again about the superlative importance of setting an AFTI (*Aim For The Ideal*) Goal. Admittedly we are fitting our arguments to the situation with the benefit of hindsight but, hypothetically, if BP had envisaged a Problem Solution that merely mitigated the Problem Cause—for instance, sought to achieve a "Manageable Public Disaster"—it is doubtful they would have been so innovative in their response. But by seeking such a radical outcome—where an intrinsically shocking incident could somehow be turned into something admirable—an imaginative, counter-intuitive remedy was conceived.

Other Stories of the Nullify Way

A herbicide producer, whose product is designed to help crop farmers control or kill unwanted vegetation, becomes aware that many users are wary of it. Their concern arises from instances where the herbicide—when not applied carefully—harms healthy crops as well as weeds. In high-volume spraying, the harm done from inadvertent application can be extensive and costly.

The inherent dilemma is that if the herbicide supplier weakens the product to minimize its harmful effects on a healthy harvest, it also reduces its effectiveness to control unwelcome growth. Training in product use helps if customers take it up but not many do due to time and productivity pressures.

And sometimes, damage is done even after purpose-built training has been carried out.

Ultimately, the herbicide manufacturer resorts to the Nullify way of innovating through their problem. They focus on the object of unintentional poisoning—the intended crops—and work with the producers of crop seeds to determine how these can be strengthened against the effects of the herbicide instead of weakening the herbicide itself. The enhanced crop seeds are then made available to growers who use the brand of herbicide with greater confidence to promote the growth of crops that are now more resilient. This Nullify strategy ensures that productive crop growth—the Problem Object previously susceptible to chemical damage—is shielded against it.

In a similar vein—but more succinctly—a comparable illustration involves a producer of weed killer who partners with a lawn supplier to fortify grass against the weed killer instead of reducing the product's effectiveness or imposing impractical instructions for its use.

Nullifying can be a most satisfactory, innovative solution in such situations.

Let's move from the rural to the urban community.

Among the many responsibilities governments bear on behalf of their constituents, keeping them safe is at the top of the list. Outside of war, this typically involves ensuring citizens are protected from harm as they go about their daily lives. A common threat to such safety lurks on streets and roads—more so in urban communities—because thousands of vehicles are in motion—conveying people and things from A to B.

Regulating such traffic flows so accidents are minimized is an ongoing challenge.

For the purposes of the illustration, we will get more specific. One of the more problematic traffic challenges involves motorcycles because—unlike cars and other larger road users—their relatively smaller stature escapes notice. Car drivers—conditioned to the bulk of standard traffic—frequently fail to notice the presence of motorcycles and collisions are the inevitable outcome.

After exhausting the regulatory options to reduce car-motor bike crashes—attempts at prevention have fallen short—a local authority decides to relax the noise regulations, allowing motorcycles to be engineered to produce a sound louder than ambient levels when ridden. Their rationale: louder motorcycles are more likely to be noticed by motorists.

Injuries caused by cars colliding with motorcyclists are less likely now because motor vehicle drivers are much more aware of the motorcyclists' presence thanks to the louder noise their bikes emit.

While not of universal relevance, this example is a good demonstration of the Nullify way. Dealing with the Problem Cause through traffic laws and fines works to a certain extent, but "near enough is not good enough" when lives are at stake. Accidents still occur. The Problem Cause of "Unaware Motorists" is still there—but the effect of that unawareness is significantly mitigated, because the Problem Object it would normally harm announces its presence before any damage is done. In essence, the effect is nullified—it is emasculated and no longer has its usual *effect*—because its intended object has been sheltered from it.

As an aside, it is worth noting that the gravity or scale of the problem does not determine whether a particular way can be used. All six ways of innovating through a problem are neutral with respect to the size or significance of the problem. What matters is not the magnitude of the challenge, but whether the right conditions exist to implement the strategy effectively.

Here is a less consequential example illustrating the Nullify way.

The proprietor of a small coffee bar becomes concerned at peak times when customers just picking up a takeout drink—and who comprise a sizable portion of his daily earnings—must wait an unreasonably long time before their beverage is ready. As the unequal flow of patrons is not something that can be easily regulated to a meaningful extent, the proprietor concentrates on the Problem Object—the waiting customers—and pursues a Nullify strategy.

How can they be insulated from the extended delay?

The coffee shop owner devises a plan to set aside a space for waiting takeout customers, centered around a small table. On it sit two or three partially completed jigsaw puzzles. Often, waiting clients engage with the puzzles, adding pieces when they can. This activity takes their minds off the wait, reducing their sensitivity to it.

In true Nullify fashion, queuing patrons—the Problem Object—are buttressed from the tedium of waiting and, for some, the jigsaw diversion adds to the appeal of the coffee bar.

Finally, a manufacturer of laundry detergent encounters a misconception among consumers of its product who believe that once clothes are washed with the detergent, they don't look clean, even though technically they are completely clean. This Problem Cause proves to be a tough perception to correct through conventional marketing communication channels.

Eventually, their focus turns to the Problem Object—the washed clothes—and a Nullify strategy is conceived. The detergent producer reformulates its product, adding optical brighteners—compounds that reflect the light. The detergent now not only washes clothes but also makes them appear brighter and whiter and therefore cleaner to people.

When all conventional attempts to deal with the Problem Cause fall short, bolstering the Problem Object is a sensible innovative choice.

It's Not for the Glamor

Chris Crawford—a pioneer in video game development and a key contributor to innovative design thinking—presides over this chapter with his recommendation:

When you can't work through a problem, go over its head

His sentiment captures the essence of the Nullify way. When a problem cannot be confronted, the Nullify strategy doesn't stop it from occurring—it simply rises above it, remaining aloof and suppressing its usual effect. The problem is left to follow its course, but its power to cause harm is blunted.

We emulate this attitude when we venture to cancel the effect of a problem. This gets the job despite the problem—disrespecting its usual potency—anesthetizing against its potential sting.

It can do its worst, but we know how to handle its worst.

We might not even be noticed.

Like its cousins—the Prevent and Avoid ways—the Nullify way wants for glamor.

When it succeeds, the result is a non-event and most of the time the nullification goes undiscovered and unheralded. The need to dredge up the largely unknown story of the initial BP oil spill is a reminder of this irony. Competence in averting a calamity—ensuring it does not occur—is rarely celebrated, even though such competence often deserves the highest praise.

Sometimes, evidence of the Nullify way's effectiveness only becomes widely recognized many years after the fact—as was the case with German industrialist Oskar Schindler, who quietly saved around 1,200 Jews from the Holocaust by employing them in his factories during the Second World War. His actions were subtle and indirect, dodging confrontation with the brutal system while protecting those under his care.

In stark contrast—the swashbuckling American Colonel George Armstrong Custer—was the very embodiment of bold, aggressive action. Celebrated for his daring cavalry charge at the 1863 Battle of Gettysburg during the American Civil War, Custer was impossible to ignore. Yet his brashness and recklessness often escalated conflicts—including during the Indian Wars—where his own provocations contributed directly to the battles that led to his demise at the Battle of Little Big Horn. Unlike Schindler's quiet, protective approach, Custer's exploits drew enthusiastic public praise—even as they fueled the very dangers he faced.

When we opt for the Nullify way to innovate, we choose the unobtrusive effectiveness of an Oskar Schindler rather than the buckle and bravado of a Colonel Custer.

12

THE WAY TO PREEMPT A PROBLEM

Get your retaliation in first

MRS MERTON (CAROLINE AHERNE)
THE MRS MERTON SHOW, 1997

Apart from the wicked barb above from Caroline Aherne (in the guise of the fictional Mrs Merton), we will enlist the help of Zentsūji—a small city on Japan's Shikoku Island—to get us into the spirit of the Preempt way of innovating through problems.

While Zentsūji is situated in the tiniest prefecture in Japan—Kagawa Prefecture—and can claim the distinction of being the only city there that does not face the sea, its innovating prowess far overshadows these rather mundane facts. In the 1970s, local watermelon farmers turned their attention to the logistical problems arising from their product: round watermelons are hard to stack, prone to rolling, inefficient to pack in fridges, difficult to store in warehouses, and awkward to load into shipping crates.

Problems that stem from nature are difficult to tackle head-on. They are, in a sense, immutable. As such, they are classic candidates for the Preempt way of innovating through problems. When the Problem Cause is too difficult to deal with directly, it makes more sense to try to head it off before it exists.

This is exactly what the Zentsūji farmers did—they got their retaliation in first.

The farmers retaliated against the physical characteristics of the watermelons—which were the root of their logistical problems. They reasoned that transforming the round shape of the watermelons into one more conducive to storing, packing, and shipping would solve their logistical headaches.

Square watermelons would do the trick.

So, they began growing the fruit in square glass boxes, letting them naturally assume the shape of the receptacle.

The result?

Square watermelons—and a perfect preemptive strike against the problem.

Conditions that Point to the Preempt Way

At this stage in each of the previous five problem way chapters, we have imported the Problem Way Decision Matrix to unpack the specific way being studied.

But not this time.

The main distinguishing feature of the Preempt way is that it precedes the cause-and-effect trajectory of a problem—it initiates *ahead of* any Problem Cause or Problem Effect—and therefore cannot be understood within the canopy of that framework.

Accordingly, it doesn't fit into the Problem Way Decision Matrix.

The Preempt way calls for a different type of analysis—one suited to its forward-looking nature—one that does not hinge on the modifiability of the Problem Obstacle or Problem Object. It is designed to head off a Problem Cause before it can come into existence. There is no subsequent Problem Effect—because it just cannot happen.

Are there any "Stop Signs"—conditions that would block choosing the Preempt way—that rule it out from the outset?

There is only one—and it is an obvious one: if the Problem Cause has already manifested and is not a repeatable event—then attempting to preempt it is clearly futile. Both exclusion criteria—the cause having already occurred and its non-reoccurrence—must be met to rule the Preempt way out.

Conversely, if the Problem Cause is still pending or is recurrent—like the Japanese watermelons that are grown every year—the Preempt way is feasible, because the opportunity to address the Problem Cause still exists, or a missed opportunity to address it is simply replaced by a fresh one.

As the Preempt way sits outside the Problem Way Decision Matrix, the Problem Cause (with its Problem Obstacle) and the Problem Effect (with its Problem Object) are irrelevant to our efforts. The cause-and-effect trajectory they represent is meaningless—because the Preempt way ensures it does not exist. This leads us to a new concept—one that lies upstream of the usual chain of events. It recognizes that before a Problem Cause can show itself, certain conditions are already conspiring to bring it about.

We will refer to these as Precursor Conditions.

Precursor Conditions are the circumstances or factors already in place that precede the cause-and-effect trajectory. They enable the Problem Cause by turning the Problem Obstacle into a harmful Problem Effect. As such, they are the fuel for the Preempt way. Neutralizing these enabling conditions can make it impossible for the Problem Cause to emerge—and without it of course, there can be no cause-and-effect trajectory.

Against the backdrop of this book—where the trajectory from Problem Cause to Problem Effect has been foundational to all the problem ways discussed to date—

what I have just said in dismissing that trajectory may be a touch disconcerting.

So let me approach the issue from another angle.

Of the five ways we have learned about so far—the Prevent, Avoid, Eliminate, Transform, and Nullify ways—four rely on the existence of a Problem Cause, and one relies on the existence of a Problem Effect. At the core of the Preempt way's underlying nature is that it deals with the cause and effect of a problem before they even exist. More precisely, the Preempt way stops the cause from occurring.

The effect then cannot be.

This discussion may seem paradoxical—even surreal—because it treats the anatomy of a problem as if it were real, only to deny its reality once the Preempt way has done its job. But it is precisely this counterfactual clarity—the ability to reason about what would exist, if not for intervention—that enables us to plan to deploy the Preempt way, forestalling the Problem Cause and Problem Effect.

The case for bypassing the Problem Way Decision Matrix—and its inherent cause and effect trajectory—when choosing the Preempt way should now be convincing.

But we cannot bypass the *Problem PhotoBox*.

The *Problem PhotoBox* remains the most essential steppingstone when we innovate. We cannot innovate without it.

That is the reason why—to implement the Preempt way—we still need to know what the Problem Cause and Problem Effect are—even if they have yet to materialize.

From here, our approach is markedly different from the previous five ways.

So, Precursor Conditions take center stage—and for our present purposes, we will focus specifically on those faced by the Japanese farmers growing the watermelons.

Let's pull up the *Problem PhotoBox*:

WATERMELONS PROBLEM PHOTOBOX		
Problem Obstacle	**Watermelons**	
Problem Cause	**Spherical Watermelons**	
Problem Solution	**Non-Spherical Watermelons**	**AFTI Goal**
Problem Object	**Logistics Operation**	
Problem Effect	**Unwieldy Logistics Operation**	

Apparently, watermelons naturally grow into a round or oval shape because of how cells expand evenly in all directions during fruit development. This spherical form is dictated by internal turgor pressure and genetics (so the scientists say), and the fruit's need to optimize space and nutrient distribution as it matures on the vine.

From the AFTI Problem Solution generated by the *Problem PhotoBox*—"Non-Spherical Watermelons"—the farmers necessarily focused on the conditions that enable the round shapes and planned to establish new conditions that would have an effect geometrically opposite to roundness.

They needed a way to deny the watermelon's natural biological tendency to become round.

To grow a square watermelon, the farmers had to carefully consider this inherent genetic tendency. The fruit's natural roundness means it resists external forces that try to deform it. Forcing the fruit into a square shape requires applying uniform pressure early enough in the growth cycle without damaging the fruit or stunting its development. Getting it right no doubt took some experimentation.

Identifying the Precursor Conditions, understanding them and working out how to modify them appropriately was required.

I do sense some raised hands from readers of a culinary disposition. You are wondering how such an aggressive intervention in the watermelon growing cycle affects taste and edibility.

No need to worry. These watermelons are grown for ornamental purposes and are said to be quite expensive.

They are not intended to be eaten.

The Potency of the Problem PhotoBox

What the Japanese watermelon farmers did is so exorbitantly novel, it is easy to dismiss it as one of those rare events that occasionally arise among millions of people engaged in millions of diverse activities, and trying millions of different things. Chance alone ensures even freakish occurrences arise from time to time.

Yet it is precisely this assumption that allows us to appreciate, once again, the true power of the *Problem PhotoBox* when we use it to innovate. I know I have made the point several times already, but its effectiveness in this case is simply too striking to pass up.

When an ideal Problem Solution takes shape not by ingenuity, but because it is the perfect opposite of the Problem Cause, radically novel possibilities emerge naturally. Once "Spherical Watermelons" were named in the *Problem PhotoBox* as the Problem Cause, the idea of pursuing "Non-Spherical Watermelons" was no longer a flash of genius or a whacky idea that seemed to come out of nowhere.

As the AFTI Goal, it was the next logical—and practically inevitable—step.

Yet again, we see the dynamic impact of the *Problem PhotoBox* when we use it to innovate.

Some Guidance on Isolating Precursor Conditions

We have already explored how to identify and understand Precursor Conditions—

the upstream circumstances that innately allow a problem to arise. In most cases, recognizing them doesn't require a great leap of imagination. They are usually visible enough.

But when they are not, a bit of structured guidance can make all the difference.

One useful approach is to borrow from an ancient philosophical idea called *via negativa*[5]—a method of understanding something by considering what must be lacking for it *not* to come into being.

Instead of asking what causes a problem, we pose a different kind of question:

QUESTION TO IDENTIFY PRECURSOR CONDITIONS

What must be removed or rendered inoperative for the problem never to occur in the first place?

This way of thinking about problems—and the Preempt approach more broadly—marks a clear shift—from reactive to proactive. Instead of chasing consequences, we focus on neutralizing the conditions that give rise to them.

Back to the *Problem PhotoBox* and the Japanese watermelon farmers.

The Problem Obstacle is: "Watermelons"; the Problem Cause is their shape: "Spherical Watermelons".

Their shape causes logistical problems with their stacking, storing and transportation.

To isolate the enabling Precursor Conditions, we apply *via negativa*:

What must be removed or rendered inoperative for "Spherical Watermelons" never to grow in the first place?

This naturally leads us to consider mirror-image circumstances—those that independently and unobtrusively shape the problem in the background, such as:

- The tradition that watermelons should be round

- The fact that watermelons grow according to their natural surroundings

- The absence of any environmental constraints to prevent roundness

These are Precursor Conditions—not causes in the usual sense, but passive default

---

5   *Via negativa* is a Latin phrase meaning "by way of negation." The idea comes from ancient philosophical and religious traditions—particularly those that tried to describe the divine not by what it is, but by what it is not. One of its earliest and most influential proponents was Plotinus (204–270). In our context, the method helps us understand something by identifying the conditions that must be absent for it *not* to exist.

states that allow the Problem Cause to emerge. Left alone, they lead to the downstream Problem Effect: "Unwieldy Logistics Operation."

By isolating these underlying conditions—seeing what needs to be *not* there—the farmers gained leverage for new thinking:

- Why not abandon traditional thinking about round watermelons?

- Why accept surroundings that are only natural?

- Why not introduce constraints that reshape roundness?

Using this leverage, they didn't merely fix the logistics issue—they rendered the Precursor Conditions ineffective for round watermelons and paved the way for growing square ones.

They didn't solve the problem—they preempted it.

Other Stories of the Preempt Way

The Preempt way may seem sophisticated and rare because of the foresight it requires.

Yet—as with so many of the innovative examples illustrated in this book— its results are so common that their origins in preempt-type thinking are usually overlooked. Many products and services that evolved as a result of a strategy which preempted a Problem Cause are an unquestioned part of everyday life.

Here is a short, random list:

- Prepaid phone cards preempt the need to issue invoices for call charges

- Prepaid travel cards preempt the need for banks to bill tourists after their trip

- Customer payment against a purchase order preempts the need to issue an invoice

- Robot vacuums preempt the need to schedule or manually carry out routine cleaning

- Self-checkout kiosks preempt the need for cashiers at supermarkets

- Cars with run-flat tires preempt the need to stop and change a tire after a puncture

- Spam filters preempt the need for users to manually sort through unwanted email

- Flight check-in apps preempt queues at airport counters

- Voice assistants (e.g. Siri, Alexa) preempt the need to use hands or navigate menus to perform simple tasks

Let's flesh the Preempt way out a bit further with a more descriptive and illustrative example.

A fledgling software company develops a powerful spam filter—but now faces a daunting challenge: how to compete with established players in a crowded market.

Traditional marketing campaigns would cost far more than they can afford.

Instead of trying to solve this problem head-on, they preempt it.

They turn to the users they already have—a small but loyal group—and utilize software to design a way for the product to market itself. Every time a customer sends a normal email to their habitual recipients, a small line is automatically appended to the footer:

> *[Spam Brand] blocked 627 spam messages and set aside 13 newsletters for me. Try it at www.spambrand.com*

This subtle, data-rich message—with numbers that grow over time—does what ads often cannot do: it proves the product works—right in front of the recipient's eyes.

And because it's attached to emails between friends, associates and colleagues, it carries credibility and relevance.

People catch on, notice the results, visit the company's site, and sign up. Without spending heavily on ads, the company gains traction—and *preempts* the costliest part of its go-to-market strategy. By designing a system where visibility and credibility grow organically, the company doesn't just reduce marketing costs—it renders them unnecessary.

Should there still be a belief that the Japanese watermelon story is no more an unusual outlier, another example of the Preempt way—likewise favoring square over round—offers a compelling parallel.

This time we move from Japan to Israel.

A major Israeli distributor of bottled water recognizes that the conventional cylindrical shape of its bottles is responsible for a range of persistent friction points: inefficient use of cold storage space, poor stackability, instability during transport and awkwardness for consumers carrying the bottles as they move about.

Rather than tackling these problems piecemeal, the company preempts them.

They reengineer their bottles into cubic forms, optimizing them for storage, stacking and portability. These new shapes don't just respond to known issues—they abolish the conditions that give rise to them. By doing so, they ensure the previous problems don't arise at all. They preempt them.

Many organizations have embraced the Preempt way of thinking to improve recruitment outcomes—particularly in response to the all-too-common problem of unsuccessful appointments—even after rigorous screening and interviews. The failure of traditional methods has shifted attention upstream—toward factors that exist *before* the job even begins.

One major factor is the candidate's personal circumstances—especially when these conflict with the real demands of the role. Such misalignments often become apparent only after the appointment is made, leading to early dissatisfaction, disengagement, and departure.

To reshape these Precursor Conditions, some employers are adopting more innovative, *preemptive* approaches.

Just three examples:

- A company gifts the successful candidate a vacation voucher to use with family or friends *before* starting the job—an early gesture that tangibly acknowledges the impact the role may later have on their personal life

- An employer reverses the usual interview dynamic, staging a session where the candidate's entire family is invited to question the employer about the role, the workplace, and its likely impact on the candidate's life. In effect, the employer becomes the one being interviewed. By including the family in the acceptance decision, later work-life tensions are more easily understood and reconciled

- A business awards any successful appointee who has been unemployed prior to their new role a generous cash sum in recognition of their period of non-earning—offering concrete acknowledgment that personal circumstances matter and preempting future resentment if work demands begin to feel unfairly dominant over life outside of work.

There are many possibilities in the hiring context. What unites them is a deliberate attempt to preempt dissatisfaction—not by refining the role or selection process after things go wrong—but by acknowledging the conflict early and acting to reshape the conditions that might give rise to it.

Elsewhere, and more generically, businesses have used customer feedback data to construct algorithms that warn them when a customer is at risk of switching to a competitor. And companies serving the travel sector preempt future difficulties for travelers by ensuring their website informs people if, for instance, their rental car booking and airport don't match.

This is the Preempt way—getting ahead of the cause before it becomes a problem—and in doing so, removing the need to solve it later.

The Case for Preemptive Healthcare

The standard model in medical insurance is reactive: the patient receives treatment for an illness or injury, then gets reimbursed. One large health insurer breaks with this convention by adopting a preemptive approach. Instead of simply paying for treatment, they double the length of standard doctor appointments they will reimburse—encouraging physicians to spend more time thoroughly assessing and managing their patients. They also introduce incentives for practitioners who successfully prevent disease progression in at-risk individuals.

For example, when patients are diagnosed with pre-diabetes but their physicians manage their care so the condition doesn't develop into full-blown diabetes, the doctors are rewarded for each period of time the patient's health remains stable. In essence, doctors are compensated for what doesn't happen.

This is clearly better for the patient—and, over time, preempting illness proves more cost-effective than treating it after the fact.

The Ways of the Family

Before we get to the usual chapter summing up—this time for the latest member in the group—the Preempt way—it will serve us well to recall all the problem-solving ways that belong to the problem-fighting family.

Back in Chapter 6, we introduced the six problem-solving ways, framed as military—or warlike—strategies. Together, they represent distinct modes of response: confronting the problem head-on, skirting around it, anticipating it, charging straight into battle, outflanking it, nullifying it entirely, or acting early enough to stop it before it begins.

Now that the full family of warriors is gathered around the table, let's bring them to life—each a distinct personality, with their own outlook, instincts, and approach—so we can commit them to memory, each with their own *way*:

- Here sits Avoid, often mistaken for a coward—but simply wise enough to walk around a fight rather than into one

- Here sits Prevent, more like a seasoned firefighter—admired not for dousing flames, but for making sure there aren't any to start with

- Here sits Eliminate, who may seem ruthless—but prefers no enemy at the start, to a hard-won victory later

- Here sits Transform, an admired turncoat—ready to become a helpful cause rather than a harmful one—to unblock the path to victory

- Here sits Nullify, modest and often overlooked—but quietly shielding against the threat already in play

- And in the final seat is Preempt, who doesn't wait for fair play—preferring to strike before a punch is even thrown

Together, they form the complete arsenal—each distinct, each providing its own path, and all united by one purpose: innovating through problems.

Retaliate First

Meeting in the proverbial dark alley to do business with Mrs Merton—the character who propels us into this chapter—is not a welcome thought.

We don't expect polite introductions or "by your leave" preliminaries.

What needs to be done will be done.

She comes at you:

Unannounced.

Unapologetically.

Uncompromisingly.

Well okay, unfairly too.

These traits suit Mrs Merton, but they would make a fitting "Wanted Poster" for the Preempt way as well.

We can certainly appreciate that—even though it is the last problem-solving strategy—the Preempt way is by no means a fallback.

Like Mrs Merton, it isn't about playing nice.

Before we conclude our study of the Preempt way, there is an important point to address.

For readers for whom the logic of order is a mental itch, the treatment of the Preempt way as the sixth and final problem-solving method may raise objections.

I hear you.

You are quite right to point out that if the Preempt way intervenes and makes its contribution before any cause-and-effect trajectory has even become a reality, shouldn't it come first?

It's a logical challenge.

And here is a logical response.

Understanding when to choose the Preempt way requires counterfactual thinking—treating the anatomy and trajectory of a problem as if they are real—only to then deny they are real as a direct consequence of the Preempt way.

That is no small mental leap—but it is not unreasonable.

It is not unreasonable because of the extensive cause-and-effect discussion that comes before it—the discussion already carried by the five other ways. Knowing the nature of their engagement with the cause-and-effect trajectory is the necessary backdrop for a discussion of the Preempt way—a way that precedes any cause-and-effect trajectory.

The same argument can be put more generally.

Counterfactual analysis only makes sense when you have a firm grasp of the factual analysis it overturns. It is not easily understandable if it has *not* been ushered in by the factual analysis it challenges.

Logic suggests the Preempt way should come first.

But deeper logic insists it come last.

There is order behind the apparent disorder.

PART 3

INNOVATE THROUGH COPYING

There are two modes of innovating: Copying and Originating.

Innovating through copying happens more often than you realize. You already do it without instruction. This is because you benefit from serendipity—those unexpected moments when chance encounters—or stray observations—suddenly converge with a need you have. This leads to an innovative breakthrough you could not have triggered by conventional thinking.

But serendipity doesn't have to be left to chance. You can deliberately place yourself in its path.

A sneak preview: the key is to form—and hold in your mind—a mental picture of the sort of solution you are seeking. When you randomly stumble across something that overlaps with this previsualized image, it is probable you will be able to adapt what you have experienced to innovate.

You copy.

In this part of the book, you will learn how to do this—through the metaphor of climbing a mountain.

Neither the copying mode—nor the originating mode—is superior. They are not rivals, but partners.

And they can and should be exercised together—simultaneously even.

Baseball Hall-of-Famer and accidental philosopher, Yogi Berra, has helped us once, and can again.

When it comes to endorsing both the copying and originating modes of innovating, we borrow from the advice he supposedly gave to visitors to help them find his house:

When you come to a fork in the road, take it

13

COPYING TO INNOVATE

Imitation is the sincerest form of flattery that mediocrity can pay to greatness

OSCAR WILDE

Among the many pop-rock bands that emerged during the 1960s—often considered the most influential decade in pop-rock music—were *The Monkees,* a four-member American band of Peter Tork, Micky Dolenz, Michael Nesmith, and Davy Jones. Interestingly, they did not evolve in the manner typical of their contemporaries. They were conceived as a fictitious band for a television sitcom but—despite their manufactured pedigree—they went on to make it in real-life and became one of the most successful bands in the world in those days.

While her guitar-playing son and his companions were establishing what would be a substantial legacy, Bette Nesmith Graham was quietly establishing a legacy of her own—one that is in many ways much more pervasive—even if it lacks the glamor of musical celebrity.

Bette Nesmith Graham was a commercial artist who later worked as an executive typist. This was around 1950. Although proficient with her electric typewriter, Nesmith Graham became increasingly frustrated by how difficult it was to correct a typing mistake once it was made. She was constantly thinking about this and her artistic background kept nagging at her. Unlike typists, artists—those brandishing a palette, not a guitar—did not seem to have this problem. They didn't screw up their canvas like a typewriter page and throw it away. They simply painted over any mistakes they made and carried on.

That simple contrast sparked an idea.

In seeking to reproduce what artists did, Nesmith Graham started experimenting in her kitchen with a common kitchen blender and went on to develop a paper-colored paint-on liquid—the iconic Liquid Paper—which typists the world over began to use to paint over their mistakes. Initially, she called the product "Mistake Out," renamed it Liquid Paper, and in 1979 sold the business to the Gillette Corporation for US$47.5 million.

With the adoption of computers for word processing, the need for Liquid Paper—also known as correction fluid—has, of course, diminished but this does not detract from the impact it had up until the 1980s and 1990s. Baby boomers will remember and appreciate the Liquid Paper phenomenon, but Generation X, Millennials and Generation Z may wonder what all the fuss was about.

If you are in one of these latter groups, may I politely ask you to take my word for—there was a fuss.

What Bette Nesmith Graham did—in generalizing from the ability of artists to paint over their mistakes to typists being able to do the same—is the essence of Copying as a mode of innovating.

Nesmith Graham was engaging in something called "mental association" or, more formally, "the association of ideas."

This is not an exclusive technique reserved for a privileged few. We can all do it—and we do.

Connecting the Mental Dots

There is a huge body of philosophical and psychological literature that underpins the concepts of mental association and association of ideas. Although there are subtle differences between the two terms, it suits our purposes to use them interchangeably. John Locke (1632–1704) is regarded as a pioneer in the field—with others such as David Hume building on his groundwork to develop associationist psychology in the late 19th and early 20th century.

We won't delve into the technicalities of the theories they developed but—by way of a quick, non-technical explanation—having ideas *by association* occurs because typically, the mind organizes information into categories. One of these categories can then link to something else in such a way that a completely new thought is formed—even though the two thoughts are not necessarily connected with each other.

Cognitive neuroscientist, Dr. Barry J. Gordon separates our memory into two domains: our "ordinary memory," which is conscious and relatively slow, and our "intelligent memory," which is usually unconscious, but fast and effortless. Our ordinary memory is where we store specific facts—whereas our intelligent memory is responsible for what we do with our senses, minds, and muscles. It drives our intelligence—thus its name.

In a helpful explanation, Dr Gordon uses the metaphor of connecting dots and says:

The dots are pieces or ideas, the lines between them are your connections or associations. That's what happens when ideas or concepts 'pop' into your mind

When the idea to copy what artists do to correct their mistakes "popped" into Bette Nesmith Graham's mind, she was drawing a line—mentally associating—between creating a painted image on canvas with a brush and producing a word image on paper with her electric typewriter.

She was able to combine two previously unrelated experiences to create something truly innovative.

As comforting as it may be to be reminded that associating mentally is something we are all able to do, it can still seem somewhat ethereal, somewhat out of practical reach. After all, not only does it rely upon our brains mysteriously connecting previously unconnected thoughts and ideas, serendipity—the element of happy chance—plays a part as well.

And that raises a crucial question: if the links inherent in mental association are so unpredictable, can we really learn to innovate through Copying?

Or is it merely a romantic notion?

In their 2011 book, *The Innovator's DNA*, respected authors Jeff Dyer, Hal Gregersen, and Clayton M. Christensen tackled this exact issue. They identify five "discovery skills" that are integral to the ability to innovate: Associating, Questioning, Observing, Networking, and Experimenting. All five skills reinforce each other to spark and sustain innovation, but the authors do home in on Associating (mental association) as being central, because it enables seemingly unrelated connections to be made between entities to generate a desired breakthrough—the very essence of creating innovative value.

The well-regarded findings of Dyer, Gregersen and Christensen add some intellectual rigor and support to our contention that mentally associating is not merely a homegrown conceptual construct. It is a viable mental framework for innovating as well.

As evidence that the phenomenon of mental association is neither obscure—nor unfamiliar—we need look no further than the word association game many of us have played. In this activity, a person starts by saying a word and the next person responds with the first word that comes to their mind based on their own mental association. The sequence continues as each person responds to the previous word with a word that it reminds them of. It can be fun to experience where the chain of associations leads—often unexpectedly far from where it began.

The Role of Serendipity

But apart from its use as a fun pastime, the association of ideas is not something we engage in with purposeful intent, and the reason is that the thoughts and ideas produced through mental association are unexpected—accidental even. Therefore, the notion of being able to control the cerebral process to generate valuable ideas is not realistic.

Chance comes into it.

To understand how and why this is the case, let's consider another historical example of association that led to the creation of an iconic product—one now also ubiquitous in the world of personal efficiency.

I am talking about the Post-It Note—those multi-colored, adhesive-backed, easily removable pieces of paper commonly used everywhere to temporarily attach notes to documents and other surfaces.

I am confident these straddle generational boundaries much better than Liquid Paper.

The contrast between the emergence of Post-It Notes and Liquid Paper gives us a useful trigger for mastering the use of mental association to innovate through Copying.

In 1968, Spencer Silver—a chemist employed in the consumer goods section of the American multinational corporation 3M—was attempting to develop a super-strong adhesive, but instead, he accidentally created a weak "temporary" one. Sometime later, a colleague, Arthur Fry was casually looking for a bookmark that would stick yet be removable without damaging the pages or leaving any residue. Fry remembered Silver's "failed experiment" and associated the accidental, temporary adhesive with his bookmark need and the widely popular Post-It Note was born.

On the surface, the experiences of Bette Nesmith Graham and the Spencer Silver–Arthur Fry pairing seem pretty much the same. A person has mentally associated a competence or ability from an unrelated domain to develop a highly effective and convenient personal productivity aid. A basic skill of artistic painters and the seemingly useless outcome of a failed experiment were translated into spectacularly ubiquitous products.

But we need to notice a crucial distinction. It is the key to innovating through Copying.

Nesmith Graham had a general impression of the capability she needed *in mind*. This helped her to associate with what painters do.

Spencer Silver wasn't thinking of a weak adhesive. In fact, he was seeking the opposite. The development of a mild bonding agent was completely unintended. It was a beneficial surprise–although its value didn't become apparent until later when Arthur Fry made the connection with his need for a particular kind of bookmark.

What happened was *serendipitous*.

When such a fortunate outcome arises, it is referred to as "serendipity"—a profitable occurrence that emerges from seemingly unrelated events—even though it is not being explicitly sought.

Serendipity is a nice word. It lilts. It carries the promise of exotic adventure—with a dose of mystery thrown in. It became part of our vocabulary as far back as 1754, when it was coined by Horace Walpole who was taken by a myth about three Princes of Serendip (which we know today as Sri Lanka). These princes roamed the world in the manner of ancient explorers, but with the intriguing twist that they solved mysteries and made discovery after discovery of things they were *not* looking for.

All of this was apparently due to their keen observational skills and their talent for connecting seemingly unrelated happenings.

Walpole's label of "serendipity" caught on and serendipity now tends to be regarded as a human aptitude—albeit an unintentional one. The *Oxford English Dictionary* for instance defines serendipity as:

> *The faculty of making happy and unexpected discoveries by accident*

Less reverently, Julius Comroe Jr said,

> *Serendipity is looking in a haystack for a needle and discovering a farmer's daughter*

However, we tend to routinely underestimate the value of serendipity as a human skill because of its unpredictability—its susceptibility to chance or good fortune.

But it is possible for us to become modern Princes of Serendip and avoid being entirely at the whim of serendipity.

We can exploit it to innovate by putting ourselves in its path.

Bette Nesmith Graham did exactly this. She had a general—yet relevant—understanding of what she needed to solve her problem. In doing so, she positioned herself in the path of serendipity. This removed the element of chance and ensured the innovative solution she came up with was not only possible, but ultimately inevitable.

We will look step by step at how she did this by utilizing a mountain metaphor.

Mountain Climbing with Bette

As an alternative to neuroscientist Barry J. Gordon's analogy with connecting dots, another way to picture what happens when we mentally associate is to imagine climbing up one side of a mountain—pausing to reflect—and then traveling down the other side. We can replicate what Bette Nesmith Graham did in inventing Liquid Paper by telling her story as a mountain climb.

We will call it a *Copying Mountain*, because instead of simply regarding mental association as an accidental, passive encounter over which we have no control, our thesis is that we can exploit the phenomenon to spawn something new—purposefully—by copying from someone or something else:

Copying Mountain for Liquid Paper

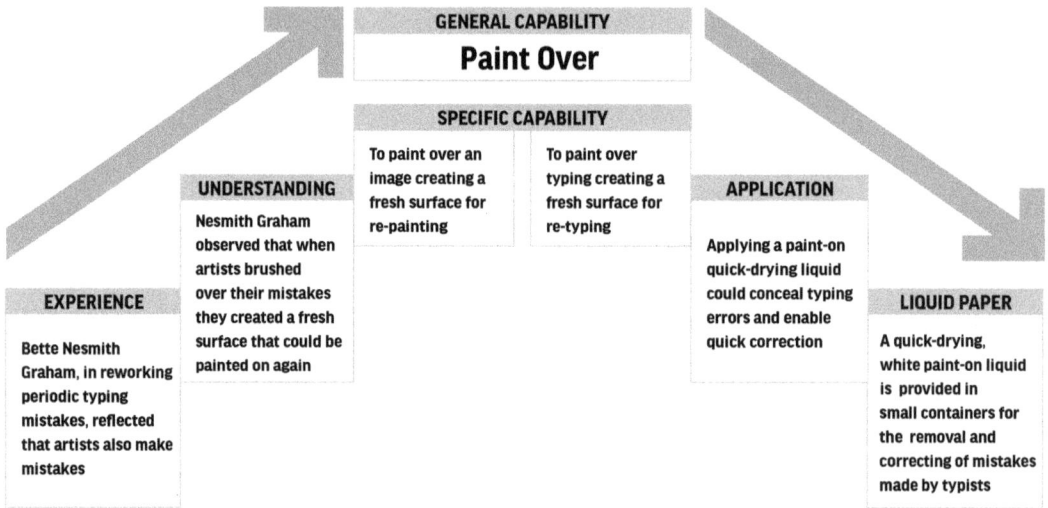

GENERAL CAPABILITY
Paint Over

SPECIFIC CAPABILITY

To paint over an image creating a fresh surface for re-painting

To paint over typing creating a fresh surface for re-typing

UNDERSTANDING

Nesmith Graham observed that when artists brushed over their mistakes they created a fresh surface that could be painted on again

APPLICATION

Applying a paint-on quick-drying liquid could conceal typing errors and enable quick correction

EXPERIENCE

Bette Nesmith Graham, in reworking periodic typing mistakes, reflected that artists also make mistakes

LIQUID PAPER

A quick-drying, white paint-on liquid is provided in small containers for the removal and correcting of mistakes made by typists

The image is reasonably self-explanatory with the details at each stage spelled out, but basically Bette Nesmith Graham's mountain climb goes like this:

- In going up the left-hand side of the mountain, she climbs from Experience, to Understanding, and to recognizing a Specific Capability—that of painting over an image to create a clean surface for re-painting

- From there, she moves to the summit and more broadly, she identifies the General Capability—"Paint Over"—a sort of a mountain-top perspective if you like

- She then starts to move back down the other side of the mountain to a comparable Specific Capability at work—that of painting over typing to allow re-typing

- Traveling further down, she descends through Application, where the "Painting Over" idea is sharpened, and then refines it further into the setting that is her focus—the invention of Liquid Paper

In other words, the essence of copying to innovate is to *generalize* from a *specific* experience that has been recognized as potentially valuable and then—having identified the general capability at work—*specializing* down from that *general* capability to apply it narrowly again, but in a different situation.

In case the idea of deliberately stepping into serendipity's path still feels elusive—or too abstract to rely on—let me, before turning to the specific strategies we can use to innovate through copying, show how I have made that concept more practical in my own work.

As noted in the Preface, the thousands of innovative ideas I have gathered over the years—used to build and test the theory in this book—are freely available at Sebir.com. But their usefulness lies not just in their content, but in how they are engaged with. From the outset, I deliberately structured the method of access to help users place themselves in the path of serendipity. Visitors begin by identifying the kind of problem they are trying to resolve. They are then presented with examples of innovative ideas that solved problems similar to theirs.

As a result, serendipity is no longer a matter of luck alone. The ideas illustrated are not just random—they are innovative solutions shaped by relevance. Because they have already solved similar problems, the chances of a visitor being able to successfully adapt and implement them rise significantly. Placement in serendipity's path has occurred—and the odds of a rewarding innovative result are sharply improved.

The Two Strategies for Copying to Innovate

In the two chapters that follow, we will look in depth at the dual strategies available for Copying to Innovate. For now, I will just introduce them. The distinction between the two pivots on who or what is being copied.

The two strategies are:

1. Copy by Observing People
2. Copy by Observing Things

Copy by Observing People

The field of human endeavor is vast and is expanding continuously (as if we needed reminding).

While some people—usually acting individually—pioneer activities that are genuinely new and untried, millions of others are acting out activities that have been established and embedded in everyday life. Usually these are actions that were once new but are now so routine that they are exercised automatically, without forethought.

And, through repetition and correction based on experience, proficiency in the actions and tasks involved is being constantly improved. Human skills routinely progress from competence to mastery.

We have already have an example of a customary practice which has been around for centuries—artists painting over brush strokes that are not exactly as intended so they can be redone.

Bette Nesmith Graham was able to copy this.

But—although what creative painters do remedially is well-established and relatively unchanging—sometimes it seems there is no limit to the degree of excellence that can be achieved in an activity—even though logic suggests there must be one eventually.

The most obvious examples are in the field of sport, where athletes continue to break records, even though when the previous record was set, many thought it could not be broken.

At least, not for a long time.

The relevance of this backdrop to copying by observing people is that once we convert what is required to overcome a goal-blocking obstacle into a human competence, we can go looking for that competence—usually a more general and best representative example of it—and then seek to reproduce it.

Once we find that broader capability, we look to apply it specifically to the particular need we have.

The people competence we are seeking can be an individual skill or talent someone has developed to a very high level.

Or it can be a form of expertise in which a team has acquired unmatched excellence.

Finally, we can observe ourselves—the person we spend most time with and know most intimately. We obviously spend a lot of mental energy thinking about ourselves. If we hold in mind a picture of a broad personal competence that we require to deal with a problem we are facing, sometimes aspects of what we are and do can be applied to that same problem outside ourselves.

We will unpack this in the next chapter when we look at precise illustrations of learning to innovate by copying others and ourselves.

Copy by Observing Things

Most of the points made in the previous section about Copying by Observing People —finding an instance of relevant, superlative competence we can emulate—apply equally to inanimate things. These often showcase the kind of elite performance we happen to be on the lookout for. Once we become attuned to such instances, the possibilities are virtually endless, as the number of things within the orbit of our experience borders on the infinite.

Once again, the basic premise is this: if we have been pondering a problem and can picture a broad version of the solution we need, that mental focus increases the chance of an innovative overlap. This occurs when what we are thinking about coincides with what we observe—when we come across some *thing* that contains hints—albeit generally—of the solution we are seeking.

We can then descend from an understanding of what is happening generally—of what is common to what we are observing and to what we need—to innovate to a specific innovative solution to our problem.

Allow me to emphasize something we have seen before—what we are learning here is not radically new thinking. Like so many of the foundational principles in this book, what we are learning to apply is no more than an adaptation or conversion of something we already do, or that someone else is already doing.

The practice of seeking and locating a method or technique that has proven to be unsurpassed in achieving a desired result in a defined situation is the essence of "best practice," a discipline adopted by organizations (mainly) and individuals all over the world. Frame what you need to do in clear terms, and then find who or what does exactly that—but does it better than anyone else.

When we copy by observing things—and people for that matter—we are seeking the acknowledged best practice, so we can understand it and then emulate it.

There is no shortage of examples of best practice, and we will check out lots of them in Chapter 15: Copy by Observing Things.

Let's Flatter

A lot of the observations attributed to the intruder at the start of this chapter, the flamboyant Irish poet, playwright novelist—and, so it seems, philosopher—Oscar Wilde, contain subtleties that may belie their ostensible meaning. It is therefore possible, in praising imitation as "the sincerest form of flattery," Wilde was also in a backhanded way, implying copying is an inferior mode of innovating, or—more accurately in his circles—of being creative.

But do we care?

If we follow the well-trodden path of someone who has been there before us—someone who has clearly defeated the trolls typically lurking under the bridges along that route—why not tread those very same footsteps if it enables us to generate the innovative solution we need?

And it doesn't require a lot of mental effort of our part. Our brains associate quite naturally with experiences we would not select of our own volition. Rather than remaining indifferent to this phenomenon, we encourage it. We put ourselves in the path of serendipity—as did Bette Nesmith Graham—when she pictured what would be required to solve her problem with typing mistakes.

This led her to copy from her artist friends.

Acquiring a picture of what it takes to innovatively deal with some problem is easier if our view is sweeping and expansive, like climbing to the top of a mountain. From there we gain an overarching perspective of what lies below us. The specifics of a problem morph into a general commonness—a broad capability—that can then be the father of a different specific solution, when we go down the other side of the mountain.

From the mountaintop, we can see people and inanimate entities, natural and man-made. We will be particularly drawn to anything whose nature or characteristics overlap with the general mental picture we retain of our need.

We then can imitate that broad capability but, in copying it, we will reduce and shape it into the specific innovative solution we require.

And if we must flatter, we do so shamelessly.

Coming second is a small price to pay for eventually joining the ranks of the best.

14

COPY BY OBSERVING PEOPLE

Good artists copy; great artists steal

PABLO PICASSO

Immature poets imitate; mature poets steal

T.S. ELIOT

The notion of copying can carry with it a fear of being unoriginal—of being the very opposite of what we need to be to innovate. But no apology is called for. The expression "steal shamelessly"—a stance we embraced at the close of the previous chapter—is commonly seen and heard in support of innovative endeavors that copy from others, and that do so without hesitation.

It is a sentiment shared in artistic communities as well, as evidenced by the introductory comments of Messrs. Picasso and Eliot, masters in their respective fields.

And—as we will see shortly—Giacomo Puccini, regarded as one of Italy's foremost operatic composers, was a disciple of the practice too.

Putting aside any sensitivities for the moment, it is difficult to argue with the logic. If you can find someone doing something you want to do and they are doing it exceptionally well, it is natural to study what they do and to try to emulate it with the aim of achieving comparable results.

Opportunities to innovate through Copying by Observing People occur on three levels:

1. Copying Individuals

2. Copying Teams

3. Copying Ourselves

Copying Individuals

During the 5th century BC, the military strategist, Sun Tzu—whose penetrating insights helped shape our thinking earlier—decreed in his masterpiece, *The Art of War:*

All warfare is based on deception

Then, and since then, misleading and deceiving the enemy has been a fundamental preoccupation of those who—willingly or unwillingly—are engaged in military conflicts.

Fast-forward to a 2007 publication by the United States Office of the Director of National Intelligence—entitled the *Textbook of Political-Military Counterdeception: Basic Principles & Methods*. In it, the authors, Barton Whaley and Susan Stratton, note in the 1970s:

> *Conjurors had evolved theories and principles of deception and*
> *counter-deception that were substantially more advanced than*
> *currently used by political or military intelligence analysts*

This finding prompted military surveillance organizations—and eventually, of course, political parties—to study the skills of magicians to gain insights into how to deceive adversaries, how to become much better at concealing intentions, and disguising military and political initiatives.

The progression of the conventional tactics of magicians in creating illusions and manipulating audiences from the entertainment arena to the military and political spheres is an excellent illustration of innovating by copying what people do.

More precisely, it draws attention to mastery in individual people skills—those who are uniquely expert in their craft.

Shortly, we will also look at how team skills can be emulated to innovate.

In many professions, individuals perform the competence embedded in a particular occupation to the highest level achievable—or at least to a level well beyond anyone not engaged in that vocation. The setting and surpassing of records in sport is the obvious reference point. What people achieve is nearly always the result of thousands of hours of training, learning and practice. When we observe what they have done and are able to copy it, innovative value is generated because the effort invested in reaching such a high level of proficiency can often be bypassed. Simply imitating what such champions have learned—through much exertion—to do, can be a valuable shortcut to doing something similar.

Not quite so straightforward in the sports arena of course, but the principle still holds more broadly. The tactic of copying relevant individual people can be exercised without restriction. It is prevalent in sport and business and—as we have seen—in the military and political arenas.

But copying from experts occurs against the backdrop of more genteel pursuits as well.

One such example of copying individual excellence to innovate comes from 1896 and the celebrated Italian composer Giacomo Puccini. He occupies a rare position in the history of opera, being ranked with Mozart and Verdi between 2004 and 2018 in the top three when it comes to the number of performances of their operas worldwide. Impressively, he had three of his operas (*La Bohème*, *Tosca*, and *Madama Butterfly*) amongst the ten most frequently performed operas globally.

Puccini obviously possessed prodigious talent in composing music, but it seems he was conscious this talent was not matched by his ability to write the best words to accompany that music. To address this problem, he innovated.

In pursuit of the perfect libretto—the text or words of an opera—he sought out experts in another field of artistic composition: poetry, where superior expertise lay in the craft of putting words together. In the creation of *La Bohème*, he engaged two poets to compose the words. He wanted the words to be concise and evocative—and to flow beautifully together with the music—like a conversation with his audience.

Poets were good at this.

Puccini's innovative resourcefulness seems to have paid off. *La Bohème* was and continues to be an outstanding success. To most observers, it is Puccini's best opera.

Copying Teams

In 2005, staff at London's Great Ormond Street Hospital were becoming increasingly concerned at the strain on their life-saving processes due to high patient volumes and the wide range of complex medical emergencies they faced. In such a hectic environment, the risks of serious patient error were very high.

Around the same time, a senior member of the pediatric intensive care unit gained a key insight while watching motor racing on TV—specifically, by observing a Ferrari Formula One pit crew. He was impressed by their skill in completing complex tasks quickly and with remarkable precision under intense pressure. It occurred to him that their seamless transition process paralleled the accuracy required in intricate healthcare transitions.

Subsequently, a Ferrari pit crew was contacted, consulted, and asked to coach the hospital staff involved in critical patient treatment. The precisely sequenced performance of a well-orchestrated racing team was translated into new behaviors that were adopted by the people involved in intensive care delivery. By mapping out the tasks and timing for every role, the need for discussion was minimized, flowing on to valuable gains in speed and rigor. A much-enhanced level of overall operational effectiveness and patient safety was achieved.

In November, 2006, it was reported in the *Wall Street Journal* that the Ferrari-inspired changes at the hospital reduced technical errors by 42% and information handover errors by 49%.

In the pursuit of greater efficiency, precision and teamwork, Great Ormond Street

Hospital generated an innovative solution by imitating people who were engaged in what was essentially parallel behavior—but in a completely unrelated field.

This is a classic example of copying by observing people performing together as a team.

Copying Ourselves

In 1962, an American engineer and inventor—Bob Kearns—was driving in the rain in Detroit, Michigan, in the USA. As his eyesight was partially impaired, the relentless movement of the wiper blades—even when the rain was not falling—meant he was struggling to see. While enduring this quandary, he began thinking about how the human eye cleans itself like a windscreen wiper when it blinks—but it only does so when it needs to.

He moved on from this insight to contemplate the broader phenomenon—the capability of something to clean itself. He then began to reason that this *self-cleaning* capability should also be able to be applied to windscreens. This would mean a wiper cleaned the windscreen only when rain fell on it.

The mental mulling Bob Kearns went through led him to invent the intermittent windscreen wiper—a standard amenity now in virtually all modern cars.

With the reliable benefit of hindsight, we can say Bob Kearns was employing the innovative tactic of copying ourselves.

Many products and services we now take for granted had their origins in the skill of copying ourselves.

We will look at another one that goes back quite a long way—the invention of the telephone—and a more recent one: how the ubiquitous social media website *Twitter* (renamed *X* in July 2023, when it was acquired by the world's richest man, Elon Musk) got its original name.

Around 1875, the eminent scientist—Alexander Graham Bell—was conducting research into the nature of sound and how to transmit it. As part of this research, he started to think about how he was able to hear.

What physically happened within his ear when he heard something?

Among other things, he noted his eardrum vibrated when hearing sound. Determined to replicate its capability, he engineered a vibrating metal diaphragm that quivered just like his ear in response to sound waves and embedded it in a groundbreaking device. Echoing his ear's sensitivity, the device was able to detect sounds with remarkable clarity.

By observing an aspect of himself, Alexander Graham Bell gave the world the telephone.

More recently, in 2006, an American software developer—Noah Glass—was trying to think of a name for an embryonic online social network. Although various accounts differ on the exact details, one version recalls an incident where his cell phone rang and vibrated, prompting him to associate the sensation with involuntary twitches of the body. Following this chain of mental association, he briefly considered the word "vibrate," but found himself drawn instead to "twitch."

Consulting a dictionary as part of his name-seeking mission, he explored related words and ideas—particularly ones that captured the essence of the site's function: short, quick bursts of communication. Following the train of his mind and the word links, he eventually landed on the word "twitter," which evoked birds chirping—an apt metaphor for the kind of rapid, lightweight interaction the platform aimed to foster.

The *Twitter* name was adopted, quickly embraced, and soon became globally recognized.

Although it's unlikely he was aware of it at the time, Noah Glass had effectively arrived at a brilliant, innovative name by copying himself.

Thieves on a Mission

We don't know if Pablo Picasso and T.S. Eliot—our hosts at the head of this chapter—knew each other well enough to have arrived at a shared belief: stealing in a creative sense is acceptable.

Not only that—they both also seem to imply it is downright beneficial.

Their lives did overlap in the early 20th century, particularly in Bohemian Paris from 1910 onwards. Perhaps they did frequent the same cafes as novelists such as Ernest Hemingway and Gertrude Stein, and the renowned French painter, Henri Matisse. Both Picasso and Eliot were prominent in their fields and participated in innovative art and literature movements, often at the cutting edge. They would have been aware of each other's work and presumably brushed shoulders at artistic gatherings.

Whether they did or did not confer, we don't know. But I think we have their blessing—even if independently bestowed—to take what other people do best and to seek to replicate it.

More than that, to better it.

Typically, such imitation is not mirror-image copying. The mountain metaphor teaches us that we must generalize from the specific to the broader capability involved—gaining from our lofty position an understanding of the general conditions that overlap with what we are seeking.

For instance, we might identify the conditions that enable a successful piece of deception—such as a magician's trick—or flawless teamwork under extreme pressure—such as in a Formula One pit stop. Once we understand these general conditions, we can fashion our own piece of deception or exemplary team performance under them.

When we copy from others to innovate, mostly we are not doing so specifically, but drawing from the broader structure that shapes the activity of interest—a concept we can liken to a box. We are not "stealing" the contents; we are simply appropriating the box they came in.

That box may have been created by individuals, by teams, or even by us.

15

COPY BY OBSERVING THINGS

The simple secret of my success is that I created something new out of the ideas and inventions of others

HENRY FORD

In 1941, a Swiss agricultural engineer, George de Mestral, went for a walk with his dog in the Jura Mountains of Switzerland. On their return, he noticed many burs from the cocklebur plant were stuck fast to his trousers and to the dog's coat.

Although probably regarded as no more than an irritating experience by most of us, de Mestral put these burs under a microscope and discovered they contained tiny hooks that had caught in the loops of his clothes and in his dog's hair. He began to think about the more general capability suggested by cocklebur plants—that of something adhering reciprocally to something else by means of hooks and loops. This led him to fabricate artificial hooks and loops embedded in man-made materials to achieve a reciprocal binding mechanism.

Some years later, Velcro made its market debut.

As was the case in Chapter 14—when we addressed the strategy of learning to innovate by observing people and surveyed examples of this happening—there was an element of serendipity involved in de Mestral's discovery. However, his chances of making such a discovery were boosted by his innate curiosity and predisposition to inventing things. De Mestral applied for his first patent when he was only 12 years of age—for a toy airplane he had designed. It was in his makeup to observe things around him and then seek to understand why they were what they were.

Unsurprisingly, the area of copying by observing things is extremely broad, embracing not only man-made things but, as we have just seen, things in the natural world as well. In his book *The Shark's Paintbrush*, Jay Harman investigates the practice of biomimicry, and acknowledges:

Forward looking companies that are releasing ingenious products that mirror innovations found in nature

He argues that solutions for challenges that require sustainable technologies can be discovered through emulating nature's designs.

The examples Harman gives include sunscreen that replicates hippos' protective sweat (presumably without the odor) and hospital wall coatings that emulate the antimicrobial properties contained in sharkskin. He also talks about more efficient wind turbine designs that emerged by imitating the shape of a whale's fin.

And, in discussing organisms in the natural world, he relates how the configuration of a termite mound resulted in innovations in building ventilation systems.

But—as the invention of Velcro demonstrates—innovating from observing what occurs in nature is not just a recently discovered skill.

Mountain Climbing with George

As we did in the previous chapter, we can depict the experience of George de Mestral that led to the invention of Velcro through the metaphor of mountain climbing. (The fact that he was walking in *mountains* may pique our curiosity a little, but let's not get excited—it's coincidental, not part of the lesson. A small brush with serendipity!)

Revisiting the mountain climbing imagery is worthwhile because it reinforces how we can become more adept at innovating through copying—how we can intentionally place ourselves in the path of serendipity, instead of just crossing our fingers and wishing for a lucky break.

George de Mestral's mountain climb would look like this:

Copying Mountain for Velcro

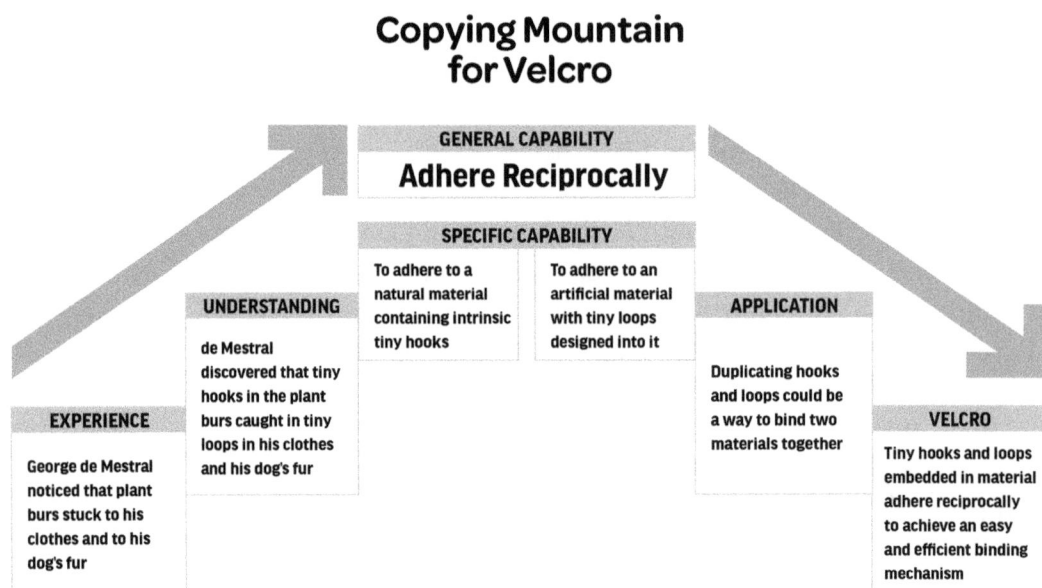

GENERAL CAPABILITY
Adhere Reciprocally

SPECIFIC CAPABILITY

To adhere to a natural material containing intrinsic tiny hooks

To adhere to an artificial material with tiny loops designed into it

UNDERSTANDING

de Mestral discovered that tiny hooks in the plant burs caught in tiny loops in his clothes and his dog's fur

APPLICATION

Duplicating hooks and loops could be a way to bind two materials together

EXPERIENCE

George de Mestral noticed that plant burs stuck to his clothes and to his dog's fur

VELCRO

Tiny hooks and loops embedded in material adhere reciprocally to achieve an easy and efficient binding mechanism

What happened to George de Mestral was quite random. While out walking, he encountered some prickly little plant bodies and noticed they stuck not only to his trousers, but also to his dog's fur. He ascended one side of the mountain from this specific experience to a more general understanding of what happened—tiny hooks embedded in the plant were responsible.

Moving mentally higher up the mountain, he discerned that tiny hooks will adhere to tiny loops if they are brought together

Then, on the mountain top, he reflected on a more general capability—a form of reciprocal adherence: where two items each play a part—albeit a slightly different one—in attaching to each other. Later, by utilizing a microscope, he confirmed minute hooks and loops were indeed behind the stickability which had made its claim on both him and his dog.

How could this capability of "Adhering Reciprocally" be replicated?

De Mestral then traveled down the other side of his cerebral mountain, and through seeking to emulate the general adhering capability of the hooks and loops, he eventually developed a material—Velcro—that does exactly that—specifically by replicating what the cocklebur plant does, but in another realm altogether.

He innovated through the strategy of copying by observing things.

Around about the same time as George de Mestral was perfecting the fabrication of Velcro, an American, Edward Gelsthorpe was also innovating by observing things. He was studying the ballpoint pen that had been patented in 1938 by the Hungarian Argentine journalist, Lazlo Biro, and was now enjoying worldwide popularity. Readers of my vintage will probably relate to the surname "Biro"—the eponym of the writing instrument we eagerly embraced as a supremely convenient successor to the fountain pen.

Gelsthorpe—who worked in sales and product development for Bristol Myers, an American maker of consumer health and personal care products—was notably curious about the rotating ball mechanism at the tip of each biro that rolled ink smoothly onto a writing surface.

In 1952, he had been ruminating about how the imprecise and messy application of deodorants to the skin might be improved. In his mulling over the operation of the biro, he eventually ascended from contemplation of the pen to the notion of a "Roll-On Liquid" capability in general. As we now know, this led him to the design of a dispenser containing a ball that had the capability to roll deodorant thoroughly and evenly onto human skin.

Roll-on deodorant took its place in the daily life of millions.

As I begin a final, historic copying tale—this time featuring animals—I'm struck by an ontological dilemma: do they fall under Copying by Observing People or Copying by Observing Things? They are animate but non-human, so they don't fit neatly under People. Yet they are far from inanimate, so putting them with Things feels wrong too.

Let's toss a coin.

Heads says they stay here under Copying by Observing Things.

Anyway, the place has been warmed by George de Mestral's cocklebur plants. In attacking his trousers and his dog without consent, they are certainly not inanimate either.

Around 1838, Samuel Morse—the soon-to-be inventor of Morse Code—was traveling by stagecoach across the USA. At the time, he was grappling with a major obstacle: electrically transmitted information could not travel long distances without fading—a limitation that threatened the very viability of Morse Code as a breakthrough communications technology.

During a stop at one of the "stage" stations, he noticed fresh horses were being tethered to the coach. Each changeover replaced tired animals with rested ones, ensuring the journey could continue with renewed physical energy. This realization caused Morse to think more broadly about the capability of "Boosting Energy"—if fresh horses could extend a physical journey, could fresh bursts of energy extend an electrical one? This thought caused him to conceive of a series of relay stations that would boost electrical energy over long distances.

Copying by observing animals helped solve a critical technical problem. And with that barrier overcome, Morse Code went on to revolutionize human communication.

The Practice of Best Practice

Seeking to do what someone else is doing exceptionally well by copying how they are doing it is a very natural human instinct. Many thousands of self-help books, podcasts and video tutorials attest to the popularity of such an aspiration. This type of thinking—identifying what is needed and locating where that relevant activity is being executed with unmatched mastery so it can be copied—is the essence of what is called "best practice."

Overwhelmingly, the best practice technique is utilized in the business world. The reasons for its attractiveness are compelling. It is an extremely valuable alternative to incremental improvement based on in-house learning and experience and is the preferred route for those seeking faster progress. Success is achieved through locating an organization in another field for whom the identified competence or capability is usually critical and at which they have therefore become expert. This includes those with parallel expertise in products or services in quite different industries and—as the story of the military copying from magicians demonstrates—also those in quite unrelated fields.

One of the better-known examples of best practice includes Kaizen—the system of continuous improvement that originated in Japan just after the Second World War. An American, Dr. W. Edwards Deming, helped Japanese companies adopt quality management practices in the 1950s and, over the next 10–15 years, to set previously unthinkable standards for waste reduction and operational advancement. That Japan rapidly rose from post-war devastation to become a global industrial powerhouse—driven by a relentless focus on quality and efficiency—is a testament not only to the value of emulating what others have achieved but also to the possibility of surpassing them.

Thirty years later, an American Company—Motorola, Inc, an early manufacturer of mobile phones (as they were called then)—raised the bar even higher with the Six Sigma methodology. Six Sigma established it was possible to aim for and achieve no more than 3.4 defects or errors for every one million operations or tasks.

Forget being 99% efficient—best practice became being 99.99966% efficient.

Such standards have been adopted extensively in manufacturing since then.

But—as we saw with the medical professionals at Great Ormond Street Hospital, who became Formula One pitmen in Chapter 14—best practice is also pursued in healthcare to ensure patient safety. It is mobilized in various other non-business fields as well. Best practice is certainly not confined to designated industries and disciplines.

Often best practice is pursued by organizations under the guise of *benchmarking*. For instance, companies can study similar processes or functions in industries quite unrelated to their own to establish what the "benchmark"—or best practice—is for that activity. It doesn't matter who is doing it; what matters is who or what *does it best*. Studying how it is performed at benchmark level and copying the *how*, can lead to new and rewarding innovative practices.

Although there have been spectacular advances in the practice of best practice during the past 50 to 100 years, the discipline goes back a long way—at least until 1450—and to Johannes Gutenberg and the invention of the printing press. While engaged in designing the printing press, Gutenberg needed to know the frequency with which letters were used so he could calculate the quantities of each individual letter to cast in metal.

To do this, he engaged in some best-practice-type thinking.

After some rumination, he concluded that the recorded documents that were most in demand during his time—religious texts, popular literature, and legal documents existing prior to the printing press—would be an accurate representation of the frequency with which specific letters appeared in recorded information. By studying them, he felt he could gauge which letters were more prevalent than others, and in which contexts.

Through careful observation of these existing written materials and the letter usage reflected in them, Gutenberg was able to solve his problem. He determined the quantities and ratios of individual letterforms he needed to cast for his printing press.

He established the incidence of each through benchmarking.

In talking about best practice, it is practically helpful to understand the important way in which it differs from the other copying tactics we have studied. The latter contain a much greater element of chance, because they rely upon us retaining a mental picture of the desired solution that is general only—a broad impression of the competence needed to solve our problem. An answer materializes when we happen upon a specific application under the same broad competence we have in mind, prompting us to innovate to a parallel, specific solution to our need.

This is what happened with Edward Gelsthorpe in the invention of roll-on deodorant. He was visualizing the unmet need to roll a liquefied substance smoothly onto the human body and discovered that a similar roll-on capability was already present in the ballpoint pen. He moved from a roll-on dispenser of ink to a roll-on dispenser of deodorant.

But when we are pursuing a best practice solution, we have a narrower, specific competence or capability in mind than Gelsthorpe did, right from the outset. We might want to halve defects in the manufacturing of a widget. Or eliminate late deliveries of that widget. With such specific and clear goals in mind, we can then purposefully seek out who or what meets them—the most efficient widget manufacturer or the most reliable widget deliverer—without relying on a chance encounter that happens to fall under the broad mental canopy of the solution we have in our minds.

The best practice framework automatically establishes the specifics of what we are looking to copy.

Who Are the Champions?

I don't know if the founder of the Ford Motor Company—Henry Ford—dreamed of making motor vehicles that were inexpensive and plentiful, and was alert to experiences that aligned with such a vision—but it seems he was proactive in observing what was going on around him.

And—from his introduction to this chapter—he certainly was not shy about copying anything that he observed and could use.

Simply observing how things function can help us to innovate—especially if we have been pondering a problem and casting around for a solution. Having a picture in our minds that broadly represents the answer we need increases the chances of an innovative overlap when we happen to notice something that, in general terms, meshes with that mental picture.

There is an umbrella function—a broad capability—that is shared by what we are observing and what we need.

Often, we stumble upon excellence of interest to us by accident. This is what happened to George de Mestral on his way to inventing Velcro. The affinity his clothes had for a particular plant led him to discover the presence of tiny hooks and loops, and then to discern—on the mountaintop—that a system of reciprocal adherence was at work. He replicated this system on two fabric strips—one containing hooks, the other loops, to create Velcro.

Serendipity played a part in the emergence of Velcro and this is gratifying when it happens. But, as our desire is to innovate purposefully to achieve a goal right now, it is better to take the element of chance out of the equation.

We can do this in two ways.

First, we can reduce the chance factor inherent in serendipity by carrying a thought-picture of what we need around in our heads—primed to recognize a fortuitous occurrence.

Or, second—with greater certainty—we can tread a more structured path: the path of best practice.

With best practice—we formally define, rather than merely visualize—the general expertise we need and then go look for it. The broad proficiency we require will be in operation somewhere and, more pertinently, in one of those places, it will be being exercised with unmatched mastery.

Every activity—whether a sport or an activity which is not conventionally competitive—has a champion that excels—is the best in its category.

And such a champion is not necessarily a person. As we learned from the development of roll-on deodorant, Edward Gelsthorpe's "champion" was something as humble as the ballpoint pen.

Whatever or whoever our champion—when we find them—we channel that champion to innovate.

PART 4

INNOVATE THROUGH ORIGINATING

Originating to Innovate is the partner of Copying to Innovate. Together they form the two core modes of innovating.

They complement each other.

The sublime insight at the heart of innovating through originating is that you don't have to originate at all.

You innovate because everything that already exists is not completely consumed or utilized. By tapping into this unused value—available value that does not need to be recreated—you gain something not only valuable but, in a real sense, free.

The three input resources that form the foundation of the Sebir Model—and the Innovative Value they unlock—frame the originating mode of innovating like this:

1. Relevant unused value is unleashed from the Initiator Resource

2. Desired behavior or performance that is already predisposed to emerge, is triggered from the Responder Resource

3. The Initiator and Responder are automatically drawn to each other by the makeup and positioning of the Connector Resource

To innovate through originating is to liberate value, not create it.

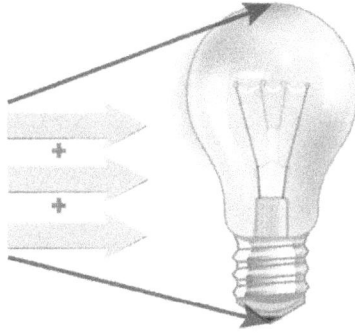

16

ORIGINATING TO INNOVATE

*Ideas are like rabbits. You get a couple and learn how to handle them,
and pretty soon you have a dozen*

JOHN STEINBECK

In 1420, Filippo Brunelleschi—considered by many to be the father of Renaissance architecture—was facing his greatest ever challenge: designing and building the Cathedral of Santa Maria del Fiore in Florence, Italy, with its large dome. The construction of a dome with such a wide span, unsupported by any centering structure, had never been successfully achieved.

Ultimately Brunelleschi's engineering brilliance won through, but on the way to a solution he considered several innovative possibilities.

The one of interest to us is where Brunelleschi toyed with the idea of supporting the dome by filling what would be the interior space of the cathedral with earth and building the dome on top of it until it became self-supporting.

A major problem Brunelleschi anticipated with this idea was removing the soil once the structure was completed. This would have to be done from within, little-by-little. Larger, more efficient excavation would not be possible.

In other words, unavoidable, piecemeal extraction was likely to be very expensive and extremely protracted.

What resources were available to him at relatively low cost—existing within the orbit of his experience and possessing some applicable, unused value—that could be brought to bear on the problem of removing the load-bearing dirt once it had done its job?

Brunelleschi's pondering led him to think about the street children of Florence—their poverty, and their basic needs. He visualized that the earth used to fill the open interior of the cathedral structure could be liberally seeded with a copper coin—the *quattrino*. Word would spread to the Florentine urchins that thousands of *quattrinos* were buried in the mound of earth, and they would be invited to bring small containers to collect the soil—and keep whatever coins they found within.

This scheme did not eventuate because ultimately Brunelleschi came up with a workable lightweight building structure, incorporating a double-shelled dome with an inner and outer layer. The accompanying brickwork was fabricated in a herringbone pattern that added to the stability of the dome.

Job done.

Notwithstanding Brunelleschi's construction breakthrough, our business is with the idea that didn't happen—the opportunity lost to the poor Florentine children. Although Brunelleschi was steeped in the fields of architecture, engineering, mathematics, and design, his thinking was not constrained by these in seeking innovative answers for his considerable construction problem. He was open to any possibility in the locale in which he lived and worked.

Brunelleschi seems to have acquired this instinct amid his impressive array of other talents.

Interestingly, his thoughts ran to a relevant resource known for its paucity—and by implication—its cheapness. It was *economico*. In this sense it was potentially undervalued. Originating to Innovate relies completely on identifying a resource that possesses untapped value that will solve a problem and extracting that unused value from the resource.

The thought experiment attributed to Brunelleschi does a good job in illustrating the type of unfettered thinking we should model in identifying the resources in our orbit when originating to innovate.

But cards on the table. I cannot be sure Brunelleschi really did consider such an option because my scant record of it does not credit a source I can verify. And it didn't literally happen. It didn't get tested. It was reported as a thought only—albeit a highly imaginative one.

But we won't let the facts spoil a great tale.

Although we must reluctantly leave Brunelleschi and his illuminating exploits, we can be grateful to him for leading us to the quintessential form of personal innovating: originating.

When we originate, we do not borrow and adapt from a parallel solution as we do when we innovate through copying. We innovate from first principles. The solution is constructed specifically for the problem at hand—personal innovating in its purest mode.

Because of its empirically grounded origin, the theory that underpins originating has identifiable roots that we will uncover. Yet what is gratifying—and perhaps unexpected—is that those roots explain behaviour that is thoroughly familiar. They sit below the surface of everyday activity, which is why we have never had reason to think about them.

Once we become aware of these roots and the role they play, however, we can begin to apply the sources of that everyday behaviour deliberately—replacing instinct with intentional innovative activity. The roots themselves may be new knowledge to us, but the behaviours they already shape are not. Recognising this places us in a strong position to use them consciously to innovate.

Unpacking these two perspectives—taking on buried knowledge and using it to explain familiar behaviour—asks more of this chapter than any other in the book. Accordingly, these two perspectives are framed separately below to make the distinction clear.

BELOW THE SURFACE

What follows is an attempt to make sense of what we already do—but in a way that reveals a deeper route to personal innovating.

From Copying to Innovate to Originating to Innovate

We were introduced to the first mode of innovating in Chapter 13: Copying to Innovate, and learned how to practice it in the following two chapters dedicated to the two main copying strategies: Copying People and Copying Things.

Before turning to the originating strategies available to us—there are three—a quick refresher on the fundamental distinction between the two modes of innovating could be useful:

1. Copying to Innovate involves comprehending the general working principles of an innovative solution elsewhere and then applying a more specific version of it to solve our problem

2. Originating to Innovate involves coming up with our own solution by locating and tapping into a relevant resource that possesses unused, embedded value that will solve our problem

Although they are obviously different, these two modes have the same grounding. Both are seeking a capability that contains the means to innovatively deal with our difficulty. The key challenge is locating that capability—the required Problem-Solving Value—and the two modes differ in the way in which they find it.

Inventions such as Roll-on Deodorant and Morse Code emerged from the Copying to Innovate mode, as we saw in Chapter 15. Most innovations however—as distinct from inventions—tend to be generated through Originating to Innovate.

Although it may sound paradoxical, the underlying reason is this: when we innovate through copying, a new resource is usually created. While the basis of copying is often a general capability—such as the ability to "Roll-on Liquid" or to "Boost Energy"—the result is a new instance of that capability. For example, the pen casing of a biro becomes a dispenser for roll-on deodorant. Or, with Morse Code, the physical boost provided by fresh horses at stagecoach relay stations is reinterpreted to create electrical relay stations that boost a telegraphic signal. These are new resources, and typically, inventions.

By contrast, when we innovate by originating, no new resource is created. Instead, an existing resource is tapped for the residual value it already possesses. That value is what is needed to overcome a problem blocking the achievement of a goal. The key is the value doesn't have to be generated—it simply has to be accessed. The result is an innovative solution, but not an inventive one.

So while Copying to Innovate can produce both inventions and innovations, Originating to Innovate is typically limited to generating innovations. In theory, it cannot be relied upon to produce inventions.

Before proceeding, I am conscious that the next three sections contain more technical terminology than any other in this book. That is deliberate.

To ease the transition, let me reproduce a simple variation of the Sebir Model image from Chapter 2—a silhouette of which heads this chapter—to orient you to the terminology that follows:

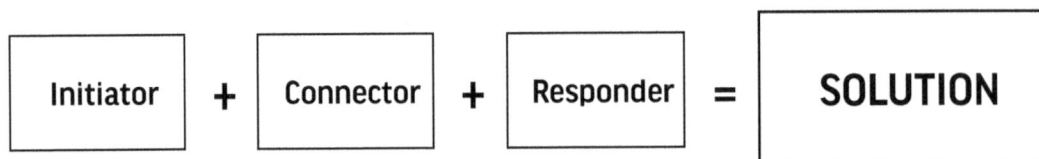

$$\boxed{\text{Initiator}} \; + \; \boxed{\text{Connector}} \; + \; \boxed{\text{Responder}} \; = \; \boxed{\textbf{SOLUTION}}$$

As you read through the following sections and encounter the repeated labels identifying each of the three input resources, regard them as you would the ingredients and instructions in a recipe—increasingly familiar as you work with them.

A quick refresh. The Sebir Model is the three-stage input-output model made up of a trio of input resources which—when added together—combine and amplify each other to generate an innovative output that well exceeds their sum. The input resources are the Initiator, the Connector, and the Responder. Each embodies a strategy we implement when we originate to innovate.

The three originating strategies birthed by the Sebir Model are:

- Originate through the Initiator Resource
- Originate through the Connector Resource
- Originate through the Responder Resource

And, as we will learn—a fourth, very useful strategy—is available to us as well:

- Originate by Renewing Processes

In the next four chapters, we will examine each strategy in depth but, for now, we will simply meet them and gain a sense of what each is about.

Before we do, it is worth pausing to address the recurring use of the term *resource*—each of the three Sebir Model elements is explicitly named as one—and the term will appear even more frequently from this point on.

In line with its conventional meaning, a resource is something that can be used to help achieve a goal. But, as discussed in Chapter 3, our use of the term goes further. In the Sebir Model, a resource is always understood to possess unused value—value that can be released with minimal effort—value that does not have to be recreated.

As we now shift our focus to *how* that value is extracted from the Initiator, the Connector, and the Responder, we will also see that every resource has inherent features or characteristics that we manipulate to innovate. These could also be called properties, but we will use the term *attributes* throughout, as it more precisely captures the specific aspects of a resource that can be identified, isolated, and modified.

Originate through the Initiator Resource

Initiator Resources are the launching element in creating Innovative Value.

The value contribution of the Initiator Resource to the total Innovative Value we generate when we innovate is designated Problem-Solving Value. This is because it converts the Problem Cause into the AFTI Problem Solution.

A straightforward Initiator example can be seen in a lighting equipment business struggling with unpredictable and irregular sales. The result is frequent cash flow problems. To fix this, the business looks for an Initiator that can turn unstable sales revenue into steady income. The owners decide to focus on their Contractual Terms as an Initiator. These trading terms have Problem-Solving Value because they shape and manage customer relationships. The company varies its trading terms to incentivize monthly leasing of lighting components and systems instead of one-time purchases by customers. This approach smooths incoming cash and makes their finances more predictable.

All Initiator Resources have distinct attributes and—once an Initiator has been selected—one or more of these can be harvested for the unused value it contains.

There are three options for tapping into the attributes of an Initiator Resource to release its unused value:

1. *Extend* an Initiator Resource to *Do More* of What it Normally Does

2. *Multiply* an Initiator Resource to *Do Something In Addition to* What it Normally Does

3. *Vary an* Initiator Resource to *Do Something Different from* What it Normally Does

Notice that the descriptions of these options are wholly consistent with the spirit of accessing the residual value that exists with Economy of Effort. This is essential if the input to any innovative project is to remain small relative to the ultimate result achieved.

Don't worry if the options seem to overlap. How each differs and is deployed will be described in Chapter 17, which explains and demonstrates practically how to innovate through Initiator Resources.

Originate through the Connector Resource

Connector Resources bring Initiator Resources and Responder Resources together to stimulate the innovative solution. They sit in the middle.

The value contribution of the Connector to the total Innovative Value we generate when we innovate is designated Attraction Value. This is because its substance and positioning are such that the Initiator Resource and Responder Resource are reflexively attracted to each other.

Here is a Connector example: a supplier of plastic storage bins eliminates the need for external packaging when shipping these items by utilizing the outermost one, with its lid in place, as an external wrapper. This is the Connector. The Initiator—the items being shipped—is connected to the Responder—required external packaging—seamlessly. The Connector ensures that packaging the storage bins for transport and shipping them happens seamlessly.

In common with Initiator Resources and Responder Resources, Connector Resources have distinct attributes that can be leveraged to maximize the chances that the selected Initiator Resource and the Responder Resource will interact instinctively.

The job of the Connector is to make the Initiator known in such a way to the Responder that the latter then behaves or performs in the desired manner. Depending on the Connector option employed, persuasion can elicit responses that range from likely to probable, and ultimately, to a guaranteed outcome.

There are four options for positioning a Connector Resource to ensure that the best possible innovative persuasion occurs between the Initiator Resource and the Responder Resource:

1. *Align* Resources to *Suggest* the Desired People Result

2. *Link* Resources to *Encourage* the Desired People Result

3. *Integrate* Resources to *Guarantee* the Desired People Result

4. *Integrate* Resources to *Guarantee* the Desired Things Result

A notable feature of these Connector options is their ability to distinguish between animate and inanimate resources. Aligning or linking resources is only effective if the Responder has some agency in the process. Human volition is essential for a response to an Align or Link Connector option. The Align and Link options for connecting are therefore only available when people are the Responder.

A machine, a conveyor belt or a piece of software, for instance, has no choice in what it is programmed to do. Therefore, the notion of suggesting or encouraging their performance is illogical.

Accordingly, the only Connector option for inanimate resources is the Integrate option. They must do as they are told.

But there are also opportunities for the Integrate option to be deployed to compel people to behave as desired. The fusing together of the Initiator Resource and the Responder Resource inherent in the Integrate Connector option always guarantees the result being sought.

How these options are put in place will be described in Chapter 18, which explains and demonstrates practically how to innovate through Connector Resources.

Originate through the Responder Resource

Responder Resources consummate the innovative result when Initiator Resources operate through Connector Resources to persuade the Responder Resources to behave or perform in the manner desired.

The value contribution of the Responder to the total Innovative Value we generate when we innovate is designated Predisposition Value. This is because the way it is stimulated to behave or perform is behavior or performance that it is *predisposed* to execute anyway.

A quick Responder example: an operator of a free carpark with a modest area for parking has a problem with drivers who leave their cars parked there for an unreasonably long time, unfairly depriving other users.

To counter this, the carpark manager introduces a directive requiring the lights of cars parked there to be left on. Cars without their lights illuminated incur a stiff financial penalty, but—more pertinently—if those car lights are left on too long, they will flatten the car's battery. Because it is in their self-interest—who wants a flat battery?—drivers are predisposed to voluntarily limit their free parking stay, improving the availability of the carpark.

The Predisposition Value of the Responder has been triggered.

In common with Initiator Resources and Connector Resources, Responder Resources have distinct attributes that can be targeted and stimulated to behave or perform in as required.

There are two options for appealing to the attributes of a Responder that maximize the chances the response received will deliver the sought-after innovative result:

1. *Stimulate People* to Do More of what they are *Already Inclined to Do*

2. *Energize Things* to Do More of what they are *Compelled to Do*

As implied in the identification of Predisposition Value, the characteristic feature of these Responder options is that they tap into behavior or performance that does what it is already predisposed to do.

Persuading people to behave in some desired manner usually requires a lot of effort—especially if they are resistant to such behavior. The innovative way to tackle this challenge is to seek something people are inclined to do anyway and mesh what you require of them with that propensity.

Things have Dispositions in the same way people have Dispositions except that with things, the inherent Disposition is unchanging in nature and reliably delivers the same result. The thing is programmed to perform in a particular way and does so unfailingly. It is therefore very worthwhile to integrate with the Disposition of a thing that is relevant to what you are trying to do. You can absolutely count on the activation of that propensity to help solve your problem and realize your goal.

How all this is brought about will be described in Chapter 19 which explains and demonstrates practically how to innovate through Responder Resources.

Before we finish, there is a final feature possessed by the Responder that is so distinct from the Initiator and Connector that it warrants mention now. It applies at the implementation stage—when we are working step-by-step toward an innovative solution. We have learned that untapped innovative value is latent in all resources. That is the easy part. The hard part is finding accessible and relevant resources but—in practice—we only need to find two: an Initiator and a Connector.

We don't need to find the Responder because we know immediately who or what the Responder is. We know as soon as we decide to innovate—as soon as we acknowledge there is a problem blocking something we want to achieve. The Responder refers to the people or things that must behave or perform in a specific way that equates to achievement of our goal. Their identity is revealed by the problem itself, which implicitly shows who or what they are. Their behavior or performance will deliver the sought-after innovative result.

This characteristic of the Responder manifests in PART 5: "How-To" Roadmap—the Sebir Ladder. Although the Responder is logically third in sequence in the Sebir

Model, it is engaged with first in the "How-To" climb of the Sebir Ladder—before the Initiator and Responder. Its visibility demands it be an early step, and knowing who or what it is decisively helps the search for the Initiator and Connector.

Originate by Renewing Processes

This strategy is not an identifiable element of the Sebir Model, but rather encompasses the entirety of it.

Throughout this book, the thinking and techniques we are learning pivot on the anatomy of the problem that has triggered the need for a solution. The makeup of that anatomy—and its cause-and-effect trajectory—determines the way forward and guides us through it.

The innovative solution is shaped by the problem that demands it.

But, there is also another route we can take.

It is possible to innovate irrespective of the nature or specifics of the problem.

This valuable alternative is accessed by focusing on the process that provides context for the situational circumstances rather than the circumstances themselves.

It is a powerful option because, as we will see, it can be applied to any situation—encompassing one or multiple problems—and its effectiveness is virtually guaranteed, thanks to its grounding in mathematical theory.

There are three options for originating by Renewing Processes:

1. *Perfect* the First Process Step

2. *Eliminate* Process Steps

3. *Squeeze* Individual Process Steps

These will be discussed in Chapter 20 which discloses the theoretical foundation of the three options and explains and demonstrates practically how to innovate by renewing processes.

How to Find Suitable Resources

Innovating through originating is resource dependent.

Finding resources that contain unused value we can draw upon to innovate is essential—specifically, we need to be able to find Initiator Resources and Connector Resources.

Responder Resources do not have to be located because—as we have learned—these are self-evident. The Responder is always the person or thing responsible for behaving or performing as needed, to solve our problem and achieve our goal. Therefore, we know who or what they are as soon as we decide to innovate.

But finding suitable Initiator and Connector resources presents us with a dilemma.

We saw from the exploits of Filippo Brunelleschi and his uninhibited thinking early in this chapter that the possibilities extend beyond the boundaries of conventional thinking. We must be careful not to impose what might appear to be sensible limits on the scope of what we should consider, or we risk shutting ourselves off from highly promising resource opportunities.

This, then, is our predicament. If the parameters for our quest are practically boundless, how can we locate a resource that is remedially relevant when the search space is impractically vast?

To answer this question in a way that is both lucid and memorable, I will borrow two innovation-related concepts that—while distinct—intersect sufficiently for both to be useful in the search for suitable resources. These enable us to cast the net wide at first and then, once it is full, to draw it tight, filtering the catch down to the most promising.

The two concepts address the resource dimensions of accessibility and relevance.

Accessibility

The first concept is "bricolage", from the French *bricoler*. It refers to the creative process of tinkering to construct or assemble something from a diverse range of available resources but using whatever is *at hand* to solve problems. Such resources need not have any distinguishing features—nor have anything in common for that matter—other than that they are within reach.

They are simply accessible.

Being proximate is an obvious pointer to accessibility.

Bricolage calls to mind the creation of the ubiquitous Caesar salad in 1924 by the Italian–American chef Caesar Cardini, who is said to have invented it in Tijuana, Mexico. He owned a restaurant there that was popular with Americans evading the restrictions of prohibition in the USA. One especially busy Fourth of July weekend— when his regular food supplies were virtually exhausted—he was forced to improvise and did so by grabbing whatever ingredients were available to mix a salad. These were romaine lettuce, eggs, Worcestershire sauce, olive oil, lemon juice, Parmesan cheese, and croutons.

Presto—the *Caesar* Salad!

And, as the saying goes, the rest is history.

Incidentally, accessibility does not merely mean physical proximity. In the way we are harnessing the concept, it also incorporates non-physical aspects, such as relational proximity.

For instance, a steel manufacturing business may import a primary raw material— coal—from a supplier in another country who, geographically, is not physically close. However, by virtue of their long-standing supply arrangement, both parties know each other very well and this means their respective resources and capabilities are accessible to each other as a matter of course.

Relevance

Although the criterion of accessibility does go some way toward limiting the extent of resources available, those within reach can still amount to a sizable list that requires filtering. This is where the second concept—the "adjacent possible"—comes in. The label was coined by theoretical biologist Stuart Kauffman. While its mathematical intricacies are beyond me, its essence is compelling: new ideas emerge from next-step opportunities that are a logical transition—are "adjacent"—to what is already in existence.

As part of a TED Talk in 2023 titled "*The 'Adjacent Possible'—And How It Explains Human Innovation*," Dr. Kauffman outlined the broad principle behind this concept. He argued that innovation progresses by building upon the resources that already exist—a foundational principle we endorsed strongly in Chapter 3: Where Does Innovative Value Come From?—but only in directions that are a natural progression from the current state. This means that what is possible next is constrained and shaped by what exists now. Expansion is only into resource possibilities that are a natural value extension from the prevailing situation. As we shall see shortly, this principle can be employed very efficiently to cull a pool of available resources. Any resource possibilities that don't flow naturally from an established starting point are ruled out as a matter of course.

Perceptive readers will have already detected the overlap between the concept of the adjacent possible and our earlier discussion of mental association in Chapter 13: Copying to Innovate. Associative thinking uncovers innovative solutions by linking previously unconnected thoughts. Similarly, the adjacent possible recognizes the emergence of new ideas from an existing state. The difference is this: mental association makes intuitive leaps to create novel connections, while the adjacent possible unfolds through a step-by-step progression from what is directly precedes it.

Accessibility and Relevance in Action

With the concept of "bricolage" in mind, first let's deal with the role of accessibility in finding suitable resources.

Once we decide to innovate through a problem and require an Initiator Resource and Connector Resource, the initial practical step to locate useful resources is through brainstorming. Setting aside questions of apparent suitability, a team recalls all the resources accessible to them and their organization, compiling a list as they go.[6] This collection of resources can grow very quickly and once the exercise is complete, grouping the list of resource items into practical categories is helpful.

---

6   Instead of team brainstorming, a properly instructed AI tool can be very effective—especially in the initial stages of resource list compilation.

For instance—from the perspective of an organization—two useful subheadings are "Internal" versus "External" resources. Another handy filter is resources that are "Tangible" versus those that are "Intangible."

The curated list constitutes the pool of accessible resources.

From accessibility, we move to the role of relevance—where we draw upon Kauffman's concept of "adjacency."

It has two functions in the search for suitable resources, and they are opposing ones.

To start with, adjacency adds potential resources to the pool. The brainstorming team considers both the accessibility of resources and those that have a logical connection to the problem being solved.

This is how we would proceed to find an Initiator Resource. The required contribution—which we have identified as Problem-Solving Value—is the capability a resource must possess to help solve the problem by realizing the AFTI Goal. Adding resources that potentially contain this value makes good sense.

Later—once brainstorming is exhausted, and the resource pool is complete—the concept of adjacency takes on a sorting role.

Having already included resources that represent a credible value progression from the Problem-Solving Value we are seeking, we do an about-face: we use that same criterion to exclude any that lack a clear connection to the specified Problem-Solving Value. The focus shifts to the subset of resources that originally qualified based on their accessibility. These are now narrowed down to the most promising ones. Those that plausibly have a connection with the stated Problem-Solving Value are retained; those that do not are culled.

Finally, the shortened, filtered list is evaluated utilizing reasoning grounded in proprietary knowledge—the experience and insight of those doing the innovating.

Don't worry if there is detail that seems to escape you at this stage. This evaluation process—including finding a Connector Resource—can be seen in action in the implementation example worked through in PART 5: "How-To" Roadmap—the Sebir Ladder.

ABOVE THE SURFACE

So much for the search logic. Now let's look at what this kind of value-extraction looks like when we do it naturally—often without noticing.

To Get Started, Watch Your Language

Hearing about acts of innovating can be uplifting and motivating, especially when what has been achieved is truly sublime. Not only is the ratio of effort to result appealing, but the innovative deed itself is often novel, clever and elegant. It possesses attractive symmetry.

Experiencing this vicariously can inspire—but at the same time it can discourage—because we may feel the chances of doing something comparable are remote. That utopia can seem hopelessly out of reach. Brunelleschi, for instance, was obviously exceptionally brilliant.

How could mere mortals like us expect to emulate him?

This is a mindset we can discard.

Although striking innovative examples give the appearance of being singular and remarkable, their manifestation can disguise their underpinning by principles that are unremarkable. These principles are often hiding in plain sight. In fact, most of us already employ the principles of purposeful innovating in our everyday language.

We innovate when we speak and write.

As we have emphasized many times already, we innovate successfully when the end we achieve outstrips the means we employed to achieve it. *Small effort→big result*.

We generate Innovative Value with Economy of Effort.

When we speak or write, we often generate additional value from the language we use. This can be demonstrated readily enough, starting with a pun. A pun is typically a similar sounding word with two or more meanings. Puns cleverly convey a new meaning as well as the normal meaning—without the need for extra words.

Just as innovating generates value from what already exists, a pun makes the most of what already exists in language. We don't exhaust ourselves searching for a pun to use—although there is still some mental effort involved.

Comedians do this sort of thing far more frequently than we do. They are skillful at regularly extracting value from words and phrases additional to the meaning normally expected—and in a manner calculated to be humorous.

To see what we can learn, it is worth looking at exactly how comedians innovate with language. They use at least two different innovative techniques that merit closer examination, because fundamentally, these techniques are comparable in principle to what happens when someone generates an Innovative Idea.

We have already acknowledged the best-known language-enhancing technique—puns. They cleverly exploit words to generate multiple meanings. Here are some:

- Jokes about German sausages are the wurst

- I'm addicted to brake fluid but I can stop whenever I want

- A good pun is its own reword

- I'm reading a book on anti-gravity. I can't put it down

- All the toilets in London police stations have been stolen. Police say they have nothing to go on

- This girl said she recognized me from the vegetarian club, but I'd never met herbivore

- They told me I had type-A blood, but it was a type-O

- Nostalgia is not what it used to be

- I went to a theatrical performance about puns. It was a play on words

While puns are usually associated with casual or playful language, they can be surprisingly effective in business settings—especially when used to disarm skepticism, create memorability, or draw attention to a serious proposal—as the following example shows.

An infrastructure construction firm seeks to be considered as a builder of road bridges commissioned by a local government authority. However, as a newcomer to the industry it faces a significant obstacle: getting its tender taken seriously. In practice, municipal managers rarely look beyond the first page of proposals from companies without a track record.

To stand out, BridgCo incorporates a visual pun. They redesign the cover of their submission, so the border resembles a briefcase lying on its side. Across the front page, in bold letters, appears the headline: "The Case for BridgCo."

This obvious yet clever play on words—packaging a professional pitch with a touch of wit—is enough to catch the reviewers' attention and make it more likely the bid is given genuine consideration.

Sometimes, comedians go one better than a pun by using a paraprosdokian.

A paraprosdokian is a figure of speech or rhetorical device in which the latter part of a sentence or phrase is surprising or unexpected. It usually causes the reader or hearer to re-interpret the first part.

Here is a selection of paraprosdokians:

- I want to die peacefully in my sleep, like my grandfather, not screaming and yelling like the passengers in his car

- A computer once beat me at chess, but it was no match for me at kickboxing

- If at first you don't succeed, skydiving is not for you

- I found a book called *How to Solve 50% of Your Problems*. So, I bought two

- My favorite uncle has the heart of a lion, and a lifetime ban from the zoo

- The key to success in life is authenticity. If you can fake that, you've got it made

These paraprosdokians—and the puns that preceded them—plus a few extras, are tucked into Appendix B for a touch of levity.

> **Innovate Through a Single Letter**
> This is a thought experiment. I want to establish a maxim that accurately conveys the frustration experienced by someone who is running late for a meeting and cannot find somewhere to park their car. The recollection of several of these experiences leads to the conclusion that as the time available reduces, the difficulty in finding a parking space increases.
>
> How can this experience be memorably documented?
>
> A survey of existing, comparable maxims identifies Parkinson's Law which states:
>
> "Work expands to fill the time available for its completion."
>
> I can innovate by adding the letter "g" to create Parkin**g**son's Law which states: "The time required to find a car parking space expands in inverse proportion to the time available to find one."

It is obvious from examples of puns and paraprosdokians why comedians like them. They are often humorous. So, when comedians innovate by using them, they are innovating on two levels—on the level of extracting additional meanings from the same words and simultaneously, on the level of sparking comic amusement.

I hope it is not too great a segue, but perhaps the most famous recorded example of extracting maximum value from the minimum number of words is a short story generally attributed to Ernest Hemingway. It had only six words: "For sale: baby shoes, never worn." This ability to hint at or imply a much larger story is innovative in the way it releases additional meaning with masterly Economy of Effort.

But we all do it. Not of course on the same level as an accomplished comedian or a Hemingway, but we innovate regularly through the language we use. Around the time I was recording these observations about puns and paraprosdokians, I met a person in an elevator who advised they were "going to ground". As I exited that elevator and went on my way, I mused about the different meanings "going to ground" could convey. I made up something that I think falls somewhere between being a pun and a paraprosdokian:

- I met a fugitive in an elevator. He said that he was going to ground

Or maybe it was a barista who said that he was "going to ground … [coffee]" but the last word was lost in the closing of the elevator doors?

While perhaps not such a big deal, tinkering with these wordplay musings can be fun—more pertinently, playing with them can help us develop greater sensitivity to the realization that all resources—even those as seemingly trivial as a word or phrase, or even a letter—contain latent, unused value that can be tapped to innovate.

It is not a huge leap from there to learning to innovate to solve a pressing problem. We are taking that leap in this book.

Using Language to Innovate in Business

Innovating by means of language is prevalent in business communications—whether it's a retailer advertising wallpaper with the line "Avoid ugly scenes in the bedroom," or naming your new accounting startup with a tagline that promises more than the literal words—"Abacus: You can count on us." And by going with the provocative brand moniker—"Fcuk"—the British-based fashion chain French Connection UK shows it knows how to innovate via words.

Accessible and Relevant

Originating to Innovate is not superior to Copying to Innovate. They are merely different. The difference between them lies in the way they locate the Problem-Solving Value—the unused capability that can be tapped to innovatively convert the Problem Cause into the AFTI Problem Solution.

In the case of Copying to Innovate, the proficiency to solve a problem is recognized as operating in a different setting—albeit more generally—and is copied and adapted to a new setting. Back in Chapter 14 we saw spies imitate magicians to deceive better, and surgeons channel race car drivers to achieve life-saving precision amidst fast-moving complexity.

This chapter—Originating to Innovate—demonstrates how the potential to solve a problem is extracted from a selected resource that contains latent, usable value—value that is applicable to that problem.

We have learned that originating to innovate closely follows the structure of the Sebir Model. Each of its three stages underpins a strategy—one each for the Initiator, Connector and Responder Resources—and under each of these are several high impact options.

Future chapters unpack these options and show how they are harnessed.

Originating to Innovate can imply a need for original thinking that is rare—the domain of the genius—but this misreads what is required. Most innovative ideas represent something analogous to the creative use of language. Additional value is extracted from an available resource—a word or a string of words—with relatively little effort.

And, speaking and writing are hardly exclusive.

Most of us resort to puns every now and then in dialogue with others—or when texting or otherwise expressing ourselves—and, apart from some sense of self-satisfaction we might feel, we don't dwell on where the thought came from.

We don't envisage a future as a stand-up comedian or renowned novelist.

We certainly don't realize we are innovating.

But we are.

If we can innovate with the language we use, we can innovate.

Conjuring up a pun evokes a feeling of relaxation and a sense of freedom. As Brunelleschi's imagination taught us when it gravitated to the street waifs of Florence, there are no acknowledged limits to what resources can be contemplated when we want to innovate our way through a problem. At first glance, this can be good news—until it is realized that having a resource pool that is unlimited is not much more useful than having no resources at all.

How do we find resources whose unused value is innovatively suited to our problem?

Two concepts found within the broader field of innovation can be yoked into service:

- "Bricolage," which involves the harvesting of diverse but accessible resources in novel ways

- The "adjacent possible," which connotes notions not only of proximity, but also of resource relevance

Traveling mentally to the intersection of these two concepts will expose resources that are both accessible and relevant.

But, the two concepts are just training wheels.

As the American author John Steinbeck advocates to open this chapter, *learning* can come quickly once *doing* is underway. His comments reflect how the creative process can multiply and reproduce "like rabbits." The foundational stages of personal innovating may seem challenging, but once you begin grasping the core tenets—and realize that you already innovate—the required way of thinking rapidly becomes second nature.

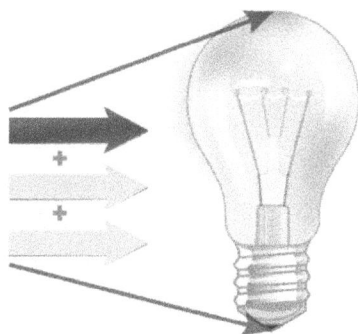

17

ORIGINATE THROUGH THE INITIATOR RESOURCE

I can fix a bad page. I can't fix a blank one

NORA ROBERTS

In 1982, the creators of a new board game, *Trivial Pursuit*—Canadian journalists, Scott Abbott and Chris Haney—faced a problem: no one knew about their creation. And that did not look like it would change any time soon. They didn't have much money for advertising and accordingly faced the dilemma of getting the game widely known without a budget for doing so. They were limited to relying on word-of-mouth promotion and demonstrating *Trivial Pursuit* at local pubs and gatherings in their hometown of Montreal, Canada.

To boost word-of-mouth activity, Abbott and Haney focused on the board game itself and, more specifically, on its central attribute, which was the Questions & Answers (Q&A) that were integral to playing the game. They added to the thousands of Q&As already existing to include questions and answers about famous people—Hollywood celebrities and other high-public-profile individuals.

They then sent the Q&As to those well-known people.

The latter welcomed the attention and started discussing the game through the lens of their own experiences, generating valuable social chatter that established awareness of *Trivial Pursuit*.

This simple extension of the dominant Q&A attribute of the game to deliver very fruitful word-of-mouth advertising is an excellent example of the first of three options that can be employed to originate through Initiator Resources—extending them to do more of what they normally do.

More on all three options shortly.

It is worth noting that the *Trivial Pursuit* innovative idea also possesses the qualitative characteristic of self-reinforcing symmetry found in many innovative ideas—the celebrities talked about *Trivial Pursuit* while talking about themselves.

Back in Chapter 2, we first heard about Initiator Resources when the model we are following—the Sebir Model—was introduced and overviewed. They are the first of the three input elements that originate the innovative solution to a problem.

The other two input elements are Connector Resources and Responder Resources.

For ease of communication and recall, we are frequently condensing them to the Initiator, the Connector and the Responder—but sometimes adding the term "resource" where it amplifies the clarity of what is being said.

How to Get the Most Out of the Initiator

Initiator Resources are the launching element we employ to innovate. They precede the Connector and Responder Resources in the Sebir Model. As resources, they are ubiquitous and contain unused Problem-Solving Value that can be unlocked with Economy of Effort.

Problem-Solving Value is the value that translates a Problem Cause into the AFTI Problem Solution, which has been ideally imagined in the *Problem PhotoBox*. Connector Resources contribute Attraction Value and Responder Resources contribute Predisposition Value.

There are three options to harvest an Initiator Resource to unlock its unused value:

1. *Extend* an Initiator Resource to *Do More* of What it Normally Does

2. *Multiply* an Initiator Resource to *Do Something in Addition to* What it Normally Does

3. *Vary* an Initiator Resource to *Do Something Different from* What it Normally Does

At first sight, the option descriptions can appear very similar but as we discuss them in more detail—especially with examples—their distinctive qualities will become clearer.

The critical point to note about these options is that they do not change the Initiator itself but rather "tweak" it—modifying one of its attributes—so it releases extra value without major investment of effort. The fundamental structure of the

Initiator remains intact; only the selected attribute is modified.

And—as the released value already exists and does not have to be recreated—it is practically costless.

By their very nature in executing minor modifications, the three Initiator options release free, residual value from the selected Initiator with Economy of Effort and, by so doing, contribute tangibly to the total value that an innovative solution to a problem delivers.

Extending the Initiator to Do More Than Normal

Extending the Initiator Resource to do more of what it normally does is the first option that focuses on an attribute of the selected Initiator.

We can word this option another way: if we innovatively extend the Initiator, it not only operates in accordance with its primary purpose, but—with the investment of minimal additional effort—it can deliver more of that exact same value.

All Initiator Resources have distinct attributes and—once the Initiator Resource has been selected—one or more of these can be tapped for the unrealized value it contains.

We can *extend* a chosen attribute to release that value innovatively.

We have already seen this option at work in the launch of *Trivial Pursuit*. The inventors zeroed in on an attribute foundational to the game itself—its questions and answers—and extended those Q&As to include famous people with whom they then engaged. The Initiator they utilized—the board game—was not changed fundamentally at all. Through one of its attributes, it was simply made to do more of what it was doing anyway—matching questions with answers. As a result, the selected Initiator provided an innovative solution for the predictably expensive marketing problem of gaining awareness for the new game.

Two further examples.

A common problem faced by airlines and other public transportation enterprises is that passengers do not pay attention to the pre-travel safety video, often ignoring it altogether. One airline—taking the safety video as their Initiator—concentrated on its content attribute and extended it by integrating various interesting and light-hearted lifestyle stories into the safety narrative. This secured the desired attention of travelers. The innovative extension of video content—which must be produced anyway—to include engaging human tales, got an important safety message across to those who needed to hear it.

An operator of car parking facilities in a major city faces the problem of the prohibitive cost of establishing new car parking capacity to meet demand that has outstripped supply. Taking the car parking owned by residents near the CBD as an Initiator, the carpark manager negotiates with them and provides a smartphone app through which residents can rent out—for a fee—car parking spaces they own, but don't use during the day. The residents can then make these available to daytime visitors to the CBD area. An extension of the normal use of private—but available—parking spaces innovatively frees up additional car parking capacity, benefiting all participants.

Well-known contemporary examples of an Initiator Resource being extended are Uber and Airbnb, whose innovative exploits we have encountered twice already. Uber has extended car utilization beyond normal personal use to the carriage of anonymous paying passengers whereas Airbnb has extended the occupation of privately owned dwellings to include users unrelated to the normal inhabitants. In both cases, the core utility remains unchanged; what has changed is that the same value is being enjoyed to a much greater extent.

Extending the primary purpose of an Initiator by means of one of its attributes—where the value it contributes has been utilized in the normal fashion but not exhausted—is the essence of innovating by extending an Initiator to do more than it normally does.

Multiplying the Initiator to Do Something Additional

Multiplying the Initiator Resource to do something in addition to what it normally does is the second option that focuses on an attribute of the selected Initiator.

It is subtly different from the first Initiator option, and we can describe this one more fully like this.

If we innovatively multiply the Initiator, it not only carries out the purpose for which it was designed, but—with the investment of minimal additional effort—it can deliver an extra beneficial result as well. Instead of manipulating an attribute of the selected Initiator so it does more of the same (the first option), multiplying the Initiator taps into another attribute that it possesses and activates that also.

The Initiator now delivers value in two different ways—one for which it was primarily designed plus a new one that is part of the innovative solution being formulated. The added value is simply the release of what is already present but, until now, unused in that way.

This is not an obscure concept. Tapping into another attribute of a resource to multiply value is commonplace. A case in point: the primary attribute of a car—its seating—is to carry passengers while its boot, a secondary attribute, can be used to transport cargo as well. Conversely, the deck of a pickup truck facilitates the primary carriage of cargo: its spare seating attribute means it can also carry passengers. Neither the car nor the truck is changed but more value is realized. Employing this principle—tapping into the secondary attributes of a resource, but in less obvious ways—is at the heart of multiplying the Initiator innovatively.

As such, being able to enjoy something approaching double the normal value is a reasonable expectation from employing this option.

An illustration.

Let's say we have a working office cramped for space, and this unfortunately rules out equipping it with a whiteboard for teamwork and visual group brainstorming.

What can be done?

In our search for an Initiator, we note there are storage cupboards along a wall. Selecting these cupboards as our Initiator—and focusing more specifically on an intrinsic attribute of those cupboards—their doors—we can multiply the usefulness of the cupboards beyond their primary purpose of enclosing what they contain.

We can write on the cupboard door surfaces—just like we would on a whiteboard.

If they are not already suitable for writing on, we can paint or otherwise treat the cupboard door surfaces so they can be written on—and thereby function as a whiteboard.

We have doubled the utility of our chosen Initiator—office cupboards—and have innovatively sidestepped the cramped space barrier to collaborative teamwork.

Multiplying the primary purpose of an Initiator by means of one of its attributes—whereby it does something on top of what it normally does—is the essence of innovating by multiplying an Initiator Resource. An additional innovative outcome is achieved with minimal effort because the same resource is doing something extra without being changed in any material way.

Varying the Initiator to Do Something Different

Varying the Initiator Resource to do something different from what it normally does is the third option that harnesses an attribute of the selected Initiator.

In practice this means that when we innovatively *vary* an attribute of the Initiator, its primary purpose is supplanted and the Initiator does something different instead—without any fundamental change to what it is. Because an existing but latent attribute is exploited, minimal effort is required to release this *different* innovative value.

Putting it another way, to solve the problem being faced, the chosen Initiator is manipulated to do something different from that for which it was originally created.

Now an example of an Initiator being varied to do something else instead of what it normally does.

Consider a confectionery manufacturer facing a frequent production problem where the integral hot runny filling is sometimes hotter than it should be. When this occurs, it melts the chocolate casing into which it is being poured, significantly disrupting the production run of infused chocolates.

The confectioner selects the production process as an Initiator Resource, and focuses on the infusion attribute of it—where the filling is introduced into the chocolate shell.

Soon, an effective remedial plan is devised that can be implemented at a modest cost. Instead of injecting the hot ingredient into the chocolate shell, the manufacturer varies that activity so the chocolate is melted, and the filling ingredient is frozen and dipped into the chocolate instead. Freezing rather than filling is the innovative answer.

By varying an attribute of the Initiator—the filling injection activity in the production process—a different but dramatic improvement is secured that results in permanent elimination of a frequent stoppage.

No Longer Weeds

A scenic town, whose appeal to many tourists lies in its natural, unspoiled state—especially its historic walls—faces an ongoing problem: weeds defacing the walls and marring their appearance.

The town managers decide to focus on the weeds and select them as their Initiator Resource. They trim the largest and most prominent batch into the shape of a swan and the other weeds into figures that complement the natural contours of the growth. These shapes are then maintained as part of the town's upkeep.

The role of the weeds is reimagined—so they become part of the attraction of the historic walls, rather than a blight on them. The weeds' visual attribute is *varied* and the appearance of the walls is transformed.

Varying the primary purpose of an Initiator by means of one of its attributes so what it now does replaces what it previously did is the essence of innovating by varying an Initiator. A different innovative result is achieved effortlessly because the Initiator itself essentially remains intact, fulfilling a different purpose, without having to be fundamentally modified in any way.

Don't Start with a Blank Page

When we intentionally innovate, we follow the Sebir Model. We know who the Responder is from the moment we decide to innovate and so the next step is to find and select an Initiator Resource from what exists in our environment. We identify it as having latent, unconsumed value that will help us innovate through the problem we are facing.

This is Problem-Solving Value.

To obtain this value, we manipulate the Initiator to the minimum extent—we tweak it—when coercing it to give up the residual value we have targeted. One of its attributes is chosen and once it is chosen, we manipulate it to extend, multiply or vary what the Initiator does, so it does something extra.

To put it another way, we modify an attribute of the Initiator without changing the fundamental nature of the Initiator itself. A major change of the Initiator would involve significant effort, the cost of which would undermine the very basis of how we innovate. We would violate the imperative of Economy of Effort. Essentially, the Initiator remains invariant while an innovative adjustment to one of its attributes causes it to do *more* than the usual, do something *in addition* to the usual or do something *different* from the usual.

There is a final, quite fundamental point to be made about innovating through Initiator Resources—one the American novelist, Nora Roberts reminds us of in introducing this chapter. One that is easily overlooked.

It is the implicit recognition that it is always easier to augment something that already exists rather than to start from scratch.

Or in the parlance of her profession, start with a flawed page rather than a blank one.

What Nora Roberts says does reinforce that an Initiator Resource gives us a significant leg-up when we innovate. Work that contributes to our innovative solution has already been done and is possessed by the selected Initiator. All we need to do is to access that work by unlocking the latent value that remains. Crucially, we do this by means of the three options we have just finished studying. They are the embodiment of Economy of Effort.

These options expose a relevant attribute of the Initiator and, once the Initiator is so primed, it is ready to be presented—by means of the Connector—to the Responder.

This is what the next chapter is about.

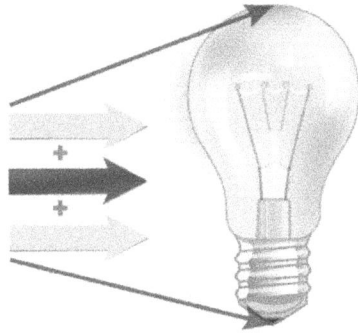

18

ORIGINATE THROUGH THE CONNECTOR RESOURCE

Creativity is connecting things

STEVE JOBS

In his book *How to Get Ideas*, Jack Foster recounts the following story.

A telephone company operating in the American mid-west in the early 1950s was grappling with a serious problem involving the training of their supervisors. The firm were very good at this particular training and an outcome was that once they were fully trained, many supervisors were poached. They left the company when competitors offered them higher compensation and other benefits for their acknowledged, superior expertise. No matter what the company did—increasing supervisor pay, introducing impressive-sounding managerial titles, thoughtfully sending flowers to spouses on various occasions, and so on—their competitors just matched or bettered it.

At a meeting after yet another departure, one of their managers exclaimed in exasperation, "I'd like to chop their damn legs off—then they couldn't leave!" In a wonderful example of the mysterious workings of the associative memory (explored in Chapter 13), this comment led the telephone company to revolutionize its hiring policy, giving priority to employing people with physical disabilities. They customized their working facilities and put in place appropriate measures to support their new recruiting practice of employing people with limited mobility. They re-equipped toilets, modified entrance ways and elevators, did what was needed to accommodate wheelchairs, modified cars and ensured appropriate medical support was always on hand.

A clear effect of this policy change was that organizations with whom the telephone company was competing could no longer justify hiring the telephone company's supervisors. The costs and problems of such employment were now prohibitive—for a variety of obvious, practical reasons.

The scheme proved very effective in terms of employee retention and was obviously commendable in community-minded respects as well.

Admittedly, there is a healthy dose of serendipity involved, but the "chop their damn legs off" tale does a good job of demonstrating just how potent the innovative positioning of a Connector Resource can be. Its ultimate effectiveness is achieved when the act of connecting the Initiator Resource and the Responder Resource guarantees what the Responder does. In the story just related, changing the hiring policy (the Initiator) to recruit only employees with disabilities (the Connector) simultaneously attains the company's goal of retaining highly trained employees (the Responder) and ensures they won't be lured away by a competitor.

In practice, we innovate most effectively when the Initiator is connected with the Responder so synergistically that no other result than the one hoped-for is possible.

How to Get the Most Out of the Connector

Connector Resources bring Initiator Resources and Responder Resources together to consummate an innovative initiative. They are in the middle stage of the three-stage Sebir Model. Like their two cousins, they are readily available resources and contain unused Attraction Value that can be unlocked with Economy of Effort.

Attraction Value is the value that ensures mutual pull between the Initiator and Responder. Initiator Resources contribute Problem-Solving Value and Responder Resources contribute Predisposition Value.

To achieve an innovative result, something must be primed—the Initiator—with the intention of eliciting the desired behavior or performance from someone or something—the Responder. The Initiator must then be presented to the Responder if anything is to happen, and this is done via the Connector. If done innovatively, minimal exertion of effort is required, because the Connector and its positioning make it highly probable the Initiator and Responder will engage with each other spontaneously.

So, how do we make this happen?

There are four options we can employ to mobilize the Connector so it ensures the desired interaction between the Initiator and Responder. It is helpful to separate situations that involve living, thinking beings—mainly people, but sometimes animals, as we will soon discover—from those where the Responder is inanimate—where it is a tangible or intangible thing of some sort.

There is a sound reason for this separation. Three of the options assume the Responder has a choice about whether to respond. This clearly rules out any lifeless resources such as a production facility, service amenity or some electronic apparatus we want to optimize.

They usually do what we instruct—or program them—to do.

The four Connector options are distinguished by their commencing action verbs and the vitality of the response stimulus for each:

1. *Align* the Connector to *Suggest* the Desired Response from People

2. *Link* the Connector to *Encourage* the Desired Response from People

3. *Integrate* the Connector to *Guarantee* the Desired Response from People

4. *Integrate* the Connector to *Guarantee* the Desired Response from Things

The sought-after response from people is usually the specific *behavior* that meets a goal, whereas the sought-after response from things is usually the specific level or type of *performance* desired.

Closer examination of the four Connector alternatives reveals they are in ascending order of potency. The least assured option—that of aligning the Initiator with the Responder—merely suggests the people from whom some desired behavior is required act that way. We then advance to encouraging and, ultimately, to guaranteeing the desired behavior.

Aligning the Connector to Suggest that People Respond

Aligning the Initiator with a People Responder is the most passive of the four Connector options.

When it is employed, it is often because circumstances preclude proximity between the Initiator and the human Responder, ruling out the linking or integrating options. They could be separated by distance, or some other physical or conceptual barrier. For instance, we will shortly learn how an internet-based retailer utilizes an align option to solve a problem because negotiating with thousands of their suppliers about a specific issue in good time is not practically possible.

When such segregation exists, all that can be done is to align the Initiator and Responder. We must then trust that the modified Initiator gets noticed and is sufficiently attractive to entice the desired response from the target audience (the Responder). The more innovative the alignment, the more likely it is the required result will be achieved.

The major drawback of this option is that aligning an Initiator provides no assurance the target person or people group—the Responder—will become aware of what is being presented.

But employing this option is better than no option at all.

And it does work.

An online middleman who supplies thousands of consumer items, sourced from multiple suppliers, encounters frequent complaints from buyers when some of those suppliers add delivery charges to advertised prices. Contacting thousands of their merchants to discuss and hopefully resolve the problem is unrealistic, so the web retailer innovates through the delivery charge problem by utilizing the Connector alignment option.

The retailer installs an algorithm that gives priority in listing to businesses that deliver free. Browsing customers will see the free delivery sellers before those who don't.

Most suppliers soon become aware of the policy change reflected in the algorithm because its *alignment* on the retailer's website is conspicuous enough and its message is unequivocally clear. Most of them act in their own best interests and implement free delivery arrangements for their merchandise, falling in line with the online vendor's goal.

Almost always, the align option and the other two Connector options that target respondents who have some discretion are employed when people are the focus. But really, any animate being—even non-human ones—can be the target of an innovative undertaking as the following account demonstrates.

A frequent task faced by a rabbit farmer is that of regularly relocating the rabbit enclosures so the rabbits can eat fresh grass. Doing this is unavoidable, and, ultimately, the farmer contemplates the appeal of not having to do it. He applies his mind to this problem and adopts the option of aligning the Initiator (the enclosures) with the Responder (the rabbits).

Invoking his understanding of the behavior of the rabbits, the farmer mounts the cages they occupy on wheels, with the intent that the rabbits can instinctively push against the sides of their cages to move them over fresh, adjacent grass. The alignment of the now mobile rabbit hutches with the rabbits—and specifically their desire for food—ensures the need for human intervention is significantly reduced.

The farmer simultaneously enjoys a healthy boost to rabbit-farming efficiency.

Let's look at another example from the business world.

Although a hotel chain devotes considerable attention to its recruitment processes, it experiences a lot of employee churn because many new hires fail to meet the performance standards required of them. To address this, the organization decides to identify and record the success attributes of those employees who have fitted in, carried out their jobs well, and appear likely to stay.

Using this information, the hotelier commissions the development of an evaluation system containing candidate questions designed to reflect these key abilities and utilizes them in interviews of job applicants.

By aligning the Initiator—the recruitment interview and a selected attribute, the questions reflecting preferred employee indicators—with the Responder—the responses of interviewees—the hotel organization achieves a much higher incidence of successful and enduring appointments.

Using Connector Theory to Innovate

The theory behind the innovative positioning of a Connector Resource is that it should maximize the likelihood that the Responder Resource behaves or performs as required to solve a problem and achieve the implicit goal. Applying this theory, I can formulate an Innovative Idea. I am unaware that anything like the following has occurred but for any organization seeking donations, an elemental problem is getting potential donors literally to take money out of their pockets. The theory informs me that to innovate, I should locate people who are already obliged *to take money out of their pockets* and bring a Connector into play.

Travelers passing through security checkpoints typically must remove money from their pockets before security screening. Aligning donation collection containers (the Connector) with people passing through the security point at the stage where they retrieve their money but before they put it back in their pockets could be an initiative worth trying. Admittedly as we move closer to a cashless environment, this idea is likely to be less applicable, but the inherent Connector principle it embodies is still instructive.

Linking the Connector to Encourage People to Respond

Linking the Initiator to the Responder is not a passive option. It does more than suggest a response from people; it encourages them to behave in a specific way. Once the Initiator has been innovatively primed to attract the people Responder, it is linked to the intended audience, who become aware of it and then, ideally, behave as needed.

The exact response of the target people group is not guaranteed for the simple reason that the linking option allows a choice. However, because the people from whom some desired behavior is required at least know about the scheme being mounted, the linking option is more assured than the aligning one. The former exposes the choice;

the latter merely creates the choice which may or may not then be noticed.

In an inspirational attempt to create an incomparable dining-out event, a restaurant operator envisages "dining in the dark," where the focus is on fostering heightened sensory engagement for diners without visual distractions. With the restaurant in complete darkness, an immediate and obvious issue is the multitude of problems that arise for diners navigating the experience without sight.

What can be done to connect them reliably and safely with their unique dining adventure?

In a radical use of the option of linking the Connector to encourage people to respond, the restaurateur employs visually impaired people to guide diners through the entire experience. This novel approach cleverly links the darkened restaurant with the sightless, but expectant, diners and their food. Drawing upon the inherent awareness and intuition of the employees who are functionally blind, this innovation succeeds in delivering a special eating out occasion that benefits not only patrons but provides fulfilling employment for those with no or low vision as well.

Another illustration of linking that encourages people to respond can be seen in the innovative scheme employed by an inter-city train operator.

The current booking system relies on fixed travel timetables with set passenger departure times. However, train occupancy is often lower than capacity because many travelers are unsure of their schedules and hesitate to book in advance for fear of wasting money.

As a result, trains often run below capacity leading to a significant issue: lower occupancy per train means more trains are needed overall.

To overcome this problem, a new policy is introduced allowing passengers to use their smartphones to go online and opt to travel earlier or later than their scheduled time with their existing ticket. Tickets for the original time can then be resold to others who are traveling at a time other than they first intended. Linking people to such an option means more of them use the inter-city train, attracted by the greater flexibility on offer at no or minimal extra cost.

When it is possible to establish a direct connection between an Initiating Resource and the people it is designed to influence, the option of linking to encourage the desired response is apt. Unlike the option of aligning, it brings with it the comfort of knowing that the target Responder is at least aware of the initiative. This allows full emphasis to be placed on tapping into an inclination of that audience which will lead to the desired behavior.

Linking the Initiator and Responder is the essential step but the more novel the linking option—using visually impaired guides in a darkened restaurant for instance—the more certain and rewarding the result achieved.

Integrating the Connector to Guarantee That People Respond

Integrating the Initiator Resource with the Responder Resource is the ultimate and most preferred Connector option because it practically guarantees the result that satisfies the desired goal. And this occurs irrespective of whether the Responder is people or things. However, although an assured outcome is the ideal, this does not always happen—no matter how strong the compulsion—because people are still free to choose.

Nevertheless, it is possible to integrate the Initiator and Responder in ways to compel people to behave as desired—despite the discretion they have.

Once again, we can draw on the "chop their damn legs off" story. It demonstrates that judicious use of the Connector is a powerful innovative strategy—especially when it absolutely secures the intended result. Ensuring that the people with physical disabilities will not be recruited by a competing organization is virtually guaranteed. The Connector option—a new employment policy—is so integrated with the Responder audience—the well-trained employees—that their behavior is equivalent to the simultaneous realization of the telephone company's employee retention goal. (Once again, symmetry that feeds upon itself.)

Consider a common situation in organizations where the process of dealing with complaints from their many customers is exceptionally cumbersome. This not only upsets and loses those customers but is also very stressful for the employees on the receiving end of such complaints. They become the meat in the sandwich between aggravated clients and an unwieldy complaints resolution system.

In an innovative use of integrating the Connector option so its employees will invariably respond in a customer-pleasing manner, a large supplier of consumer electronics solves such a complaint predicament. After ascertaining the average cost of settling most legitimate complaints, the merchant authorizes all staff members in the organization to settle any customer complaint as quickly as possible to a maximum value of $500—if they consider it justified. This integration of the complaint decision-making process with employee roles results in prompt, often instantaneous rectification of complaints.

And there is no surge in costs for the resolution of customer grievances. The tendency of many people to look after others' affairs more responsibly than their own becomes evident. The employees concerned respond to the uncommon trust placed in them by deciding on complaints astutely and with great maturity. They are often more decisive and uncompromising than the previous administrators, from whom they sought an approval that was inevitably slow in coming.

Integrating the Connector to Guarantee That Things Respond

There is a very simple reason why there is only one option for connecting the Initiator with the Responder when the responder is things, versus three options when the Responder is people. People have a choice when they are stimulated to respond; things do not. Things do what they are told—whether it be physically, chemically, electronically or conceptually—and this reality frames our options for connecting with them.

And—outside of some sort of disruption of the normal situation—things respond unvaryingly when the connection is innovative.

Connecting Physically

Things like a machine or a piece of equipment can be engineered to carry out a specific physical task. Once set in motion, the functioning unit will keep producing what it has been designed to produce unless it breaks down or is deactivated.

But connecting to things physically does not apply only to man-made objects. It can be effective in nature and wildlife settings as well. After all, nature itself is governed by the same physical forces—like gravity—that we harness in industrial settings.

In Chapter 9, we learned how a metal products manufacturing business integrated with the invariably predictable law of gravity. The enterprise reinstalled its productive equipment upside down so previously disruptive metal waste offcuts no longer accumulated harmfully on the machinery, but fell continuously to the floor instead.

And wildlife continues to do what it usually does—physically.

Snails can destroy an entire crop if unchecked. Runner ducks like nothing more than a diet of snails. A farmer faced with the threat of a plague of snails introduces runner ducks to his crop growing areas. The runner ducks gobble up the snails before they can do any significant damage. He also brings in some geese. The geese in turn protect the ducks from other predators such as owls and mongooses. The ducks and geese do what is physically natural to them and protect the farmer's harvest while they are at it.

The laws of the natural world can work as very effective physical connectors.

Connecting Chemically

Many familiar food products result from underlying chemical reactions. Bread, pizza dough and pastries are predictably created when yeast converts sugar into carbon dioxide and ethanol. The carbon dioxide ensures the dough rises.

Similarly, the rust proofing of cars and appliances culminates when zinc reacts with oxygen and carbon dioxide to form the protective layer of zinc carbonate that prevents rust. Soap and detergents are a consequence of a chemical process known as a saponification reaction.

There are more inspiring chemical connections as well. An international aid organization aims to improve water quality in an undeveloped country. They compile a practical guide filled with simple tips on purifying drinking water—but they don't stop there. The pages of the book are specially treated with silver or copper—metals known for their antimicrobial properties. When water is poured through the pages, 99% of bacteria are eliminated. Remarkably, the entire book can filter one person's water supply for up to four years. In this way, the pages connect chemically with the water to purify it.

So, applying chemical science is also an assured way of connecting to things— especially when elemental reactive compounds are involved.

Connecting Electronically

Countless digital devices that we take for granted—smartphones, computers, tablets, televisions—perform electronically exactly as programmed, repeatedly, as prescribed by the software inside them.

Radio Frequency Identification (RFID) is a widely used form of electronic connection that relies on electromagnetic fields to automatically identify, and track tags attached to objects. These tags contain electronically stored data that can be read remotely by RFID readers. RFID is widely used to track products in warehouses and retail stores, manage access control (such as building keycards), and support public transportation card systems.

A more specific example can be found in a popular family theme park that upgrades its standard admittance wristbands to RFID-enabled ones. These smart wristbands not only grant entry but also allow visitors to access individual attractions without delay, reserve fast passes to avoid queues, and order food in advance. The result is a seamless experience in which guests enjoy far more of what the park has to offer, thanks to immediate and automated access to services—a marked improvement in ease and convenience.

Software is a powerful and unwavering Connector in contemporary life.

Connecting Conceptually

At first glance, the notion of connecting with something conceptually may sound odd and seem confusing, but don't be put off by the terminology. The underlying message is likely something we know intuitively—so familiar, in fact, that we have never seen it put into words.

In a business setting, many abstract ideas or mental constructs ("concepts") drive decision-making. For instance, operating costs is a concept that represents a general category of the expenses of a business, rather than a specific transaction. Even though operating costs are not a physical entity, they actively influence behavior and choices simply because of what they reveal.

Operating costs can *conceptually* shape and steer decisions and actions, as we saw with the men's clothing retailer who abandoned his retail store in favor of a temporary warehouse in Chapter 9.

There are many similar concepts that permeate the business world and play a very significant role. In addition to operating costs, common examples would include market demand, customer satisfaction, profit margins, brand profile, employee engagement, income and revenue streams, operational efficiency, and sustainability policies.

There are many such conceptual paradigms—essentially forms of metrics—that guide choices and decisions in commerce.

A jeweler finds that keeping the store open seven days a week results in excessive expenses. After analyzing sales data, the merchant discovers over 85% of weekly revenue is generated between Thursday and Saturday.

In response to unsustainable fixed, operating costs, the store reduces its opening days—from seven to just those three high-performing days. Although revenue is no longer earned on the days the shop is closed, the significant savings in operating expenses more than compensate for that loss. The result is striking. Operating the business for only part of the week has a much greater proportionate impact on expenses than on sales, leading to a noticeable boost in profitability.

Arguably, such a revolutionary change would not have occurred had the unacceptable level of overheads costs not *conceptually* compelled it.

A Creative Connection

I'm taking a little license in opening this chapter with a remark by the late Steve Jobs, co-founder and visionary leader of Apple Inc., whose innovative prowess transformed entire industries—from computing and phones to music and animated films.

Jobs declares: "creativity is connecting things."

Given that his ground-breaking exploits are now regarded as symbols of authentic innovation, I trust he wouldn't mind if I equated "creativity" with "innovation" for our purposes—on just this occasion.

When we innovate, we also connect things—although we use the term a little more broadly to include people.

We use the Connector Resource creatively to innovate.

The Connector sits in the middle of the trifecta of resources embedded in the Sebir Model. This is natural and fitting because the Connector brings the Initiator and Responder together to ensure our innovative initiative is consummated.

The true power of the Connector is its ability to spark interaction between the

Initiator and the Responder. Because minimal coercion is required—often in reality, no coercion at all—innovative value is generated relatively effortlessly. The Initiator and Responder get together because they want to—they are innovatively attracted to each other.

Attraction Value in action.

A fundamental distinction we recognize in employing any of the four Connector options is the distinction between Responders that are living and those that are not. This distinction may seem obvious, but it's operationally important. It is a recognition that drawing upon a Connector option when the Responder can choose whether or how to respond gives us three opportunities to innovate—aligning, linking and integrating.

If the Responder is inanimate, we are limited to the fourth option—integrating the Connector to guarantee things respond—but can rely on the absolute certainty that the intended outcome will occur—every time.

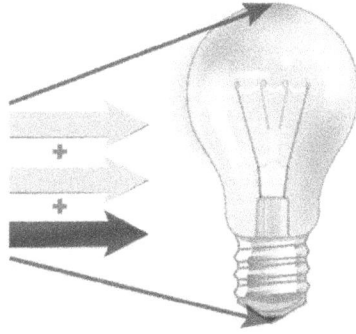

19

ORIGINATE THROUGH THE RESPONDER RESOURCE

Leadership is the art of getting someone else to do something you want done because he wants to do it

DWIGHT D EISENHOWER

Collecting donations is a tough assignment. Consumer society is built on the notion that handing over money is contingent upon getting something tangible in return. The law of contracts in most countries embodies the need for reciprocal "consideration." Each party must provide something of value—whether it be goods, services, money, or some other benefit—that is fundamental to the contract.

Any charitable organization must confront this entrenched attitude. People are reluctant to give money away without a quantifiable, matching benefit offsetting the favor. Asking people to donate to a cause—even a worthwhile one—cuts across this expectation. People are not inclined to hand over money when they get nothing tangible in return.

The humanitarian organization UNICEF faces this transactional imperative in its efforts to improve the lives of children worldwide. To boost its fundraising success, UNICEF initiated its *Change for Good* program—a partnership with various airlines to collect donations from passengers during flights. In the storage pocket of each plane seat, UNICEF places collection envelopes into which passengers can deposit coins and notes they will be unable to spend in their destination country.

In doing this, UNICEF is addressing the inconvenience air travelers face in holding currency that will be something of a headache for most of them when they land. The initiative overturns the prevalent inclination against donating by tapping into another disposition—that of people needing to get rid of a potential nuisance. UNICEF provides an opportunity for travelers to deal with the inconvenience of unwanted currency. People who may not normally be inclined to donate—unwilling donors—are transformed into willing donors because of this.

Stated plainly, UNICEF succeeds in raising significant donations when people give away money because they want to give away money.

How to Get the Most Out of the Responder

Responder Resources are the third element of the Sebir Model—following on from the Initiator and Connector Resources. They contain Predisposition Value that can be tapped with Economy of Effort.

Predisposition Value is, by definition, both latent and available—it reflects behavior or performance that is already poised to express itself. Initiator Resources contribute Problem-Solving Value and Connector Resources contribute Attraction Value.

The account of innovating by UNICEF is an excellent introduction to the Responder Resource. It highlights very nicely the principle of stimulating the Responder in an innovative undertaking to behave in the manner desired because that is what they desire to do anyway.

In the UNICEF illustration, the Responder is people. (We will get to the necessary distinction between people and things in a moment.) The inherent principle—that of stimulating a sought-after but latent response from otherwise indifferent people—is shrewdly articulated by the 34th president of the USA, Dwight Eisenhower, with his comment on leadership to open this chapter.

Get someone to do what you want done by innovatively shaping conditions so they want to do it.

But don't overlook the more basic point here. When we set about innovating, we must be crystal-clear about who or what needs to respond, and how they need to respond if the problem blocking our goal is to be solved.

From there, we can identify a Disposition—which, from now on, we will refer to as a Capability if the Responder is inanimate—that harmonizes with our desired result.

To put it another way, we locate a disposition or capability that, when activated, represents the behavior or performance that embodies the achievement of our goal.

The final step is to ignite that applicable tendency—a relevant readiness to behave or perform—so that it does.

The way in which the activation of a disposition or capability of a Responder simultaneously achieves a goal is worthy of further elaboration.

A simple example illustrates this overlay of triggered behavior and goal achievement.

An appliance retailer who is seeking to raise the awareness of a new product range without paying for expensive advertising, designs an engaging Christmas Card—in both physical and digital formats—and sends it to a large database of potential customers. Information about the new appliances is cleverly and humorously woven into the image and seasonal message. Recipients are enticed to open and read the card and, when they do, inevitably learn about the new products.

Their predisposition to respond to something topical and funny—like reading an engaging Christmas greeting—effectively doubles as fulfillment of the appliance business's goal of increasing customer awareness of their products inexpensively.

Disposition tapped; goal achieved.

As touched on above, the Responder can be animate—which mainly means people, but occasionally other living entities such as animals or wildlife—or things that are inanimate. Inanimate things can be tangible—like physical objects—or intangible and conceptual—like time, space, gravity and man-made concepts like money and language.

We will talk more about people before dealing with things as Responders.

When the Responder is People

If we want people to respond to our efforts, the key is to fall in line with their behavioral inclinations as UNICEF has done. Latent dispositional value always resides in people and, arguably, because they are the only category of Responder Resource that thinks and acts of its own accord, such value is much more varied and abundant than that found in non-living Responders.

On the flip side, living entities cannot simply be instructed or programmed to behave as we would like. They can exercise choice.

So, where do we find the unused potential that lies dormant in people—behavior that is poised to respond as we would like?

As stated already, this potential resides in the Dispositions of people—their inclinations or tendencies to behave in particular ways. Dispositions contain potential, untapped value because they already exist and are ready to express themselves. The logic is compelling. If you want people—such as your customers—to respond in a particular way to an initiative—for instance, buy the product or service you are offering—your effort is dramatically reduced if you tap into an inclination they already have to do so.

Granted, the term *Disposition* is a rather formal, technical one—one commonly found in behavioral science—but don't let that put you off. Dispositions originate from beliefs and when those beliefs graduate into dispositions, they become reliable predictors of human behavior. I have found it helpful to think of a disposition as a taper on a specific, unexpressed behavior. To activate the response we desire, we innovate by lighting that taper.

Not surprisingly—given the complexity of human nature—there are many potential dispositions. However, it is possible to distill them down to four main ones that are relevant for most situations we are likely to encounter when innovating. They tend to overlap a little, but can be described as follows:

1. People Do What *They Normally Do*
2. People Do What is *Easy and Convenient*
3. People Do What *They Think is the Right Thing To Do*
4. People Do What is *In Their Interests*

In our earlier donations raising example, we saw how UNICEF appealed to the second item on the list—the affinity of air travelers for behavior that handily resolved a pending inconvenience.

We will now look at some illustrations involving the other Dispositions.

Doing What is Normal

In business situations, persuading someone to buy your product or service if they are not interested is very difficult. Persuading them if they are indifferent is also hard. Convincing them when they are inclined to make the purchase anyway is self-evidently the most desirable option.

Take a car rental company that wants to increase the total revenue earned per vehicle hired. It knows customers typically refill the tank just before returning the car as required under the rental agreement. The company taps into this anticipated behavior by offering an optional prepaid tank of fuel at a discounted rate at the time of hire—saving customers the need to detour and pay market prices at the end of their trip.

By drawing early on the future, normal behavior of customers—refill the tank before returning the car—and making it easy and economical for them to act now, the company finds an innovative way to boost revenue per rental. Normal car renter behavior is smartly channeled to achieve the car rental firm's goal of increasing what each hirer of a vehicle spends.

Doing What is Right

At some point, most organizations try to understand how their customers perceive them and how they compare with competitors. This requires research that demands unpaid time from the chosen respondents and—with so many surveys circulating—many of those approached simply decline to participate.

To address this problem, an industrial equipment supplier that is conducting a market perception survey to see how they are doing, harnesses the disposition of people to help younger people prepare for their future careers—the preparedness of most people to do the right thing. The firm employs students studying human resources to carry out the research on their behalf.

These students are not only familiar with the workings of behavioral research because of their chosen curriculum, but their personal status as learners helps win interview time from people when they advise that the exercise is part of their studies. Many respondents are naturally inclined to assist them in their required coursework. By engaging with a common, benevolent tendency—a pro-social disposition—the recruitment company innovatively secures an above-the-norm response rate to its survey.

Doing What is in People's Interests

Spoiler alert: this is not a true story.

A beggar sits on the pavement with seven bowls in front of him labeled as follows: Christian, Muslim, Jewish, Buddhist, Hindu, Agnostic, and Atheist. Prominently displayed behind the bowls is a handwritten sign:

Which religion cares the most about the homeless?

The beggar is blessed with valuable insight. His campaign is not founded upon his needs but upon what he understands about the disposition of his various audiences. He is not simply relying on a common altruistic inclination, but is tapping into the personal interests of potential donors as well.

He lets people do what is right, but also what taps into their self-interest.

When the Responder is Things

If the Responder Resource is inanimate—say, an under-performing factory, some faulty machinery, or even an object with a single purpose that someone wishes to improve—it could be an inefficient lawn mower an inventor is tinkering with for instance—the desired, enhanced performance can usually be guaranteed through an engineering or software modification.

Things have dispositions in the same way that people have dispositions although, more appropriately—as noted earlier—we will refer to them as Capabilities. Unlike human dispositions, things do not make choices. Their capabilities do what they are told or hardwired to do.

It is therefore very worthwhile to integrate with the capability of some *thing* that—when it is exercised—is consistent with what we are trying to do. We can then absolutely count on that capability to help neutralize our problem and achieve our goal.

The capabilities of things can be relied upon to do what they normally do.

There are potentially many possibilities, but it is a quite straightforward task to generalize them into just four main options that cover most circumstances. They are simply the natural complement to the four Connector options introduced in the previous chapter. This time we look back from the vantage point of the Responder rather than looking forward from the vantage point of the Connector.

It follows then that the four main Responder options invariably expressed by things are:

1. Things do what they normally do *physically*

2. Things do what they normally do *chemically*

3. Things do what they normally do *electronically*

4. Things do what they normally do *conceptually*

A few examples will demonstrate how these options work in practice.

Responding Physically

First, an illustration of a thing doing what it normally does physically—a thing in pristine condition from nature—whose capability has never been embellished in any way.

A local government body wants to address the significant ongoing cost of maintaining its heavily used urban infrastructure. A prime candidate is pedestrian crossings that endure a lot of wear-and-tear from foot and vehicular traffic and therefore require regular painting to keep them safely visible.

So, the Responder—the thing that needs to perform differently for the municipality to achieve its maintenance goals—is the pedestrian crossings. The maintenance burden they currently impose is unacceptable. An ideal solution would be to get rid of the need for periodic repainting altogether.

Ultimately, the town council reimagines the formulation of its pedestrian crossings and begins constructing them from paving slabs that are natural. It sources black basalt paving tiles—cut to size and shape—and alternates the laying of them with white limestone ones that are similarly prepared.

No painting required—ever.

The pedestrian crossings respond physically. Integrating the fabrication of zebra crossings with the enduring physical capability of the stone components eliminates the need for maintenance and guarantees long-term performance.

Responding Chemically

Second, an illustration of a thing doing what it normally does chemically.

A paint manufacturer wants to grow but cannot raise the capital funding needed to increase the capacity of their factory. A significant bottleneck that constrains the rate of paint output is the batch production operation. Each color and variety of paint is mixed in a discrete batch and after each is finalized, the vessel in which it is mixed must be washed out with cleaning solvents in preparation for the composition of the next variety.

If this highly disruptive necessity could be eliminated with relatively little effort, paint output from the existing productive facilities would soar without the need for an expensive expansion. Continuous uninterrupted flow of paint production would see to that.

The breakthrough comes when the production people direct their attention to the cleaning solvents as the Responder—after all, these are a prime reason for the stop-start batch operation—and focus specifically on their chemical properties. They discover they can reformulate the cleaning solvents so that when they integrate them with the recipes used for paint production, they become an ingredient in the subsequent batch of paint, whatever variety it is.

Both the paint ingredients and the cleaning solvents combine exactly as their respective chemical capabilities compel them to do. This absorption of the cleaning solvents means of course they no longer need to be removed. With this disruptive task abolished, a much higher rate of paint production is achieved as a matter of course and at a relatively small cost.

Responding Electronically

Third, an illustration of a thing doing what it normally does electronically.

A building operator is receiving many complaints from the occupants of a large office building about the slowness of the elevators. Adding extra elevators is impractical due to the design of the building and would be prohibitively expensive anyway.

What to do?

The building manager chooses the standard elevator-calling mechanism as their Responder and implements a simple software change that requires lift occupants to request the floor they wish to visit instead of just pushing a button for the next available elevator. A smart algorithm then optimizes the operation of the elevators, taking account of two pieces of information: where the occupant is and where they want to go to. This dual input ensures the elevators always travel by the fastest and shortest possible loop. This significantly reduces wait times for users.

Modifying the operation of the existing elevator software enables the property overseer to innovate through ensuring the Responder performs exactly as programmed electronically.

The development of algorithms that enable computers to process data and make predictions and decisions has greatly amplified and multiplied the possibilities for innovating electronically. We have just heard of one instance. Another but different application comes from the healthcare field.

A medical practice experiencing loss of income due to patient "no-shows" analyzes the historical records it holds about its patients and, based on these, constructs a clever algorithm that predicts the patient profile most likely to miss an appointment. Whenever possible, such patients are sensitively assigned appointment times outside standard working hours—perhaps during what would be normal lunch breaks, at the end of the day, or in other discretionary time slots—when the failure to turn up has the least financial impact.

This innovative effort enables the healthcare clinic to move much closer to their goal of eliminating the reduction in earnings caused by missed appointments.

Responding Conceptually

As I encouraged during our discussion of "Connecting Conceptually" in Chapter 18, don't be unsettled by the phrase "Responding Conceptually". It may sound unusual, but it does align with the way we describe the various Connector and Responder options when they are connected to intangible as opposed to tangible things.

In common with all responses of things, the entities themselves don't choose how to respond. They simply follow the rules of the systems they are part of. This applies even more strongly when the *thing* is a concept. A conceptual response just happens. Once activated, the Responder is automatically transformed in accordance with its conceptual obligation.

In the previous chapter—looking forward from the perspective of the Connector—we saw how operating costs—specifically their scale—could compel decisions to redress them. The costs themselves *conceptually* drive such decisions. However, looking back from the perspective of the Responder, once action is brought to bear on those costs, they then respond conceptually. They have no choice.

We saw a highly pertinent example of this in Chapter 9. A contact center, struggling with the high overhead cost of employing many telephone operators handling inbound customer service calls, begins selling the expertise of those operators, who then administer phone calls on behalf of other organizations as well. The revenue generated offsets the overhead costs. Costs that eroded profitability now generate income instead. To the extent this transformation occurs, the overhead costs respond by *conceptually diminishing*, becoming a source of value rather than loss.

Converging Passions

As the third element of the triumvirate of resources that comprise the Sebir Model, the Responder Resource is the consummating resource. It delivers the behavior—if the

Responder is a living entity—or the performance—if the Responder is inanimate—that is required for a goal to be achieved innovatively.

We know the total Innovative Value we generate is attributable to the imperative of Economy of Effort that suffuses the Sebir Model and its three elements. The contribution of the Responder to the total Economy of Effort at work is Predisposition Value—the behavior or performance that will solve our problem and realize our goal is behavior or performance that the Responder is predisposed or compelled to execute anyway.

Influencing people so they do something that helps you meet a particular objective can be a significant challenge, especially if they are not merely uninterested, but are opposed to such behavior. This challenge is far less formidable if you put yourself in the position of persuading people to do something that they are already inclined to do. Embracing a predisposition to act by stimulating it in a manner that naturally discharges that act is a sure path to follow.

In selecting the Responder and stimulating the response we need, we are essentially joining a ride that has already been scheduled and paid for. We trigger it and participate in an activity that is mutually beneficial.

I have already referred to Dwight Eisenhower's shrewd observation at the launch of this chapter. He noted that falling in line with what someone wants to do is very insightful if that happens to coincide with what you want them to do. He was talking about leadership, a concept that attracts innumerable definitions. It is a concept perhaps easier to define when it is absent than when it is present.

Although there are many descriptions and definitions of effective leadership, Eisenhower's one is reminiscent of another that accords with the spirit of this chapter:

Superlative leadership consists of getting people to do what you want them to do because they want to do it

This definition is quite sublime. Whatever claims someone might make about effective leadership, here is an unvarnished test of their veracity. If a leader is truly empowering people, the proof lies not just in what an organization achieves—especially when measured solely in financial terms. The deeper, more exacting test is this:

Do the people being led genuinely want what the leader wants?

This rare overlap—where intent and response are reciprocally fused—embodies the core insight of innovating through the Responder Resource.

20

ORIGINATE BY RENEWING PROCESSES

Great innovations are the result of structured processes that allow for experimentation

ERIC RIES

In comparing the effectiveness of community welfare programs between countries, one of the more puzzling humanitarian juxtapositions is the disparity in the rate of voluntary organ donation between Germany and Austria. According to information available in 2022, Germany has an organ donation consent rate less than 15% while Austria has an organ donation consent rate of nearly 100%.

The huge imbalance is baffling, because the countries both appear to have similar enthusiasm for voluntary organ donation—an initiative that saves and improves many lives—and support its encouragement.

In addition to a shared goal regarding organ transplantation, the two countries are neighbors, German is the official language of both, they have intersecting histories and share a similar cultural heritage in literature, music, art, and cuisine.

And they experience comparable economic circumstances.

If we regard the promotion of voluntary organ donation as a process with inputs and an output, the societal inputs of both countries are much the same, but the output for each is strikingly different.

Why such a dramatic divergence?

The answer lies in the design of the system: Austria innovates in this instance—Germany does not.

Although a high-level look at the organ donation process of each country suggests the input steps are comparable, there is a small but critical difference in the details. It all comes down the first real step in the process—the step when people decide whether to commit to donating their organs.

In making their appeals, Germany employs an explicit consent system. It asks prospective donors to "opt-in." Austria, on the other hand, uses a presumed consent system. If you do not wish to donate your organs, you must "opt out." Unless the contributor formally declines, voluntary donation is assumed.

The result?

A single, almost imperceptible change to the first step in the organ donation process means Austria enjoys an organ donation consent rate (95% plus) more than six times that of Germany (under 15%). A simple tweak of just one detail among otherwise common inputs produces a remarkable difference in the respective outputs. The reversal of the initial approval step from opt-in to opt-out in has transformed voluntary organ donation in Austria.

When I said a little earlier that Austria innovates but Germany does not, I was probably being unfairly reductionist. There would be complexities associated with this situation that I am unaware of, but a simplified interpretation serves our purposes here: to speculate that innovating—at least the practice of innovating as championed throughout this book—has taken place. A relatively minor change to the inputs of a process has resulted in a strikingly disproportionate increase in the output.

More precisely, an innovative revamp of the first step in the process—that of obtaining consent—has dramatically improved the last step—the outcome.

How to Get the Most Out of Processes

Compared with what we have been learning in previous chapters, the practice of innovating by renewing processes is more generic. Rather than extracting value from the individual input resources that comprise the Sebir Model, we manipulate the process regardless of the factors that make it up—including any inherent problems. What these factors are—what the problems are—doesn't really matter, as we will learn shortly.

Note however that what has not changed from earlier is the inviolable principle that successful innovating is evidenced by a process that is lopsided. A beneficially unequal process. *Small effort→big result.*

Processes are at the heart of the Sebir Model of innovating—especially in relation to the centrality of problems. The key process we engage with is cause-and-effect as explained in Chapter 6. The cause-and-effect process helps us determine the best path we should follow to innovate through a problem.

But there is an additional payoff we enjoy if we stay faithful to this process-minded discipline.

It is this.

Whereas the many examples we have reviewed at the various phases of our learning have pivoted on the specific problems prevailing and have instructed us accordingly, when we turn our attention to processes in their own right, we can bank on an ironclad assurance—not only can we innovate without knowledge of the specific problems we face, but we can also innovate with the result of our efforts virtually guaranteed.

This may sound improbable or an exaggeration at best. But that is only until we comprehend that innovating by renewing processes is based on a verified theorem called Little's Law, not merely on the confidence gained from wide-ranging, validated experience.

Little's Law is a theorem in queuing theory developed in 1961 by John D.C. Little, a professor at the MIT Sloan School of Management in the USA. It is based on treating any process as a series of dependent events or steps. The performance excellence of each step is dependent on the step and steps that precede it. In any process, there is at least one bottleneck that limits the process's ability to fully achieve its goals. Dealing with these bottlenecks by drawing upon the lessons of Little's Law is what liberates Innovative Value.

The insights of Little's Law—which we will get to in a moment—are extremely reliable, and not only because the Law has been used successfully in thousands of industries and settings where it has demonstrated its superlative effectiveness. More fundamentally, it can be relied upon because it is a proven mathematical truth. The conclusions we generalize from it are theoretically sound, and we can have every confidence in them when we utilize them to innovate.

What is a Process?

As the remainder of this chapter revolves around the concept of processes—a term that has become somewhat nondescript through overuse—we will spend some time here explicitly defining what we mean by a process—particularly the anatomy of a process.

We will run through a hypothetical example to do so.

The Scenario

Imagine a bistro—renowned for the quality of its coffee—that wants to increase its takeout sales. The main problem in achieving this goal? During busy periods—when dine-in customers are also ordering—coffee queues build up, and potential business is lost. Many takeaway customers are not willing to wait. They leave before placing an order.

The *Problem PhotoBox* would illuminate the problem like this:

TAKEOUT COFFEE PROBLEM PHOTOBOX		
Problem Obstacle	Takeout Coffee Production	
Problem Cause	Disrupted Takeout Coffee Production	
Problem Solution	Seamless Takeout Coffee Production	AFTI Goal
Problem Object	Takeout Coffee Customers	
Problem Effect	Deterred Takeout Coffee Customers	

The Current Takeout Process

Let's break down the current takeout process into nine distinct steps:

CURRENT TAKEOUT COFFEE PROCESS
1. Accept Customer Coffee Order
2. Process Payment and Record Customer Name
3. Place Coffee Order in Queue
4. Brew Coffee in Machine
5. Dispense Brewed Coffee into Takeaway Cup
6. Heat Milk (if required)
7. Add Heated Milk (and any other Condiments) to Takeaway Cup
8. Put Lid on Cup
9. Identify Customer and Handover Coffee

This is what a sufficiently defined process looks like. Clear and straightforward. In practice, breaking down a process into nine or ten steps works well, and it is not a complicated task: identify the main actions and use simple, verb-led labels. Doing so helps keep steps distinct and ensures they are named in line with their intended purpose.

Applying Little's Law

Once we have mapped a process of nine or ten sequential steps that lead to a desired goal, we are ready to harness Little's Law to innovate. There are three strategies—or more precisely, rules—we can apply with high confidence:

1. Perfect the First Process Step

2. Eliminate Process Steps

3. Squeeze Individual Process Steps

Each of these rules is clearly explained and illustrated in the remaining sections of this chapter, but to gain a sense of what is involved now, let's speculate about how our coffee bistro might apply them. Admittedly, we are hypothesizing somewhat for the sake of illustration, but the priority right now is clarity over exactitude.

How the Bistro Might Respond

To achieve greater sales, we will assume the bistro makes these three changes:

1. Sets up a mobile coffee cart to make coffee and locates it just outside instead of inside the premises

2. Splits coffee production into two locations: the existing facility serves dine-in customers while the cart outside serves takeaway customers

3. Compresses customer handover: takeout coffees are placed on a pickup counter, labeled with the customer's name, ready for collection

Anticipated Results Interpreted Through Little's Law

- Perfecting the First Step
  Step 1—Accept Customer Coffee Order—improves significantly. Separating takeout customers from dine-in ones allows streamlined order-taking and less queuing, preventing bottlenecks

- Eliminating Steps
  Steps 4—8—Making the Coffee—which used to vary constantly depending upon who was ordering the coffee—dine-in or takeout—are now split into two streamlined, format-specific workflows. No more switching back and forth

- Squeezing a Step
  Step 9—Identify Customer and Handover Coffee—is condensed. Instead of locating and handing the coffee to each customer, the labeled drinks are collected from a counter. Quick and frustration-free

The bistro's revised workflow shows how process innovating grounded in Little's Law—perfecting, eliminating, and condensing steps—can streamline operations, reduce delays and achieve a vastly improved result from the process which, as predetermined by the AFTI Goal in the "Takeout Coffee" *Problem PhotoBox*, is now seamless.

Incidentally, a practical hint: if you map out nine-to-ten process steps of an activity you want to improve but find that some of them are too complicated or unwieldy to focus on, extract any of those steps separately and dissect each into its own nine-to-ten-step process. Apply the rules of Little's Law to that nested process, and then reintroduce the streamlined sub-process into the flow of the original nine-to-ten-step process.

With a hypothetical primer now in place and the potential changes sketched out, we can look more closely at how to innovate through processes, taking each of the three rules from Little's Law in turn.

Innovate by Perfecting the First Process Step

The account of the startling difference in the voluntary organ donation campaigns of Austria and Germany that opens this chapter clearly demonstrates the potency of making the first step of a process as purposely focused and finely tuned as possible.

The result speaks for itself: 95% versus 15%.

Understanding that any process consists of a series of connected steps—where the effectiveness of each depends on the one before it—means for any key process step to meet expectations, the step that precedes it must do its job well.

We can take this logic further.

If, say, the performance level of Step 7 in a process is dependent upon the contribution of Step 6, and Step 6 is dependent upon what is fed to it by Step 5, and so forth, we can reason the earlier a step is located in any process, the more important is its overall contribution to the ones that follow. It has a subsequent impact on all those steps and inevitably, on the final result.

Taking this line of thinking to its inevitable conclusion, the highest priority should be given to the first step. It should be made as perfect—as fit for purpose—as possible.

Here is another example from the business world, showcasing the impressive benefits of upgrading the first step of a process.

The standard expectation of many products or services in ongoing use is that sooner or later—despite professional quality control in their production—some aspect of them will fail unexpectedly. This is obviously a serious matter for a medical equipment manufacturer, because lives could be at risk. The manufacturer needs an innovative safety net, a way to ensure its equipment never ceases to function without warning.

How can the medical device maker improve their process so there is never an apparatus failure during operation—especially when third parties use their equipment remotely?

While many factors affect the environment in which medical equipment performs—such as clean, well-suited premises, trained operators, and regular servicing—the device maker concentrates on a very early step in its production process, the design of its equipment itself. It develops and installs sensors in its medical devices that monitor key components and issue early warnings of potential failures—*before* they occur. These alerts trigger preemptive maintenance activity that is carried out before any malfunction takes place.

Just as the coffee bistro virtually eliminated customer queues through dramatically improving its first process step by installing a mobile coffee cart, the healthcare device manufacturer largely eliminates unplanned downtime and associated risks experienced by users of its equipment. This is achieved by innovatively *perfecting* the early production step of equipment design.

Innovate by Eliminating Process Steps

Given that all processes consist of several steps—and each step is dependent on the one that precedes it—it follows logically that the fewer the steps in any process, the better the outcome of that process.

To put it the other way, we can conclude that the greater the number of steps, the more difficult it is to manage how well any process performs and to ensure the acceptable quality of its output.

Therefore, if we can eliminate steps and still achieve our process goal, the result will be significantly improved and much more reliable. Done innovatively, this does not impair the output of the process—it actually improves both the quantity and quality of what it yields.

Let's look at an illustration that demonstrates the principle.

One of the final steps a manufacturer of reconstituted timber cladding faces is applying a protective coat of paint to the raw board before dispatch. This critical step ensures the expected quality prior to delivery to customers, and its role directly impacts the rate at which the finished product is made ready for sale. It is an essential activity that cannot be easily omitted.

Yet by asking how the painting step—but not its intended effect—might be eliminated, the manufacturer comes up with a way to shorten the process. They introduce a colorant solution directly into the product's liquid formulation early on in its manufacture. Once the mixture is pressed and cured, the result is finished timber cladding that comes out pre-painted. More product is now generated from the same process—simply because modifying an earlier production step removes the final painting step. It is no longer needed.

While there are thousands of examples in the business world where a step has been removed from a productive process to significantly improve it, some are especially prominent. We met one standout example back in Chapter 6 with the invention of Just-In-Time (JIT) manufacturing by car manufacturers in Japan in the early 1970s. Faced with delays and costs from inventory issues—like shortages and overstocking—car manufacturers reimagined inventory holding as a step that didn't exist. Through close coordination with suppliers, they shifted to daily deliveries of only what was needed, eliminating inventory management entirely as a step in the car production process.

A less consequential example. Consider the logistical process of shipping products for sale in supermarkets, which inherently involves high volumes and frequent activity. This creates two handling-related challenges: repetitively unpacking products for display places a physical burden on workers—risking ergonomic injuries—and the emptied packages generate packaging waste.

A supermarket operator calls on its suppliers to address these issues in the products they supply.

Instead of attempting to mitigate the issues independently, one supplier—a stretch luggage strap manufacturer—envisions a process in which the activities that generate the two logistical problems simply do not exist. To ship their product, they bundle 50 straps together, using one strap to wrap and secure the other 49. The resulting bundle becomes the shipping unit, eliminating the need for an outer shipping container— and with it, the unpacking step for workers and the waste disposal step.

The result is a significantly streamlined logistics process for luggage strap supply, where removing two activities—two steps—automatically removes the conditions that created ergonomic and waste-related issues. This is why innovating through eliminating the steps of a process is so powerful. Because the step disappears, the activities it hosts—and therefore their ability to cause problems—disappear as well.

Innovate by Squeezing Individual Process Steps

A less obvious opportunity that emerges from an appreciation of Little's Law and the inter-dependency of steps in a process, is one that concentrates on the inherent stability of each step. This stability refers to how variable a single process step is— how tightly its performance clusters around how it performs on average.

We see the manifestation of this often as a key metric in assessing the quality of public transportation. Take flight arrivals and departures. If a regular, daily flight is scheduled to arrive at 9.00 am and nearly always arrives in the range of 8.55 am to 9.05 am, the impacts on commuters heading for a meeting, or hire cars meeting the flight, or the timing of connecting flights—all the possible knock-on effects—are not very significant.

However, if the same flight sometimes arrives as early as 8.30am or as late as 9.30am, the consequences for all affected parties are obviously much greater.

Train travelers in Tokyo, Japan, are the fortunate beneficiaries of squeezed transport processes. With around 40 million commuters utilizing the city's rail system daily, on-time performance is critical to preventing bedlam. Even so, the record is impressive: in 2022, almost 99% of Tokyo Metro services arrived within five minutes of their scheduled time—an impressively narrow spread around the target.

Intuitively, being early may seem to be beneficial but it becomes problematic if early is too early. The smaller the range of variation—from *good* to *bad*—the better. Technically, being too early is just as bad as being too late.

The process rule we follow here is that of limiting the range of potential outcomes from a single process step to as tight a spread as practicable. The more we reduce such variation—the narrower the range of possible outcomes within each step—the better the quality and output of the overall process we are seeking to improve.

To put it another way, we aim to condense as much as possible the range from the best to the worst that each step can produce. Each step is *squeezed*, so it performs its assigned task with the minimum variation around what it does on average.

This principle becomes even clearer when we move from hypothesizing to some other real-world examples.

User or consumer demand in most markets is variable. For most suppliers of goods and services, the number of orders they receive is not the same each day. Occasionally, an unusually high level of daily orders comes in. On some other days an unusually low number of orders are received. But, most days, the level of orders hovers around what would be an average number for the business.

Although the variation in the number of daily orders is to be expected, the degree of variation can pose major problems.

Let's get more specific.

Sometimes—but more frequently than they would like—a large home building firm must deal with dissatisfied customers because their home completion is late due to the builder having too many homes scheduled for completion and handover in the same month. The promised completion date is always a standard six months from the date the home building contract is signed. As the number of new home orders (signed contracts) varies from month to month, this loads some months unrealistically and leaves others relatively unburdened.

Result: due to a concertina effect, the overloaded months eventually result in disappointed customers because physically completing the required number of homes within the later, more congested months—even though they are contractually due—is impossible.

By looking back through the home building process—and particularly at the order-taking step—the home builder decides to restrict the new home orders it commits to each month. More precisely, it decides to place a ceiling on the number of orders it will accept that carry the standard six-month time to build. In months of high sales orders, customers are financially incentivized to accept contractually, say, a seven-month build time and later completion date.

By adopting this approach, the home builder purposefully regulates the number of homes passing through each building process step until they are ready for occupation. An even flow of completed homes is the aim. By squeezing orders taken with standard build times into a narrow band and pushing others outside that band to a later month for completion, promised dates are achieved with customer-pleasing consistency.

Why Variation Hurts

"Variation" is a mundane term and an indeterminate one. Accordingly, it is often overlooked. Understanding it better and comprehending the value of reducing it for any process step when we innovate—shortening the distance between the two extremes—is profoundly valuable. A quirky illustration of why the extremes that define the extent of variation matter is this. I have two buckets of water—one contains freezing water and the other boiling water. I place one of my feet in each bucket. On average, do I feel OK?

A fertile business area for this squeezing aspect of innovating by renewing processes is in the management of inventory—as opposed to eliminating it altogether in the manner of the 1970s Japanese car manufacturers. This is particularly so if it is combined with the process rule of perfecting the early step of a process.

Consider an example from the manufacture of fashion clothing—where variety is of the essence but can quickly become physically uncontrollable if left to run free.

A brand supplier of knitted sweaters faces such a problem. The demand for styles and colors of sweaters explodes. Predicting precisely what customers will want and having all these items available for sale from inventory threatens to overwhelm the firm.

In response, the business innovates by focusing on an early production step for the sweaters and significantly narrows the range of possibilities at that point. They have all styles of sweaters produced in white to begin with, and store them in proximity to their established markets. Later, when demand reflects exact customer preferences, the sweaters are dyed locally according to the colors required by that market region.

Squeezing an early step of its supply chain process—white sweaters only—successfully preempts the buildup of inventories to expensive and troublesome levels.

The Silent Scaffolding

Processes tend to be unobtrusive and are rather dull in an intellectual sense, but they are central to achieving our objectives in life—no matter what those may be. It would be a rare ambition indeed if it could be achieved with a single, isolated act. There is always a starting point and an ending point—with a sequence of steps or events separating the two.

But, while processes enable and support all human activity, they fade into the background in our consciousness.

Eric Ries, an American author, is best known for *The Lean Startup: How Today's Entrepreneurs Use Continuous Innovation to Create Radically Successful Businesses*. His book has been widely used by young companies in the business world. Through his own extensive startup experience and interacting with other entrepreneurs and venture capitalists, he learned much about why startups succeed and why they fail. At the head of this chapter, he articulates a key discovery that not merely processes, but "structured" processes are essential to innovative success for aspiring new businesses.

We agree but would argue for the indispensable role of processes whenever we innovate with intent—not just when we are commencing a new venture. They provide much more than context. They are fundamental background enablers when we innovate. After all, the Sebir Model—the foundational structure we have drawn from throughout this book—is a three-stage *process*.

Processes are the scaffolding upon which we build our innovative solution.

Paying attention to the technical structure of processes and grasping that they obey mathematical laws exposes three innovative options that can be relied upon with certainty. Critical to accessing these truths is the understanding that all processes are comprised of a discrete number of steps and recognizing the reality of dependency. Every step owes its value to the preceding steps—its performance is shaped by what it inherits.

Following this line of logic to its inevitable conclusion, we grasp that maximizing the excellence of the first step, removing steps and compressing the variability of individual steps, are the unfailing keys to generating innovative value by renewing processes.

EPILOGUE

THE UNLIKELY FREEDOM TO INNOVATE

In writing in *The New Yorker* magazine in early 2014 about the Nobel Prize-winning poet, Derek Walcott, Adam Kirsch—a poet himself as well as a literary critic and journalist—marveled at what Walcott produced despite the ostensible barrenness of his environment. Derek Walcott was born on the small island of Saint Lucia[7] in the eastern Caribbean Sea in 1930, and was "doomed, or privileged, to spend a lifetime writing about the sea."

The sea surrounded him, it constrained him.

However, in reviewing what Walcott achieved, Kirsch was forced to conclude:

But, like so many great poets before him, he shows that constraints do not have to starve the imagination; they can also nourish it

Walcott died in 2017, remembered as one of the greatest poets of the 20th century.

Of salient interest to us is the metaphor of constraint alluded to by Kirsch and its counter-intuitive benefits.

For Walcott, the sea both constrained him and caused him to thrive creatively.

For us—throughout this book—our "sea" has been the imperative of Economy of Effort that permeates the Sebir Model. Constraint frames our total enterprise. We innovate only when what we have produced cannot possibly be justified by the relatively meager means that brought it about. We must consume far fewer resources than would normally be required to achieve a given end.

This is what establishes the Innovative Value gap and enables us to innovate.

Small effort→big result.

---

7   As a small, relatively unknown, island country of the West Indies in the eastern Caribbean, Saint Lucia received another boost to its profile at the 2024 Paris Olympics when Julien Alfred, a 23-year-old track star, won the gold medal in the women's 100m sprint. This was Saint Lucia's first-ever Olympic medal, a historic moment for the small nation of less than 200,000 people. The victory sparked celebrations across the island, including a watch party at Derek Walcott Square with the global media covering a further proud achievement by Saint Lucia.

More specifically, our sea constrains us in three ways:

1. We are limited to initiating resources that possess relevant, usable value that does not have to be recreated

2. We are limited to responding resources that will behave or perform as we want because it is something they are predisposed to do anyway

3. We are limited to connecting relevant initiating resources to responding resources in a manner that implicitly encourages or compels their union

Although it might seem counterintuitive—like the way it helped Derek Walcott—constraint enables us to be creative when we innovate. The concentrated focus it imposes removes the distraction of a myriad of other possibilities. In a twist of logic, when we place limits on the resources we utilize to innovate, we remove the limits on our ability to do so.

An unlikely freedom.

But this is not something completely new for us. In submitting to the sea of Economy of Effort we are not doing anything we have not done before. We often tax our imaginations by testing them with constraints. If you recently played Sudoku, you were consciously seeking a solution that constrained you to fill various grids and sub-grids so each contained *all* the digits from one to nine.

When you read or watch a detective story, you accompany the protagonist—Sherlock Holmes, Miss Marple, or these days, maybe a Hieronymus "Harry" Bosch—as they unravel their cases by treating each clue they discover as a constraint. Ultimately, they solve their case in a way that satisfies all the constraints they ferret out.

Whether playing Sudoku or vicariously playing detective, we willingly accept necessary constraints on our actions in the interest of achieving a satisfying end.

And that, in essence, is how we innovate.

We don't innovate *despite* the constraint of Economy of Effort. We innovate *because* of it.

We innovate with the liberty of constraint.

PART 5

THE SEBIR MODEL IN ACTION

"HOW-TO" ROADMAP: THE SEBIR LADDER

Accusations of mixed imagery are understandable at this implementation stage of the book. We were close to completing the journey metaphor with the *"How-To" Roadmap* as a fitting, culminating milestone.

Therefore, the introduction of the ladder metaphor may offend some sensibilities.

I would like to stick with it however, but before I submit my arguments on why the ladder metaphor resonates, I want to acknowledge another sense in which PART 5 departs from the rest of the book. Unlike PARTS 1 to 4—which aim for a more conversational style—PART 5 is organized in a structured, educational format.

We shift from an armchair chat to something more like a formal lecture.

Some readers may not want to attend this lecture—and for good reason. They may prefer to overlay their own implementation format on the concepts and propositions advanced in PARTS 1 to 4. They may also wish to independently incorporate some enhancements of their own where they feel they can improve on what has been presented.

That kind of independent engagement is not only valid—it's welcome.

Now, the case for the Sebir Ladder.

The *"How-To" Roadmap* is packed with practical instructions. These are made up of 7 major steps and 24 sub-steps. As argued in the Introduction, a schematic of the entire suite of instructions is reminiscent of the rungs and steps of a ladder. There is a clear step-by-step progression, just like climbing a ladder. Every step must be taken, one by one. The early steps—instructions—are foundational, all build on each other and the steps that come later require the preceding steps to be completed.

Finally, "Sebir Ladder" is a succinct and compelling descriptor—far easier to remember than generic labels like "Set of instructions" or "How-To Guidelines". It also integrates seamlessly, ensuring that the book's *learning*—the Sebir Model—bridges naturally into the *doing* of the Sebir Ladder.

"HOW-TO" ROADMAP: THE SEBIR LADDER

The secret of getting ahead is getting started

MARK TWAIN

There are two modes of innovating: Copying and Originating. This *"How-To" Roadmap* essentially follows the Originating mode of innovating although the directions up to and including Step 2.7 apply to the Copying mode as well. The entire Sebir Model is unpacked into a series of step-by-step instructions. The roadmap also weaves in a real-life business example from a home improvement store that shadows the end-to-end process. The example clarifies the essence of each of the numbered instructions while demonstrating their sequential implementation.

Another important exception to note is that the shadow example does not map onto the sixth Problem way—the Preempt way. The key players are already dealing with an irreversible reality, so the option of *preempting* the inherent problem is no longer available to them.

To enhance readability, the workings of the business example are always illustrated in breakout boxes.

Also, refresher tips have been added at points, to support recall and simplify implementation.

We will look over the shoulders of the owners of the home improvement business as they innovate through a significant problem. We will watch them in action and—using questions, dialogue and critical reflection—we will attempt to interpret their reasoning, explorations and decisions.

Before You Dive In:

While the objective is to explain every step clearly and thoroughly, sometimes the iterative nature of the task concerned means it is impractical to lay bare every nuance and detail. Two instances that highlight this predicament are the logical thinking routines for tackling the problem in Steps 3.2, 3.3 and 3.4 and searching for and selecting the Initiator Resource in Steps 5.2, 5.3 and 5.4. There are some others.

To signal what is coming, here is a schematic of the full suite of *How-To* instructions. This is the Sebir Ladder.:

THE SEBIR LADDER

1.0 Summarize the Situational Background and Extract Preliminary Goal
1.1 Summarize the Circumstances
1.2 Extract Preliminary Goal

2.0 Load Problem PhotoBox
2.1 Identify Problem Obstacle
2.2 Describe Problem Cause
2.3 Envision AFTI Problem Solution
2.4 Formulate AFTI Goal
2.5 Identify Problem Object
2.6 Describe Problem Effect
2.7 Showcase Problem PhotoBox

3.0 Determine Problem Way Strategy
3.1 Add Problem Obstacle and Problem Object to Problem Way Decision Matrix
3.2 Assess Modifiability of Problem Obstacle
3.3 Evaluate Problem Way Options for Tackling Problem Cause
3.4 Assess Modifiability of Problem Object
3.5 Evaluate Problem Way Options for Tackling Problem Effect

4.0 Name Responder Resource
4.1 Name Who or What Must Respond
4.2 Specify Role of Responder

5.0 Search for and Locate Initiator Resource
5.1 Specify the Problem-Solving Value Being Sought
5.2 Brainstorm Resources Available
5.3 Exclude Available Resources Not Containing Problem-Solving Value
5.4 Reduce Remaining Resources to Most Promising Initiator
5.5 Decide Initiator Harvesting Option

6.0 Search for and Locate Connector Resource
6.1 Specify What the Connector Needs to Do
6.2 Find the Connector that Possesses the Required Attraction Value

7.0 Review the Completed Innovative Project (Optional)
7.1 Validate the Distinctive Innovative Value Generated

THE SEBIR LADDER

1.0 Summarize the Situational Background and Extract Preliminary Goal

1.1 Summarize the Circumstances

Describe the situation in plain language, making clear who is unable to achieve what goal, and why.

> ### SITUATIONAL BACKGROUND [FOR SHADOW EXAMPLE]
>
> In a fast-growing city, a long-established home improvement store is under financial pressure because the leasing costs for its superlative location are rising faster than overall business profitability. While relocating to a less expensive area would reduce such costs, it would also turn away customers who value the store's centrally located, easily accessible site with abundant parking.

1.2 Extract Preliminary Goal

Refresher Tip:

The formulation of the Preliminary Goal—once distilled from the Situational Background—enables the identification of the five problem components that are required to populate the Problem PhotoBox in Step 2.0.

1.2.1 Review the situational details and translate them into the Preliminary Goal they imply.

> ### PRELIMINARY GOAL
>
> A home improvement retailer wants to halt the damaging impact of increasing premises leasing costs on business profitability.

2.0 Load Problem PhotoBox

Refresher Tip:

Every unachieved goal is blocked by a problem. The Problem PhotoBox displays the five key components that characterize the anatomy and trajectory of the problem from cause through to effect. It also ignites a penetrating insight into the ideal solution for the problem. Steps 2.1 to 2.6 bring together the five components, and the AFTI Goal.

2.1 Identify Problem Obstacle

2.1.1. Identify the obstacle blocking the achievement of the Preliminary Goal by using one or more nouns to name it.

Problem Obstacle	Premises Leasing Costs

2.2 Describe Problem Cause

2.2.1. Describe why or how the Problem Cause is blocking the achievement of the Preliminary Goal by qualifying the Problem Obstacle with one or more vivid adjectives.

Problem Cause	Profit-Damaging Premises Leasing Costs

2.3 Envision AFTI Problem Solution

Refresher Tip:

This instruction involves visualizing a perfect outcome to the problem and is accomplished by drawing upon the AFTI principle—Aim For The Ideal. The AFTI Problem Solution pictures an ideal state that is diametrically opposite to the current state (the Problem Cause). If your Problem Solution comes across as outrageously ambitious, you are on the right track.

2.3.1. Envision the Problem Solution by radically reimagining a result that is perfectly and determinedly inverse to the Problem Cause description. This can be done by using exact antonyms of the adjectives used to describe the Problem Cause. Alternatively, preface the Problem Cause description with the words "Not," "Non" or "Nil."

Problem Solution	Profit-Boosting Premises Leasing Costs

2.4 Formulate AFTI Goal

Refresher Tip:

The AFTI Goal does more than establish a goal that is the ideal. It also facilitates the creation of a mental picture in our minds of the type of remedial capability—the Problem-Solving Value—required of the Initiator Resource when we seek to locate it in Step 5.0. The AFTI Goal supersedes and replaces the Preliminary Goal.

2.4.1 Revisit the Preliminary Goal and reformulate it into an AFTI Goal by articulating what a perfect outcome would be, one that profoundly contrasts with the Problem Cause description. Something unrealistically audacious is the right nuance.

AFTI GOAL
A home improvement retailer wants to ensure the increasing costs of leasing its store location no longer erode total business profitability but rather boost it.

2.5 Identify Problem Object

2.5.1   Identify the object impacted by the Problem Cause by using one or more nouns to name it.

Problem Object	Home Improvement Business

2.6 Describe Problem Effect

2.6.1   Describe the effect of the Problem Cause on the Problem Object by qualifying the Problem Object with one or more vivid adjectives that convey how it is being harmed.

Problem Effect	Unprofitable Home Improvement Business

2.7 Showcase Problem PhotoBox

Refresher Tip:

The anatomy and trajectory of the problem and its ideal resolution are captured in the completed Problem PhotoBox.

2.7.1   Populate the *Problem PhotoBox* with the five components that have been derived from Steps 2.1 to 2.6, including the AFTI Goal in Step 2.4.1.

2.7.2   Confirm the Problem Solution reflects the AFTI principle.

PROBLEM PHOTOBOX		
Problem Obstacle	Premises Leasing Costs	
Problem Cause	Profit-Damaging Premises Leasing Costs	
Problem Solution	Profit-Boosting Premises Leasing Costs	AFTI Goal
Problem Object	Home Improvement Business	
Problem Effect	Unprofitable Home Improvement Business	

→ SIGNPOST FOR COPYING MODE

Branch into Innovating by Copying as Well

Once a mental visualization of the required Problem-Solving Value has been framed by the AFTI Goal, reinforced by the other four components, the second mode of innovating—Innovating by Copying—can be pursued concurrently. Simply having a vivid, revealing picture in our minds primes us—in the spirit and logic of mental association—to recognize a comparable situation that contains a relevant and adaptable solution, should we encounter it.

In Chapter 13, a mountain metaphor is employed to give detailed guidance on how to think when Innovating by Copying. Going up one side of the mountain parallels moving from a specific observation to generalizing a principle from it, whereas going down the other side mirrors the application of that same general principle in a specific manner again—but this time, to address a different need.

The two modes—Innovating by Copying and Innovating by Originating—can be pursued simultaneously. The actions through to and including Step 2.7 inform both modes. There is obvious benefit in traveling on two parallel tracks—placing ourselves in the path of serendipity through Copying, while also advancing along the companion track of Originating.

Win–win.

3.0 Determine Problem Way Strategy

Refresher Tip:
There are five ways to innovate through problems that utilize the Problem Way Decision Matrix—Prevent, Avoid, Eliminate, Transform and Nullify. These are displayed in Step 3.1.1. The sixth way—the Preempt way—operates outside the Problem Way Decision Matrix and, as already explained, is not an applicable option for the shadow example we are working though here.

3.1 Add Problem Obstacle and Problem Object to Problem Way Decision Matrix

Refresher Tip:
The Problem Way Decision Matrix helps us choose the best way to tackle a particular problem by evaluating the characteristics of the incumbent Problem Cause (with Obstacle) and Problem Effect (with Object) to determine their susceptibility to modification. Taking account of the Situational Background, a Logical Reasoning Routine is employed to filter the Problem way strategies until we arrive at the best one.

3.1.1   Access the Problem Way Decision Matrix and embed details of the identified Problem Obstacle and Problem Object.

PROBLEM WAY DECISION MATRIX		
	MODIFIABLE	**NON-MODIFIABLE**
PROBLEM CAUSE [contains Problem Obstacle] **"Premises Leasing Costs"**	Prevent	Avoid
	Eliminate	
	Transform	
PROBLEM EFFECT [contains Problem Object] **"Home Improvement Business"**	Nullify	Avoid

3.2 Assess Modifiability of Problem Obstacle

Refresher Tip:

To evaluate the options for tackling a particular Problem Cause, it is necessary to focus on the modifiability of the Problem Obstacle inherent in that Problem Cause.

3.2.1   Use logical reasoning to determine the susceptibility of the Problem Obstacle to being modified—manipulated, controlled or influenced—to achieve the AFTI Goal.

REASONING ROUTINE TO EVALUATE PROBLEM OBSTACLE

Note: Iterative tasks like this don't lend themselves to exhaustive, detailed elaboration.
 	
Q: Is the Problem Obstacle "Premises Leasing Costs" Modifiable?
 	
• **"Premises Leasing Costs"** are probably influenced by negotiation between the business owners and their landlord.
 	
• **Possible Modifications:**
  o The amount being paid could be reduced through negotiation.
 	
• **Limitations:**
  o This obvious negotiation has most likely been attempted already.
  o The relief achieved through any renegotiation would probably be negligible.
 	
• **Conclusion:**
  o **"Premises Leasing Costs"** are unlikely to be modified or influenced substantially enough to achieve the AFTI Goal.

3.3 Evaluate Problem Way Options for Tackling Problem Cause

3.3.1 Use logical reasoning to evaluate the options for tackling the Problem Cause.

3.3.2 Confirm the most viable Problem way.

REASONING ROUTINE FOR TACKLING PROBLEM CAUSE

Q 1: What Problem Way options are available for tackling the Problem Cause "Profit-Damaging Premises Leasing Costs"?

- **"Premises Leasing Costs" cannot be modified:**
  - This eliminates these strategies: the **Prevent, Eliminate,** and **Transform ways.**
  - The **Avoid way** is the only possibility for a non-modifiable Problem Obstacle.

Q 2: Can the Problem Cause "Profit-Damaging Premises Leasing Costs" be Avoided?

- Avoiding the **"Premises Leasing Costs"** suggests two possibilities:
  - Close the business. Clearly unacceptable based on the owners' aspirations as recorded in the Situational Background.
  - Move to cheaper premises. Also unacceptable, based on the customer-loss implications of relocating, as recorded in the Situational Background.

- **Conclusion:**
  - It is impossible to avoid the Problem Cause **"Profit-Damaging Premises Leasing Costs"** in a feasible way.
  - **Avoid** is not a viable innovative strategy.

3.4 Assess Modifiability of Problem Object

Refresher Tip:

To evaluate the options for tackling a particular Problem Effect, it is necessary to focus on the modifiability of the Problem Object that is impaired by that Problem Effect.

3.4.1 Use logical reasoning to determine the susceptibility of the Problem Object to being modified—manipulated, controlled or influenced—to achieve the AFTI Goal.

REASONING ROUTINE TO EVALUATE PROBLEM OBJECT

Q: Is the Problem Object "Home Improvement Business" Modifiable?

- **Yes, the "Home Improvement Business"** is modifiable since the proprietors own it and can make decisions about its operation.

3.5 Evaluate Problem way Options for Tackling Problem Effect

3.5.1 Use logical reasoning to evaluate the options for tackling the Problem Effect.

3.5.2 Confirm the most viable Problem way.

REASONING ROUTINE FOR TACKLING PROBLEM EFFECT

Q 1: What Problem way options are available for tackling the modifiable "Home Improvement Business"?

- **From the Problem Way Decision Matrix:**
  - o **Nullify way.**

Q 2: Can the modifiable Problem Object "Home Improvement Business" be Nullified?

- Nullifying the impact on the **"Home Improvement Business"** seems plausible given its accessibility.

- **Conclusion:**
  - o The **Nullify way** is the only viable strategy left for safeguarding the profitability of the **"Home Improvement Business"**.

4.0 Name Responder Resource

Refresher Tip:

Having established the anatomy and trajectory of the problem, and how to tackle it, we now harness the three input resources that comprise the Sebir Model to craft our innovative solution. The Responder is the third of these, but as explained just below, we engage with it first. The Responder behaves or performs as it is predisposed to do when stimulated by the Initiator via the Connector. The Responder's behavior or performance solves the prevailing problem and leads to goal achievement.

Even though it is positioned third in sequence in the Sebir Model, we start with the Responder because it is the only one of the three Sebir Model resources that we can immediately identify when we begin to innovate.

4.1 Name Who or What Must Respond

Refresher Tip:

The Innovative Value contributed by the Responder Resource is Predisposition Value. It is the People or Things that we want to behave or perform in a specifically desirable manner to achieve the AFTI Goal. The Responder behaves or performs as it is already inclined to do.

4.1.1 Name the identified People or Things whose behavior or performance is required to solve the problem.

4.1.2 Specify the behavior or performance required of the identified People or Things (derived from the AFTI Goal in Step 2.4.1).

NAME THE RESPONDER RESOURCE AND REQUIRED RESPONSE

Q 1: Who or what needs to behave or perform to solve the problem faced?

- **Responder is "Premises Leasing Costs"**
  - o Increases in these are currently endangering business profitability.

Q 2: How must "Premises Leasing Costs" respond?

- **"Premises Leasing Costs" must:**
  - o Transition from profit damagers into profit boosters.

4.2 Specify Role of Responder

Refresher Tip:

Engaging the Responder depends upon whether the Responder is People or Things. If the Responder is a Thing, there is just one option for engaging with it and that is integrating with it. This will compel a Thing to perform according to one of four predetermined tendencies. These are listed in the breakout box below.

However, if the Responder is People, there are three options for persuading them to behave as required. These range from Likely to Probable, and finally to Certain to occur. They are not relevant to our example.

4.2.1 Classify the Responder as People or Things.

4.2.2 List the options available for engaging with the Responder given its status.

4.2.3 Select the applicable Responder option.

4.2.4 Specify the Predisposition Value.

DETERMINE ROLE OF RESPONDER RESOURCE

Q 1: Do "Premises Leasing Costs" fall under the category of People or Things?

- "Premises Leasing Costs" are an inanimate, intangible item and therefore fall under Things.

Q 2: What responses are possible from "Premises Leasing Costs"?

- Things are compelled or programmed to respond via one of four main mechanisms::
  o Physically.
  o Chemically.
  o Electronically.
  o Conceptually.

Q 3: What is applicable Responder option?

- As an abstract entity, "Premises Leasing Costs" are compelled to respond Conceptually.

Q 4: What is the Predisposition Value required of "Premises Leasing Costs"?

- "Premises Leasing Costs" must diminish or disappear when connected with the Initiator Resource so that profitability is boosted.

5.0 Search for and Locate Initiator Resource

Refresher Tip:

The Initiator is the first of the three input resources that comprise the Sebir Model. It is followed by the Connector and Responder. It possesses the unused value that will solve the problem faced when it is presented to the Responder via the Connector. The Responder's behavior or performance when it embraces the Initiator ensures that the desired goal is achieved.

5.1 Specify the Problem-Solving Value Being Sought

Refresher Tip:

The Innovative Value contributed by the Initiator Resource is its Problem-Solving Value— the value that converts the Problem Cause into the AFTI Problem Solution. The Initiator ensures that the specific value required to solve the problem is harvestable and able to be presented to the Responder via the Connector. The Responder and the preferred Problem Way from the Problem Way Decision Matrix are relevant inputs to this step.

5.1.1   Revisit Step 4.1.1 to confirm Responder.

5.1.2   Revisit Step 3.5.2 to confirm the preferred Problem way.

5.1.3   Articulate what is required of the Initiator based on the confirmed Problem way and the identity of the Responder.

5.1.4   Specify the Problem-Solving Value the Initiator requires, taking account of the known circumstances.

SPECIFY PROBLEM-SOLVING VALUE REQUIRED OF INITIATOR RESOURCE

Q 1: Who is Responder?

- The Responder is **"Premises Leasing Costs"**.

Q 2: What is Preferred Problem way?

- The **Nullify way** is the only viable strategy yielded by the Problem Way Decision Matrix analysis.

Q 3: What must the Initiator empower the Nullify way to do?

- The **Nullify way** must:
  - o Buttress the profitability of the **"Home Improvement Business"** from the effect of the Problem Cause "**Profit-Damaging Leasing Costs**", and
  - o Neutralize **"Profit-Damaging Leasing Costs"** to such an extent that they boost business profitability rather than damage it.

- The Nullify Way must therefore offset part or all of **"Profit-Damaging Leasing Costs"** with some sort of income or revenue.

Q4: How does this translate into the specific Problem-Solving Value the Initiator Resource needs?

- **The Initiator Resource must contain Problem-Solving Value that:**
  - o Represents new, additional income or revenue.
  - o Is customer-generated income or revenue of some kind as the business has no other major income sources.
  - o Comes from non-traditional customers as revenue from traditional customers has probably stabilized around its natural peak.

- **Therefore, the Initiator must contain Problem-Solving Value that can be unlocked to generate "Non-Traditional Customer Revenue".**

5.2 Brainstorm Resources Available

Refresher Tip:

This exercise builds a pool of resources by amassing all those that are physically and relationally accessible, plus those that are logically connected to the Problem-Solving Value being sought.

5.2.1   Commission a team to brainstorm an array of available resources. (Alternatively, employ an AI tool which can assist in generating an initial list.)

This step involves answering two key questions, which can be addressed either in one combined brainstorming session or two separate ones:

- o What resources are accessible—either physically or through relationships?
- o What resources are plausibly related to the specified Problem-Solving Value?

5.2.2 When finished, sort the list into sensible, broad categories with appropriate sub-categories that will help their evaluation.

Example of possible sorting categories:

I.   EXTERNAL TO OUR ACTIVITY
    (i)   Tangible Resources
    (ii)   Intangible Resources
II.   INTERNAL TO OUR ACTIVITY
    (i)   Physical Resources
    (ii)   Human Resources
    (iii) Operational Resources
    (iv)   Non-Physical Resources

Note: To avoid visual overload, we will reproduce the results of the imagined brainstorming in two breakout boxes: those resources that are external to the Home Improvement Business and those resources that are internal.

BRAINSTORM ACCESSIBLE AND RELEVANT INITIATOR RESOURCES [EXTERNAL]

Q 1: What resources are accessible physically or relationally?

Q 2: What resources are related to the specified Problem-Solving Value "Non-Traditional Customer Revenue"?

Note: Answers to the two brainstorming questions have been combined although the lists are Illustrative only, not exhaustive.

EXTERNAL TO BUSINESS:

- **Tangible Resources:**
  - Local Shopping Malls and Their Customers.
  - Assorted Retailers (Grocery Stores; Gyms; Pharmacies; Beauty Salons; Restaurants; Cafes; etc.) and Their Customers.
  - Public Services (Banks; ATMs; Post Offices; Gas Stations; Parks; etc.) and Their Customers and Their Users.
  - Transportation (Bus Stops; Rail Hubs; etc.) and Their Users.
  - Building Residents (Residential Dwellings; Apartments; Offices).
  - Sports Facility Attendees.
  - Customers of Local Suppliers of Home Improvement and Related Items.
  - Local Customers of Online Suppliers of Home Improvement and Related Items.

- **Intangible Resources:**
  - Local Car and Foot Traffic.
  - Community Activities.
  - Consumer Behavior.
  - Reputation of Brands and Products Stocked and Sold
  - Neighborhood Image.

ETC.

BRAINSTORM ACCESSIBLE AND RELEVANT INITIATOR RESOURCES [INTERNAL]

Q 1: What resources are accessible physically or relationally?

Q 2: What resources are related to the specified Problem-Solving Value "Non-Traditional Customer Revenue"?

Note: Answers to the two brainstorming questions have been combined although the lists are Illustrative only, not exhaustive.

INTERNAL TO BUSINESS:

- **Physical Resources:**
  - o Store Premises.
  - o Store Land.
  - o Warehouse and Storage.
  - o Showroom Space.
  - o Fixtures, Displays and Shelving.
  - o Tools and Equipment.
  - o Business Vehicles.

- **Human Resources:**
  - o Business Owners.
  - o Skilled Tradespeople.
  - o Sales and Marketing Staff.
  - o Other Experienced Employees.

- **Operational Resources:**
  - o Merchandise for Sale.
  - o Business Website.
  - o Ecommerce Platform.
  - o Enterprise Software.

- **Non-Physical Resources:**
  - o Customers.
  - o Suppliers.
  - o Brand Reputation.
  - o Financial Leverage.
  - o Permits and Licenses.

ETC.

5.3 Exclude Available Resources Not Containing Problem-Solving Value

Refresher Tip:

Don't worry if this step seems a bit circular—that's because it is. In Steps 5.2.1 and 5.2.2, we used potential Problem-Solving Value as one of two criteria for including resources on the list of those available. Now, we are using it to exclude resources that were added only because they were accessible. In other words, we are culling any resources that are accessible but lack the specified Problem-Solving Value. Some resources, of course, will meet both criteria—they are accessible, and they contain the desired Problem-Solving Value. They will stay.

5.3.1   Retrieve the specification for Problem-Solving Value in Step 5.1.4.

5.3.2   Use the specified Problem-Solving Value to trim the list of available resources:
- o   Retain those that are likely to be associated with the specified Problem-Solving Value, and
- o   Exclude those that are unlikely to be associated with the specified Problem-Solving Value.

Use a question like this:

"Which available resources in the list plausibly contain value that could contribute to the specified Problem-Solving Value?"

USE THE PROBLEM-SOLVING VALUE CRITERION TO REDUCE RESOURCES AVAILABLE

Q 1: What is the specified Problem-Solving Value?

- **The Problem-Solving Value is "Non-Traditional Customer Revenue".**

Q 2: Which of the available resources could plausibly embody unused value that would yield "Non-Traditional Customer Revenue"?

Note: Results only, based on inferred prioritization.

- **From External Resources:**
  - o Customers of Local Suppliers of Home Improvement and Related Items.
  - o Local Customers of Online Suppliers of Home Improvement and Related items.
- **From Internal Resources::**
  - o Store Premises.
  - o Store Land.
  - o Showroom Space.
  - o Sales and Marketing Staff.
  - o Ecommerce Platform.
  - o Merchandise for Sale.

5.4 Reduce Remaining Resources to Most Promising Initiator

Refresher Tip:

This step narrows the Initiator Resources further. Each resource remaining on the list is assessed for factors likely to rule it out, rather than for reasons to keep it in. A useful approach is to look for signs of underutilization. Innovative Value is unused value embedded in all resources—although it is not always obvious. If a resource is already known to be thoroughly exploited or fully activated, its potential value as an innovative solution will obviously be reduced—although there will always be a remnant. Conversely, any resource that clearly appears to have unused capability should be considered.

5.4.1 Evaluate the resources one by one to determine which potentially contain Problem-Solving Value, with the aim of excluding the least promising until only the most prospective Initiator remains.

  Use a question like this:

  "Why is this resource unlikely to contribute to the specified Problem-Solving Value?

  (*Clue: For all practical purposes it appears to be fully utilized already.*)

EVALUATION AND REDUCTION TO THE MOST PROSPECTIVE INITIATOR RESOURCE

Q: Why might each of these resources fail to contribute to "Non-Traditional Customer Revenue"?

Note: The following evaluation doesn't cover every possibility. A representation of the type of reasoning undertaken has been imagined. Evidence of high practical use is a key factor for filtering out resources.

- **Customers of Local Suppliers of Home Improvement and Related Items:**
  - Customers are unlikely to switch suppliers without a significant cash incentive, which would be counterproductive.

- **Local Customers of Online Suppliers of Home Improvement and Related Items:**
  - Online customers are unlikely to switch to an new Ecommerce Platform without a significant cash incentive, which would be counterproductive.

- **Store Premises:**
  - These are totally utilized. There is no obvious way of generating supplemental revenue from them without significant cost—by enlarging them, for instance. Such cost would be self-defeating, and the landlord would need to agree.

- **Store Land**
  - The land adjacent to the store premises shows promise, particularly due to its spaciousness and—more specifically—the ample customer-friendly parking that is rarely fully utilized, even at peak times.

- **Showroom Space:**
  - This is fully stocked and furnished. Making the showroom bigger to present non-traditional items is the only possibility here but this would involve a substantial capital outlay (unhelpful) and would require the landlord's approval.

- **Sales and Marketing Staff:**
  - Due to extensive business development over the years, marketing and sales activities are now well-optimized. As a result, it is unlikely increasing these efforts will lead to significant spending by non-traditional customers.

- **Ecommerce Platform**
  - As part of marketing operations, the Ecommerce platform has also been fully leveraged. The potential for harvesting further revenue from customers just because they are non-traditional is minimal.

- **Merchandise for Sale:**
  - Merchandise holdings have been fine-tuned over many years. Extending them to include items of a different type is not possible without building larger premises, which would be costly, even if possible.

5.4.2 Select the most promising candidate for Initiator—the one that is most validated and least contested—according to the reasoning in Step 5.4.1.

5.4.3 Itemize the attributes of the Problem-Solving Value that the selected Initiator needs to possess.

SELECT THE MOST PROMISING INITIATOR RESOURCE AND CONFIRM ITS VALUE

Q 1: Which available resource is most promising Initiator for containing the Problem-Solving Value "Non-Traditional Customer Revenue"?

- **Conclusion from Step 5.4.1**
  - o **"Store Land"**—the spacious land on which the store is located emerges as the most promising Initiator.
  - o More precisely, the land area with unused customer-friendly parking is an obvious value source.

Q 2: What are the specific Problem-Solving Value attributes possessed by the parking on "Store Land"?

- **Attributes likely to appeal to "Non-Traditional" Customers:**
  - o Centrally located.
  - o Abundant, free parking.
  - o Conveniently accessible.
  - o Practical pickup and collection ease for items that can be bulky.

- **The Problem-Solving Value of "Store Land" is Accessible, Pickup-Friendly Parking for Non-Traditional Customers.**

5.5 Decide Initiator Harvesting Option

Refresher Tip:
There are three options for tapping into an Initiator Resource with minimum effort to release its unused value: extending it to do more of what it normally does; multiplying it to do something in addition to what it normally does or varying it to do something different from what it normally does.

5.5.1 List the options for releasing unused value from the Initiator Resource.

5.5.2 Select the applicable Initiator option.

<table>
<tr><td>

DECIDE APPLICABLE OPTION FOR HARVESTING SELECTED INITIATOR RESOURCE

Q 1: What options are available for harvesting "Store Land"?

- **There are three options for releasing Problem-Solving Value ("Non-Traditional Customer Revenue") from "Store Land":**
  - o Extending it to provide parking for more customers.
  - o Multiplying it to do something else for parking customers.
  - o Varying it to do something different altogether from providing parking for customers.

Q 2: Can "Store Land" be extended, multiplied or varied to release "Non-Traditional Customer Revenue"?

- **The normal capability of the "Store Land" is to provide Accessible, Pickup-Friendly Parking.**
- **The normal capability of "Store Land" can be extended to do more of what it usually does because it is underutilized.**
- **The value provided is a potential source of Non-Traditional Customer Revenue from alternative customers if they use the parking capacity and it is paid for.**

</td></tr>
</table>

6.0 Search for and Locate Connector Resource

Refresher Tip:
The Connector is the second of the three input resources that comprise the Sebir Model. It is preceded by the Initiator and succeeded by the Responder. It connects the Initiator to the Responder in a manner that urges or compels the behavior or performance from the Responder that will solve the problem faced. Once the problem is solved, the goal is achieved.

6.1 Specify What the Connector Needs To do

Refresher Tip:
The Innovative Value contributed by the Connector Resource is Attraction Value. The Connector ensures that the Initiator and Responder have a strong affinity for each other.

6.1.1 Recall selected Initiator Resource and its unused Problem-Solving Value from Step 5.4.3.

6.1.2 Recall Responder Resource and its Predisposition Value from Step 4.2.4.

6.1.3 Blend Problem-Solving Value and Predisposition Value to specify the required Attraction Value.

SPECIFY WHAT CONNECTOR RESOURCE NEEDS TO DO

Q 1: What is the selected Initiator and its unused Problem-Solving Value?

- **"Store Land" is the selected Initiator.**

- **Problem-Solving Value is "Non-Traditional Customer Revenue":**
  - This value must come from customers who are not normally served by the business.
  - Such customers must have a need for **Accessible, Pickup-Friendly Parking.**

Q 2: What is the identified Responder and its Predisposition Value?

- **The Responder is "Premises Leasing Costs".**

- **Premises Leasing Costs" must shift from being a drain on profitability to being a profit contributor when offset by Non-Traditional Customer Revenue.**

Q3: What Attraction Value does the Connector Resource need?

- **It needs to encourage the convergence of the buying needs of Non-Traditional Customers and Accessible, Pickup-Friendly Parking facilities.**

6.2 Find the Connector that Possesses the Required Attraction Value

6.2.1 State clearly how the Initiator and Connector are to be drawn to each other.

6.2.2 Brainstorm where the required Connector of the Initiator and the Responder can be found.

6.2.3 Decide on the most promising Connector.

FIND SUITABLE CONNECTOR RESOURCE

Q 1: How can "Non-Traditional Customer Revenue" and "Premises' Leasing Costs" be drawn to each other?

- **Non-Traditional Customers who require Accessible, Pickup-Friendly Parking must be found.**

- **Premises Leasing Costs will diminish if Non-Traditional Customers utilize and somehow pay for the Accessible, Pickup-Friendly Parking on "Store Land."**

Q 2: Brainstorm where Non-Traditional Customers who have a need for Accessible, Pickup-Friendly Parking might be found?

- **Brainstorming brief:**
  - o Consider suppliers and their local customers for home improvement products and comparable items.
  - o Focus on bulky or heavy products requiring delivery or pickup.

- **Brainstorm the possibilities:**
  - o Customers of local home improvement suppliers.
  - o Customers who buy products comparable to home improvement items and their *local* suppliers.
  - o Local customers who buy products comparable to home improvement items and their *online* suppliers.

Q 3: Who or what is the most promising Connector?

- **The most promising Connector is "Online Suppliers of Home Improvement Products and Comparable Items" who:**
  - o Require an order fulfillment service for customers who buy online.
  - o Supply products whose physical characteristics often make shipping expensive or impractical.
  - o Need a conveniently located delivery and collection point.

- **Negotiate commercial arrangements with online suppliers who require Accessible, Pickup-Friendly Parking for their customers who purchased home improvement or comparable products online.**

7.0 Review the Completed Innovative Project (Optional)

Although this seventh step is not an essential part of the Sebir Ladder, it is useful for providing learning and insights that will benefit future projects. It can also highlight oversights or omissions, and pinpoint areas where Innovative Value was not maximized. The satisfaction that comes from a job well done is also likely to be reinforced.

7.1 Validate the Distinctive Innovative Value Generated

7.1.1 Restate the problem faced.

7.1.2 Validate the Problem-Solving Value liberated from the Initiator Resource.

7.1.3 Validate the Attraction Value liberated from the Connector Resource.

7.1.4 Validate the Predisposition Value liberated from the Responder Resource.

7.1.5 Summarize the job done.

JOURNEY TO THE INNOVATIVE SOLUTION (THE SEBIR)

1. Problem:
- **Premises Leasing Costs are seriously eroding business profitability.**

2. Initiator Resource—Problem-Solving Value:
- **The under-utilized, Accessible, Pickup-Friendly Parking on "Store Land" is offered on commercial terms to online retailers of home improvement and comparable products for shipment, storage and collection by their customers.**
- **A covered carpark area will allow for the on-site storage of pickup items.**

3. Connector Resource—Attraction Value:
- **Online retailers must ensure reliable and convenient delivery of goods that their customers have purchased from them on the web by:**
  - Transporting items sold to a conveniently accessible location for pickup by their customers.
  - Instructing their customers who must:
    - pick up their internet purchases from the home improvement store;
    - visit and park at the store to collect what they have purchased online.
- **The online retailers pay a commercial usage fee to the home improvement business for the service provided.**

4. Responder Resource—Predisposition Value:
- **"Profit-Damaging Leasing Costs" are compelled to yield to the following nullifiers:**
  - The recurrent commercial fee received from online retailers, for customers collecting their purchased goods, offsets the impact of the escalating leasing costs.
  - Customers who visit the store to collect purchased items frequently buy other items while they are there, further offsetting the impact of escalating leasing costs.
- **The total additional revenue received from Non-Traditional Customers utilizing the Accessible, Pickup-Friendly Parking decisively nullifies the impact of "Profit-Damaging Leasing Costs" on business profitability.**

JOURNEY TO THE INNOVATIVE SOLUTION (THE SEBIR)

5. Summary:

A home improvement retailer addresses the problem of the damaging costs of leasing its store premises through negotiating with online suppliers who sell to similar customers and who need a means of getting the goods purchased into the hands of those customers. In return for a commercial payment, the home improvement retailer agrees to make available its store as a drop-off location, where customers of those online suppliers can visit to conveniently pick up items they have purchased via the web.

ACKNOWLEDGMENTS

Because this book has been decades in the making, I have consulted hundreds of people whose guidance I have greatly appreciated. Although attempting to list them all would be brave, I would surely forget some who are well deserving of mention.

Even if I were to take the conventional route and single out a few especially helpful contributors, my memory would favor recent conversations rather than significant ones. So, my expressions of gratitude must remain general—but they are no less sincere for that. I take comfort in knowing that—even though I haven't named names—you know who you are. How could you forget my badgering?

I can, however, highlight two areas of appreciation in particular:

First, specific thanks go to Paul Wood of *iP Edge*, who has spent more than fifteen years working with me in the design and development of Sebir.com. The website and this book have a symbiotic relationship: each has nurtured the other, and they are inseparable in their impact.

Second, I thank Kristina and Ron Proft of *Delphian Books* for the presentation of the book in its final form. They have been stalwart partners, patiently enduring my perfectionist tendencies on the way to its completion.

And third, my appreciation goes to Iryna Yermashkevich for a cover design that aptly achieves without words what I have tried to do with them.

Finally, to my wife Ruth, who was there before the first word: she rightly deserves the last one. If a single word could honor her properly, I would use it.

There isn't one.

THIS PAGE INTENTIONALLY LEFT BLANK

APPENDIX A

The essential first step to achieving a disproportionately big result, relative to the effort expended, is to complete the *Problem PhotoBox* that captures the situation faced. The template below will guide you through this task:

PROBLEM PHOTOBOX TEMPLATE		
PROBLEM OBSTACLE	[Goal-Blocking Obstacle]	
Example: Product Inventory		
PROBLEM CAUSE	[Harmful Obstacle]	
Example: Excessive Product Inventory		
PROBLEM SOLUTION	[Perfectly Opposite Obstacle State]	**AFTI Goal**
Example: No Product Inventory		
PROBLEM OBJECT	[Object Harmed]	
Example: Cashflow		
PROBLEM EFFECT	[Harmful Effect on Object]	
Example: Depleted Cashflow		

HOW TO COMPLETE EACH SECTION	
Identifying Problem Obstacle	Use one or more nouns which identify the barrier blocking the reaching of a goal
Describing Problem Cause	Use one or more adjectives that identify *how* the Problem Obstacle blocks the reaching of a goal
Framing AFTI Problem Solution	Use one or more adjectives to reframe the Problem Obstacle into a perfect or *ideal* opposite of the Problem Cause
Identifying Problem Object	Use one or more nouns which identify the object harmed by the Problem Cause
Describing Problem Effect	Use one or more adjectives to identify *how* the Problem Object is harmed by the Problem Cause

THIS PAGE INTENTIONALLY LEFT BLANK

APPENDIX B

A Collection of Puns and Paraprosdokians

PUNS

A collection of puns in which additional meanings are innovatively extracted from one or more of the words used:

- Jokes about German sausages are the wurst

- I'm addicted to brake fluid, but I can stop whenever I want

- A good pun is its own reword

- I'm reading a book on anti-gravity. I can't put it down

- All the toilets in London police stations have been stolen. Police say they have nothing to go on

- This girl said she recognized me from the vegetarian club, but I'd never met herbivore

- They told me I had type-A blood, but it was a type-O

- I went to a theatrical performance about puns. It was a play on words

- Nostalgia is not what it used to be

- I have kleptomania, but when it gets bad, I take something for it

- What does a clock do when it's hungry? It goes back four seconds

- I used to be a banker, but then I lost interest

- I dropped out of communism class because of lousy Marx

- I took the job at a bakery because I kneaded dough

- Velcro—what a rip off!

- Prediction is very difficult, especially when it is about the future

- Throckmorton knew that if he were ever to break wind in the echo chamber, he would never hear the end of it

- Cartoonist found dead in home. Details are sketchy

- I didn't say it was your fault. I said I was blaming you

- I used to be indecisive. Now, I'm not so sure
- I stayed up all night to see where the sun went. Then it dawned on me
- Just beyond the narrows, the river widens
- Although Sarah had an abnormal fear of mice, it did not keep her from eeking out a living at a local pet store
- I was going to procrastinate, but I decided to do it tomorrow
- It's déjà vu all over again

Their Own Work

- I can resist everything except temptation—Oscar Wilde
- Time flies like an arrow. Fruit flies like a banana—Groucho Marx
- Ending a sentence with a preposition is something up with which I will not put—Winston Churchill
- Denial ain't just a river in Egypt—Mark Twain
- I have nothing to declare except my genius—Oscar Wilde
- I'm not afraid of death; I just don't want to be there when it happens—Woody Allen
- My education was interrupted only by my schooling—Winston Churchill
- That's the trouble with eternity; there is no telling when it will end—Tom Stoppard

PARAPROSDOKIANS

A collection of paraprosdokians, figures of speech, in which additional meaning is innovatively extracted by crafting the latter part of a phrase or sentence so it is unexpected—and often humorous—causing the reader or listener to reinterpret the first part:

- I want to die peacefully in my sleep, like my grandfather, not screaming and yelling like the passengers in his car

- A computer once beat me at chess, but it was no match for me at kickboxing

- If at first you don't succeed, skydiving is not for you

- I found a book called *How to Solve 50% of Your Problems*. So, I bought two

- My favorite uncle has the heart of a lion, and a lifetime ban from the zoo

- The two rules of success are: 1. Never tell them everything you know...

- The key to success in life is to be authentic. If you can fake that, you've got it made

- Stanley looked quite bored and somewhat detached, but then penguins often do

- Where there's a will, I want to be in it

- Where there's a will, there's relatives

- The last thing I want to do is hurt you, but it's still on my list

- If I agreed with you, we'd both be wrong

- War does not determine who is right, only who is left

- Having more money doesn't make you happier. I have 50 million dollars but I'm no happier than I was when I had 48 million

- I asked God for a bike, but I know He doesn't work that way. So I stole a bike and asked for forgiveness

- You do not need a parachute to skydive. You only need a parachute to skydive twice

- Knowledge is knowing a tomato is a fruit; wisdom is not putting it in a fruit salad

- Behind every great man is a woman rolling her eyes

- I thought I was wrong once, but I was mistaken

- I've had a perfectly wonderful evening, but this wasn't it

- Always borrow money from a pessimist. They won't expect it back
- If you're not confused, you don't know what's going on
- Doctor to patient: "I have good news and bad news. The good news is that you are not a hypochondriac."
- Did you know that on the Canary Islands there is not one canary? And on the Virgin Islands? Same thing. Not one canary there either

Their Own Work

- I was married by a judge. I should have asked for a jury—Groucho Marx
- I was always a good housekeeper. Whenever I divorced, I always kept the house—Zsa Zsa Gabor
- I am opposed to millionaires, but it would be dangerous to offer me the position—Mark Twain
- It takes only one drink to get me drunk. The trouble is, I can't remember if it's the thirteenth, or the fourteenth—George Burns
- Youth would be an ideal state if it came a little later in life—Herbert Henry Asquith
- What would men be without women? Scarce, sir, mighty scarce—Mark Twain
- I don't feel old. I don't feel anything until noon. Then it's time for my nap—Bob Hope
- Nobody goes there anymore. It's too crowded—Yogi Berra
- I spent a lot of money on booze, birds, and fast cars. The rest I just squandered—George Best

Author's Musing

- I met a fugitive in an elevator. He said he was going to ground

GLOSSARY

The Language of How to Innovate

AFTI Goal (see also "AFTI Problem Solution" and "Problem Solution")

AFTI stands for *Aim For The Ideal* and is used to describe a goal or objective that represents the ultimate or perfect solution to a problem. For example, if the Problem Cause of reputational damage to an organization is due to an "Outrageous Public Disaster," the desirable Problem Solution (that gives rise to the AFTI Goal) would be articulated as a "Praiseworthy Public Disaster." The goal state that AFTI envisages completely inverts the problem state. This radical transformation encourages thinking well beyond conventional limits. The AFTI Goal supersedes and replaces the Preliminary Goal.

AFTI Problem Solution (see also "AFTI Goal" and "Problem Solution")

This phrase is used to highlight the radical nature of a Problem Solution—the fact that it is not only the mirror opposite of the Problem Cause, but is opposite it in the most ideally desirable sense possible. The AFTI Problem Solution is the component of the *Problem PhotoBox* from which the AFTI Goal is formulated.

Attraction Value

Attraction Value is the value that resides in a Connector Resource. This value emerges because the Connector is positioned between the Initiator Resource and Responder Resource in a way that creates conditions that naturally draw both together. It is part of the total Innovative Value generated when we innovate. Value is also extracted from the Initiator Resource and the Responder Resource. The aggregate value extracted from all three resources equals the total Innovative Value. Attraction Value advertises Problem-Solving Value so that it stimulates Predisposition Value.

Attributes

Attributes are inherent features or characteristics—properties—of selected resources that are manipulated when we innovate. An attribute is identified and isolated and then modified in such a way that the host resource containing that attribute remains essentially unchanged. This insightful modification is the epitome of a "small effort."

Brainstorming

Brainstorming is the most common approach used for creative idea generation. It involves intensive and free-wheeling group discussion with the aim of producing as many ideas as possible about the target subject. Some rules are followed, such as each participant being encouraged to think aloud and propose any ideas, no matter how outlandish or bizarre they may seem. Priority is given to quantity over quality with

241

review only when the brainstorming session is over. Brainstorming is a Divergent Thinking technique.

Capability

A Capability represents the natural performance of something inanimate that—once identified and harnessed—can enable the achievement of our goal. A Capability of things is analogous to a Disposition of people. Unlike people, the Capabilities of non-thinking things cannot choose what, when or how to perform. They do only what they are created, designed or programmed to do.

Cause-and-effect (Causality)

Cause-and-effect is the relationship we invoke when innovating through problems. It can be discerned in the trajectory followed by a Problem Cause through to its ultimate Problem Effect. Understanding the path of this trajectory—how a Problem Cause and its Problem Effect specifically impedes the achievement of a goal—helps us to decide which of six ways is the most advantageous for innovating through a particular problem.

Connector Resource

The Connector is the second of three input resources that comprise the Sebir Model. It possesses Attraction Value. It is positioned between the Initiator and the Responder and innovatively maximizes the likelihood the sought-for beneficial interaction will occur between those two.

Convergent Thinking

Convergent Thinking is a thinking technique that is most readily understood by contrasting it with Brainstorming. Instead of generating multiple potential solutions to a problem, Convergent Thinking concentrates on funneling down toward a single workable solution. Brainstorming is an example of a Divergent Thinking technique. Convergent Thinking and Divergent Thinking are opposites.

Copying Mountain

The Copying Mountain is a metaphorical representation of how mental association works when we innovate. Climbing up the mountain, we move from a specific experience to understanding it sufficiently well to comprehend what is occurring in general terms. Climbing down the mountain, we descend from our general appreciation of what is happening to being able to apply that knowledge specifically again—but this time in a different setting—to meet a need we have.

Copying to Innovate

Copying to Innovate is one of the two modes of innovating we employ. The other is Originating to Innovate. Copying to Innovate involves discerning the general working principle of a potential solution observed elsewhere. We then apply a more specific version of that principle locally to resolve our need.

Creativity

Creativity is usually regarded as an innate personal ability, not one that is learned. Although it can refer to the ability to generate new and original ideas, it is most associated with the "creative" arts. Because it is regarded as an innate talent, it is not a core feature of the Sebir Model of innovating where learning how to innovate is an ability that can be purposefully cultivated by anyone. Creative thought certainly has a place however, but the place it has is one bounded by Economy of Effort and the constraining principles associated with that imperative.

Disposition

A Disposition is the inclination or tendency of a person to behave in a particular way and this grows out of a belief. When it takes root, a Disposition becomes a reliable predictor of human behavior. We innovate when we blend with a Disposition that equates to the behavior we require to achieve our goal. A Disposition to behave is the corollary of a Capability to perform, with behavior stemming from individuals and performance from non-living things. Unlike a Capability which is certain to do its thing, a Disposition is the outworking of human choice and must be harnessed in recognition of this understanding.

Divergent Thinking

Divergent Thinking is a term applied to thinking techniques where the aim is to generate as many ideas as possible to resolve some challenge. The best-known Divergent Thinking technique is Brainstorming. Divergent Thinking is the reverse of Convergent Thinking which seeks to isolate a single, workable solution.

Economy of Effort

Economy of Effort is the essential imperative that permeates and authenticates the Sebir Model of innovating. It constrains us to innovate by limiting our choice of contributing resources so the results are beneficially disproportionate to the basic resource inputs we employ. Economy of Effort embeds three limitations. First, we can only launch an innovative effort by locating and unlocking value that already exists in a selected resource. Second, we must bring about the behavior or performance we require by connecting with behavior or performance that is already poised to occur. Third, we are bound to connect selected resources in a manner that maximizes the chance that the needed interaction will occur.

Four Foundational Axioms

The Four Foundational Axioms upon which the Sebir Model of innovating is based are:
1. Problems are welcome, and even desirable, because they reveal the pathway to Innovative Value
2. Innovative Value is the large but unwarranted, beneficial gap between effort and result

3. Innovative Value is unlocked or uncovered, not created
4. Innovative Value is ubiquitous and readily accessible, not scarce and elusive

Goal

Goal is the most used term throughout this book because, when we innovate, we are always seeking to solve a problem that is blocking the achievement of some objective. A goal is a specific and measurable end toward which we direct some purposeful, innovative effort. Without some unfulfilled objective, we have no need to innovate.

Initiator Resource

The Initiator is the first of three input resources that comprise the Sebir Model. It possesses unused value—Problem-Solving Value—that converts the Problem Cause into the AFTI Problem Solution. Once the relevant value is unlocked, the Initiator presents it to the Responder by means of the Connector.

Innovate

There is a single, defining test to determine whether we are innovating. We innovate when the solution we generate represents value that clearly and significantly exceeds the effort we expend to generate that solution. An Innovative Value gap is generated. For a relatively small amount of effort in terms of the resources we employ, we achieve a disproportionately large result. *Small effort→big result* is the test.

Innovative Idea

An Innovative Idea is a solution to a problem where the value of the solution significantly surpasses the value of the effort invested to achieve it. Because of the imperative of Economy of Effort—maximum results with minimal effort—an Innovative Idea also often exhibits appealing symmetry that can be manifested through characteristics such as novelty, simplicity, unexpectedness and inevitability. An Innovative Idea is a "Sebir".

Innovative Value

Innovative Value is the unwarranted gap that is generated between the effort invested when we innovate and the value of what we achieve. Total Innovative Value is the aggregate of Problem-Solving Value from the Initiator Resource, Attraction Value from the Connector Resource and Predisposition Value from the Responder Resource.

Law of Action and Reaction

The third of Sir Isaac Newton's Laws of Motion states that for every action there is an equal and opposite reaction. In the natural, physical world this is always true. This Law is a useful counterpoint to the Sebir Model of innovating where we envisage an action that generates an unequal but disproportionately favorable reaction. The pairing of Newton's Law with the Sebir Model evokes a memorable mental anchor.

Little's Law

Little's Law is a mathematical theorem which proves that the value of the outcome of processes is dependent on the number of discrete steps that they contain. It reveals that perfecting the first step, reducing the variation within individual steps and ensuring that a process is composed of as few steps as possible will guarantee Innovative Value is generated.

Logical Reasoning Routine

To filter the five available strategies contained in the Problem Way Decision Matrix down to the most viable one, it is necessary to engage in some logical thinking by analyzing and reasoning through what is known about the Situational Background. The recognized Problem Obstacle and Problem Object are assessed for their susceptibility (or not) to each of the Problem ways. Logical thinking is also involved in evaluating Precursor Conditions to determine the feasibility of implementing the sixth way—the Preempt way—which operates outside the Problem Way Decision Matrix.

Originating to Innovate

Originating to Innovate is one of the two modes of innovating we can employ. The other is Copying to Innovate. Originating to Innovate involves starting from scratch, independent of an analogous situation that might be copied. It taps into resources that are accessible and that contain unused value that is relevant and applicable to the solution we need.

Precursor Conditions

Precursor Conditions are the enabling conditions that give rise to the Problem Cause. These exist upstream of the familiar cause-and-effect trajectory and are responsible for converting a Problem Obstacle into something that delivers a damaging effect. By identifying and addressing these conditions early, it is possible to employ the Preempt way to achieve an innovative solution to a problem by forestalling any unwelcome downstream consequences.

Predisposition Value

Predisposition Value is the value that resides in a Responder Resource. This value emerges because the Responder is stimulated to behave or perform in a manner to which it is already inclined. It is part of the total Innovative Value generated when we innovate. Value is also extracted from the Initiator Resource and the Connector Resource. The aggregate value extracted from all three resources equals the total Innovative Value. Predisposition Value responds to Attraction Value in a manner that amounts to the goal being achieved.

Preliminary Goal

The Preliminary Goal is crafted from the prevailing situation and circumstances. Specifically, it articulates an objective that represents resolution of the problem being faced. The description of the Preliminary Goal enables the identification of the five problem components that are required to populate the *Problem PhotoBox*. It is then superseded and replaced by the AFTI Goal.

Process

A process is best seen as a series of dependent steps when we innovate. Understanding that the performance excellence of each step is dependent upon the steps that precede it leads to three powerful and unfailingly trustworthy courses of action: maximize the effectiveness of the first step, remove steps where possible and narrow the potential for variability within individual steps to the bare minimum.

Problem

A problem is a difficulty that blocks the achievement of a goal and contains within its anatomy and cause-and-effect trajectory the means of achieving that goal.

Problem Cause

This phrase—which is the mirror opposite of the Problem Solution—contains the Problem Obstacle qualified by one or more adjectives that specify how it blocks the reaching of a goal.

Problem Effect

This phrase contains the Problem Object qualified by one or more adjectives that specify how it is harmed by the effect.

Problem Object

This phrase contains one or more nouns that identify the object that is harmed by the Problem Effect.

Problem Obstacle

This phrase contains one or more nouns that identify the obstacle that blocks the reaching of a goal

Problem PhotoBox

The *Problem PhotoBox* is the lens through which we see and record the unembellished reality of the problem we are facing. It employs compact descriptions and contains five components: the Problem Obstacle, the Problem Cause, the AFTI Problem Solution, the Problem Object, and the Problem Effect. The *Problem PhotoBox* enables the succinct execution of two pivotal tasks: the AFTI (ideal) Problem Solution is established by inverting the negative image of the Problem Cause, and an understanding of the trajectory of the cause of a problem through to its effect is obtained.

Problem Solution (see also "AFTI Goal" and "AFTI Problem Solution")

This phrase—which is the mirror opposite of the Problem Cause—uses one or more adjectives to reconceptualize the Problem Obstacle, portraying it as it will be once the problem is *ideally* resolved and the goal is achieved.

Problem-Solving Value

Problem-Solving Value is the potential capability that resides in an Initiator Resource that—when released—converts the Problem Cause into the AFTI Problem Solution. It is part of the total Innovative Value generated when we innovate. Value is also extracted from the Connector Resource and the Responder Resource. The aggregate value extracted from all three resources equals the total Innovative Value. Problem-Solving Value stimulates Predisposition Value when Attraction Value is deployed.

Problem Way Decision Matrix

The Problem Way Decision Matrix helps us choose the best way to tackle a particular problem. Its four-zones framework incorporates the binary possibilities of modifiability and non-modifiability of both the Problem Cause and the Problem Effect. The Problem Cause intrinsically contains the Problem Obstacle, and the Problem Effect intrinsically contains the Problem Object. Five ways of innovating through problems are distributed over the four right-hand zones of the matrix according to the viability of each given the prevailing status of the Problem Cause and Problem Effect. A sixth Problem way—the Preempt way—operates outside the Problem Way Decision Matrix.

Resource

A resource is the fundamental input when we innovate. Three elemental input resources—the Initiator, the Connector and the Responder—are the foundation of the Sebir Model. Because resources are ever present, their essential worth is often overlooked. They always contain unused value because it is impossible to consume or utilize a resource completely or perfectly. We innovate when we tap into residual value that already exists in an undervalued resource, rather than expending effort to generate such value from scratch.

Responder Resource

The Responder is the third of three input resources that comprise the Sebir Model and possesses Predisposition Value. It completes the innovative solution and contributes to the total Innovative Value generated by behaving or performing in a manner to which it is already predisposed.

Sebir

Sebir is a loose acronym for "**S**mall **e**ffort, **b**ig **r**esult." It refers to a specific value relationship observed when we innovate:

Sebir: *a result in which the value achieved clearly exceeds the effort invested.*

It furnishes a convenient and time-saving way to recognize and identify an idea infused with Innovative Value (an Innovative Idea is a "Sebir") and to represent the methodology developed throughout this book (the "Sebir Model").

Sebir Ladder

The Sebir Ladder is the detailed set of instructions in the form of steps and sub-steps that demonstrate how to implement the Sebir Model of innovating.

Sebir Model

The Sebir Model is a three-stage process in which each of the three sequential elements is an input resource. The three input resources combine with and amplify each other to produce an innovative solution that is the output. The value of the output of the model—the innovative solution to a problem—significantly exceeds the value of the sum of the inputs.

Serendipity

Serendipity is often described as a lucky or fortunate accident, something that benefits us without any planning or intent on our part. When we Copy to Innovate, we can eliminate the natural randomness or unpredictability involved by deliberately placing ourselves in the path of Serendipity. This can be as simple as retaining a picture in our minds of the type of solution we require for an unresolved problem. By doing this, we avoid failing to notice an encounter that contains the general essence of that solution.

Situational Background

The Situational Background consists of knowledge captured in informal notes that set the scene for the required innovative solution. They describe the existing circumstances and their context. The information should be simple and succinct, as long as it clearly conveys the desired objective and highlights why it cannot currently be achieved.

Six Ways

There are six ways to innovate through problems:
1. Prevent the cause from having its effect
2. Avoid the effect of the cause
3. Eliminate the cause of the effect
4. Transform the negative cause into a positive cause
5. Nullify the effect of the cause
6. Preempt the cause and the effect

Small effort → big result

Small effort → big result is a visual shorthand used throughout the book to emphasize its core message: we innovate when the effort we invest in pursuit of a goal is greatly exceeded by the value of the result we achieve.

BIBLIOGRAPHY

GUIDES, GURUS AND GREAT MINDS THAT HELPED

A selection of references that helped shape this book and may also assist readers who want to do more of their own exploration

Anderson, Chris. (2006). *The Long Tail: Why the Future of Business Is Selling Less of More*. Hyperion.

Botsman, Rachel and Rogers, Roo. (2010). *What's Mine is Yours: The Rise of Collaborative Consumption*. Harper Business.

Brockman, John. (2013). *Thinking: The New Science of Decision-Making, Problem-Solving, and Prediction in Life and Markets*. Harper Perennial.

Cabane, Olivia Fox and Pollack, Judith. (2017). *The Net and the Butterfly: The Art and Practice of Breakthrough Thinking*. Portfolio.

Csikszentmihalyi, Mihaly. (1996). *Creativity Flow and the Psychology of Discovery and Invention*. Harper Collins.

de Bono, Edward. (1970). *Lateral Thinking: Creativity Step by Step*. Harper & Row.

de Bono, Edward. (1985). *Six Thinking Hats*. Little, Brown and Company.

de Bono, Edward. (1992). *Serious Creativity*. Harper Business.

de Brabandere, Luc and Iny, Alan. (2013). *Thinking in New Boxes*. Random House Group.

Deming, W. Edwards (1982). *Out of the Crisis*. MIT Press.

Dobelli, Rolf. (2013). *The Art of Thinking Clearly*. Sceptre, Hodder & Stoughton.

Dudgeon, Piers. (2001). *Breaking Out of the Box: The Biography of Edward de Bono*. Headline Book Publishing.

Duggan, William. (2007). *Strategic Intuition*. Columbia Business School Publishing.

Dyer, Jeff, Gregersen, Hal and Christensen, Clayton M. (2011). *The Innovator's DNA: Mastering the Five Skills of Disruptive Innovators*. Harvard Business School Publishing.

Ferriss, Timothy. (2007). *The 4-Hour Workweek: Escape 9–5, Live Anywhere, and Join the New Rich*. Crown Publishing Group.

Foer, Joshua. (2011). *Moonwalking with Einstein: The Art and Science of Remembering Everything*. Penguin Press.

Foster, Jack. (1996). *How to Get Ideas*. Berrett-Koehler Publishers.

Foster, Richard N. (1986). *Innovation: The Attacker's Advantage*. Summit Books.

Gawande, Atul. (2009). *The Checklist Manifesto: How to Get Things Right*. Metropolitan Books.

Gladwell, Malcolm. (2000). *The Tipping Point: How Little Things Can Make a Big*

Difference. Little, Brown and Company.

Glassman, Brian Scott. (2009). *Improving Idea Generation and Idea Management in Order to Better Manage the Fuzzy Front End of Innovation.* Dissertation. Purdue University.

Godin, Seth. (2003). *Purple Cow: Transform Your Business by Being Remarkable.* Portfolio.

Godin, Seth. (2006). *Small is the New Big.* Portfolio.

Gordon, B. J., & Berger, L. (2003). *Intelligent memory: Improve the memory that makes you smarter.* Viking.

Guilford, Joy Paul. (1967) *The Nature of Human Intelligence.* McGraw-Hill.

Hardy, G. H. (1940). *A Mathematician's Apology.* Cambridge University Press.

Harman, Jay. (2013). *The Shark's Paintbrush: Biomimicry and How Nature Is Inspiring Innovation.* Nicholas Brealey Publishing.

Haines-Gadd, Lilly. (2016). *TRIZ For Dummies.* John Wiley & Sons, Ltd.

Hipple, Jack. (2003). *Proactive Failure Prediction (Reverse TRIZ).* Presentation at an InfraGard™ Meeting.

Holiday, Ryan. (2015). *The Obstacle Is the Way: The Ancient Art of Turning Adversity to Advantage.* Profile Books Ltd.

Hudson, Ken. (2008). *The Idea Generator: 60 Tools for Business Growth.* Atlantic Books.

Jacobs, Alan. (2017). *How to Think: A Survival Guide for a World at Odds.* Profile Books Ltd.

Johnson, Steven. (2010). *Where Good Ideas Come From: The Natural History of Innovation.* Riverhead Books.

Kauffman, S. (2023). *The "adjacent possible"—and how it explains human innovation* [Video]. TED Conferences.

Kahneman, Daniel. (2011). *Thinking, Fast and Slow.* Farrar, Straus and Giroux.

Kelley, Tom and Kelley, David. (2013). *Creative Confidence.* Crown Business.

Kelley, Thomas. (2001). *The Art of Innovation.* Currency, Doubleday.

Kirsch, A. (2014, February 3). Full fathom five. *The New Yorker.* https://www.newyorker.com/magazine/2014/02/03/full-fathom-five-2

Koestler, Arthur. (1964). *The Act of Creation.* Macmillan.

Kourdi, Jeremy. (2008). *100 Great Business Ideas.* Marshall Cavendish Limited.

McConnell, John S. (1988), *Safer Than a Known Way.* Delaware Group.

Merton, Robert K. and Barber, Elinor (2004). *The Travels and Adventures of Serendipity.* Princeton University Press.

Moseley, David. (2005). *Frameworks for Thinking: A Handbook for Teaching and Learning.* Cambridge University Press.

Naik, G. (2006). "A hospital races to learn lessons of Ferrari pit stop." *The Wall Street Journal.* https://www.wsj.com/articles/SB116346916169622261

Nalebuff, Barry and Ayres, Ian. (2003). *Why Not? How to Use Everyday Ingenuity to*

Solve Problems Big and Small. Harvard Business Review Press.

Nussbaum, Bruce, (2013). *Creative Intelligence: Harnessing the Power to Create, Connect, and Inspire.* Harper Business.

O'Hare, Mark (1988). *Innovate!: How to Gain and Sustain Competitive Advantage.* Basil Blackwell Ltd.

Osborne, Alex F. (1942). *How to Think Up.* McGraw-Hill Book Company, Inc.

Osborne, Alex F. (1953). *Applied Imagination.* Charles Scribner's Sons.

Polya, G. (1945). *How to Solve It.* Princeton University Press.

Purdie-Smith, John. (2024). *Sebir—where Small effort→big result.* https://www.sebir.com/

Radjou, Navi and Prabhu, Jaideep. (2015). *Frugal Innovation: How to Do Better with Less.* Profile Books Ltd.

Ries, Eric. (2017). *The Startup Way: How Entrepreneurial Management Transforms Culture and Drives Growth.* Penguin Random House.

Ries, Eric. (2011). *The Lean Startup: How Today's Entrepreneurs Use Continuous Innovation to Create Radically Successful Businesses.* Crown Business.

Robinson, Alan G and Schroeder, Dean M. (2004). *Ideas Are Free: How the Idea Revolution Is Liberating People and Transforming Organizations.* Berrett-Koehler Publishers.

Rogers, Everett M. (1962). *Diffusion of Innovations.* The Free Press.

Sandman, P. M. (2019). *Risk communication strategies: Cawley 2019 class presentation.* Retrieved from https://www.psandman.com/articles/Cawley2019.htm

Sawyer, R. Keith. (2006). *Explaining Creativity: The Science of Human Innovation.* Oxford University Press.

Segall, Ken. (2016). *Think Simple: How Smart Leaders Defeat Complexity.* Portfolio.

Smith, Daniel. (2010). *Lucky Bugger's Casebook: Tales of Serendipity and Outrageous Good Fortune.* Icon Books Ltd.

Sternberg, Robert J. (1991). *Handberg of Creativity.* Cambridge University Press.

Sun Tzu. (1983). *The Art of War* (J. Clavell, Ed.). Dell Publishing.

Taleb, Nassim Nicholas. (2012). *Antifragile: Things That Gain from Disorder.* Random House.

Trott, Dave. (2015). *One + One = Three: A Masterclass in Creative Thinking.* Pan Macmillan.

Watts, Duncan J. (2011). *Everything is Obvious: Once You Know the Answer.* Crown Business.

Wallas, Graham. (1926). *The Art of Thought.* Jonathan Cape.

Whalley, Barton and Aykroyd, Susan Stratton. (2007). *Textbook of Political-Military Counterdeception: Basic Principles & Methods.* National Defense Intelligence College.

Young, James Webb. (1940). *A Technique for Producing Ideas.* Advertising Publications, Inc.

www.ingramcontent.com/pod-product-compliance
Lightning Source LLC
Chambersburg PA
CBHW052341210326
41597CB00037B/6210